OLD BRANDS AND LOST TRAILS

For my friend
& fellow Carver
Rosey
Happy Trails
Ivan Denton

Old Brands and Lost Trails

Arkansas and the Great Cattle Drives

I. Denton

THE UNIVERSITY OF ARKANSAS PRESS
FAYETTEVILLE
1991

Copyright 1992 by Ivan Denton

All rights reserved
Manufactured in the United States of America

96 95 94 93 92   5 4 3 2 1

This book was designed by Brenda Zodrow using the Janson typeface.

The paper used in this publication meets the minimum requirements of the American National Standard for Permanence of Paper for Printed Library Materials Z39.48-1984. ∞

Library of Congress Cataloging-in-Publication Data

Denton, Ivan, 1927-
  Old brands and lost trails: Arkansas and the great cattle drives.
    p.   cm.
  Includes bibliographical references.
  ISBN 1-55728-146-7. -- ISBN 1-55728-147-5 (pbk.)
  1. Cattle trails--Arkansas--History. 2. Cattle trails--West (U.S.)--History. 3. Cattle trade--Arkansas--History. 4. Cattle trade--West (U.S.)--History. 5. Arkansas--Description and travel. I. Title.
F411.D46 1992
976.7--dc20   90-48724
                                                                   CIP

This book is respectfully dedicated to
the cowboys, cowgirls, and Indians of Arkansas,
with a special tribute to those "good people,"
the Quapaw Indians, who cared for
our earliest pioneers and cattlemen,
and gave Arkansas its name.

Contents

Preface ix

Acknowledgments xiii

I From Olden Times to the Cattle Drives

1	The Land of the Old West	*3*
2	Horses Arrive	*11*
3	Cattle Arrive	*31*
4	Lost Trails West	*43*
5	The Cattle Drives	*71*
6	The Open Range Saga	*127*

II The Long Ride

7	Some of My Story: The Rocking Lazy "D"	*173*
8	The Quest	*183*
9	From Artist Point to the Oklahoma Border: The first Small Steps Were Big Ones	*189*
10	Through the Indian Territory: Oklahoma is OK!	*193*
11	Kansas: A Land of Many Trails	*201*
12	The Long Horizons: From the Colorado Plains to the Rockies	*208*

13 Wyoming: Wagon Ruts and Legends of
    the Cherokee Trail   *214*
14 Hopscotch on Four Corners: To Idaho via
    Colorado, Wyoming, Utah   *229*
15 Onward to California: High Deserts,
    Beautiful Rubies, and Wild Horses   *240*

Bibliography *259*

Preface

After several years of hard work researching and writing *Old Brands and Lost Trails*, I feel as if I have climbed a mountain. It feels something like the day I rode west out of Encampment, Wyoming, heading for the Continental Divide. I stopped the hard climb for a few moments to give my horse a rest and looked back down into Encampment and beyond to where I had been shown traces and ruts of the old Cherokee Trail. Both evidence and logic were there. To the south of this old cattle trial lay rugged mountains, more trees, better water holes. To the north lay the plains and deserts. The chosen trail had avoided these two extremes.

Looking back now, I hope that I have blazed a literary trail, and like all trailblazers I hope that my work can be improved upon. I hope others can add something to this work or at least fill in some missing spaces. However, I want to say here that by researching this story I have come to have a much deeper appreciation for truth. I have tried to avoid the pitfalls of lies, opinions, and deceptions in writing with the pen, just as I avoided pitfalls of nature riding my horse from Arkansas to California. Once, at Lone Tree, Wyoming, my horse suddenly sank in silty mud near an irrigation ditch, and it was only with much effort and fast reactions that we got out. And several times in my research I have realized that the trail was getting a little too mushy and deep, and I backed out to the more solid ground of truth.

When you are pursuing truth, you keep bumping into it because it is solid. On my cross-country ride, I met descendents of characters in my story. I did not know these people, and I was not looking for them. I bumped into them because they were there, and their stories are true. A lie is often about something that doesn't exist, so there's nothing to bump into. Truth is a straight trail; it goes somewhere, it does not leave you stranded.

I am not claiming that every statement in this book is proven, documented truth. Too much time and space are covered for this to be possible, but I have tried to keep my trail on solid ground.

Many friends have asked why I did this book on *Arkansas* of all places. Why not do a book on some other more traditional Western area? Well, if the stories told here surprise you, just rest assured. They surprised me, too. I picked up the tracks and followed the story. I gasped when I came over the rises and around the bends in the trail the same as I hope you will when you read about them.

I am not a native of Arkansas, but I believe that the role this area played in the development of the West has been too long overlooked. When we read the history of Arkansas Post and of the origins of horses and cattle in this state, when we read the advice of Captain Randolph Marcy of the U.S. Army to the the forty-niners to wait until they got to Fort Smith and Van Buren to buy horses and cattle, we feel compelled to the conclusion that Arkansas played nothing less than a key role in the development of the West. Captain Marcy commented on those "large stout ponies found among some of our frontier settlements," called "range horses," and he discovered that they did hard work eating only grass. Thomas Nuttall mentioned the range horses of eastern Arkansas in 1819 in almost these same words. Records show that this far south, horses and cattle ranged out the year round without feed or help of any kind from man, and so sizable numbers of extras were available and driven along with most wagon trains going west from Arkansas. How many wild horse herds originated along the Cherokee and other westbound trails as a result of Indian attacks or careless herding?

This book didn't start out being about cattle drives. The original idea was to document Arkansas's open range heritage, and that research led me to the stories of the great cattle drives. I have not told of all the Arkansas to California drives. Stories keep turning up, some by word of mouth, some from old letters. Sometimes one leads to the other and they verify each other.

Most of the Arkansas ranches were and are small compared to those in other western states. This does not mean that the excitement and adventure of these drives were less. The Arkansas drover period, from 1849 to 1860, was before the Civil War. The Texas drover period, from the late 1860s until fencing closed the trails, was after the Civil War. The climax of the Texas drives was the excitement of the Kansas railway shipping points. The climax of the Arkansas drives was California and the innumerable gold fever boomtowns and tent cities. To some extent, Arkansas, Oklahoma, Texas, and other areas shared involvement in both drover periods, but the purpose of this book is to document the previously overlooked part that Arkansas played in the development of the West as it revolved around the livestock industry.

It has long been my opinion that the fur and mining industries have been given more than their share of credit for blazing new trails which in reality the Indians had already pioneered and indeed were called into service as guides to help the fur traders and miners to follow them.

These Indians were "cattlemen" before the white man arrived. The Spaniard De Soto called the bison "cattle," and his chronicles referred to the Indians in what later came to be called the Arkansas Territory as "herdsmen" or "Vaqueros."

If we, for the sake of an illustration, compared the West to a large sand pile, we might say that the fur trappers, miners, and gamblers were little boys playing in the sand pile until the real builders could arrive to really build something. But I admit that this is a biased viewpoint; I have always been a cowboy at heart.

My viewpoints are not incontestable, but I hope you will

share with me through the pages of this book the excitement, romance, and adventure of mounted horsemen, cattle drives, wagon trains, and Indian attacks. This is the story of Arkansas and our nation as seen through the eyes of a cowboy. I have tried to help you see what I have seen by preparing the illustrations that appear throughout the text. I hope they are as valuable as the stories themselves.

If you enjoy reading these stories as much as I have enjoyed researching and writing them, this book will have been a double success.

Acknowledgments

I am both humbled and gratified to say that I could not have done this book alone. First, I want to thank the many county clerks and their assistants for a fine job of record keeping. I will never forget the priceless treasure of those many old "Marks and Brands" books, bound in leather and stamped in gold.

Other researchers, independent historians, and just plain friends have been innumerable and invaluable. Two groups deserve special recognition. The old-timers among us who shared many conversations over many cups of coffee and the descendents and kin of the old drovers themselves.

And I would be a worthless saddle bum if I were to overlook saluting the many cowboys and friends I met riding an old cattle trail from Arkansas to California in 1989. After I saddled up and before I mounted my pony I would shake hands, look them in the eye, and say, "I will never forget your kindness." And I never will.

The following is a list of friends that contributed toward making my cross-country ride a success.

Mrs. Sandra M. McAuliffe
Mrs. Ruth Plambeck
Mr. & Mrs. Douglas Bibby
Mr. & Mrs. Tom Curtis
Mr. Frank McAuliffe
Terry Q. Carson

Mr. & Mrs. Russell Smoker
Mr. & Mrs. Bill Fortenberry
Mr. & Mrs. Ivan Bys
Mr. & Mrs. Franklin S. Williams
Mr. & Mrs. W. Nelms
Mr. & Mrs. George H. Estelle
Aaron Davis
Mr. & Mrs. John Chaney
Mrs. Joanna Pfeffer
Mr. Bob Pfeffer
Mr. & Mrs. Robert McGill
Win Paul Rockefeller
Mr. & Mrs. Russell Blaylock
Mr. Norman L. Claybourn
Frank Sharp
Paula Broadfoot
Mr. Kit Carson
Mr. & Mrs. Charley Montooth
Steve Sharp
Mr. & Mrs. Robert J. McGinnis
Ray B. Thurston
Janet Cordell
Color Mate Photo
Cliff Lewis
Andy Anderson
Mark Roberson
Walt Rowden
Walt Kreeger, who sometimes all but held my hand to get me through some rough spots.

I

From Olden Times to the Cattle Drives

1

The Land of the Old West

The bull was huge. He would have weighed well over a ton, but scales to have weighed him, at least in this wild area, were hundreds of years away. The year was A.D. 1541, sixty-six years before the Jamestown settlement and seventy-nine years before the *Mayflower* sighted Plymouth Rock. Hundreds of years later, offspring of this bull's kind would be called "bison" and "buffalo." This one stood in lush prairie grass over six feet tall and close to a million acres of it surrounded him. Perhaps as many as fifty thousand of his kind roamed the one hundred or more miles of this prairie. It would take horsemen close to a week to traverse this great pasture. In this year, horsemen appeared for the first time on this prairie that we today call the Grand Prairie of eastern Arkansas.

Around the bull grazed several cows. Occasionally the peculiar, low grunt of their calves could be heard. When one of the Spaniards, approaching on horseback from downwind, said, *"Hay muchas vacas grandes aqui,"* there were no other beings within a thousand miles who would have understood the words. When the not-so-sharp bison eyes saw the sun reflect off steel, and the bison ears heard the sound of thunder in the clear summer sky, the bison had no way of understanding that this was the beginning of the end for its kind in this *pastura grande*, that in fact this would bring them close to total extinction on the entire American continent.

But now, through the eyes of the doomed buffalo, we see the arrival of the first Europeans, De Soto and his men, to this land of Arkansas, a land that would be called "the Far West" for the next three hundred years. As a matter of fact it was exactly three hundred years after De Soto's arrival that the German writer and world traveler, Frederich Gerstaecker, published the story of his adventures in Arkansas under the title *Wild Sports in the Far West.*

Just how much trail dust of time drifted over these prairies and through these woodlands and mountain passes before other Europeans followed De Soto is hard to say. Indian tribes were much easier to travel through before permanent settlers started to arrive, and other Spanish or French adventurers could have explored here and left no written records. Legend says they did travel through; however, there is more than enough from those who did leave a written record to give us a clear picture of what Arkansas was like before our pioneer ancestors arrived. We know that it was not all dark, somber alligator swamps or forests with trees so thick that cattle and horses could not graze. Some romantic writers have printed such a picture of this land before it was cleared, but that was not the early Arkansas. The misconception may come from the fact that De Soto's cruelty resulted in the Indians' deliberately misleading the Spaniards through dark swamps in an effort to lose them, very near where the Frenchmen later reported "most pleasant plains."

The Frenchman Marquette, who came down the Mississippi in 1673, wrote of hearing the "bellowing of great numbers of buffalo," and La Salle, nine years later, in 1682, described the Arkansas wilderness just inland from the Mississippi. John Upton Terrell quotes La Salle in *La Salle, the Life and Times of an Explorer* saying that behind the forbidding river swamps "you see the finest country in the world . . . there are vast fields of excellent land, diversified here and there with pleasing hills, lofty woods, groves through which you might ride on horseback, so clear and unobstructed are the paths."

On La Salle's last voyage from France, in 1686, he missed the mouth of the Mississippi and landed somewhere on the shores of the Gulf of Mexico considerably west of his goal. In the meantime, Henri de Tonti had established the Arkansas Post settlement near the mouth of the Arkansas River in expectation of a rendezvous with La Salle, his friend and commander. Arkansas Post thrived as the oldest white settlement west of the Mississippi and east of Santa Fe, predating the trading post at present-day St. Louis by seventy-eight years.

In 1687, La Salle, having lost all his ships to desertion and mutiny, started an overland expedition to rendezvous with De Tonti. He was skilled in the ways of the wilderness, spoke several Indian tongues, and was proficient in their sign language, but the expedition failed to reap the benefits from this experience, for he was killed by his own men early in the journey. La Salle's loyal friend Joutel kept a most revealing chronicle called *A Journal of La Salle's Last Voyage*, from which we know that a remnant of La Salle's party reached Arkansas Post.

Joutel's journal, published in French in 1713 and in English the next year, lets us see the Indians, the wildlife, and the pristine geography of the country between the Texas Gulf coast and Arkansas Post. Traveling across it meant an odyssey of roughly 600 miles, 117 years before Lewis and Clark made their famous trek.

The buffalo, called bullocks, are described by Joutel as ". . . very like ours, there are thousands of them," he writes, "but instead of hair they have a very long curl'd sort of wool." Somewhere near the Texas coast, before reaching the plains, he records that, ". . . we also met with some woods so thick, that it was requisite to hew a passage for the horses."

The French seemed to be talented at peacefully dealing with the Indians, always seemed to have a local guide to the next village, and apparently were never misdirected. Repeated mention was made of wild goats and deer. The French were probably actually seeing pronghorn antelope. Our pioneer forefathers reported antelope in Arkansas as late as the early 1800s.

By the first of April 1687 the party encountered Indians (Caddo, presumably) who knew of the French settlement at Arkansas Post. Joutel reports that according to the Indians the explorers were only about forty leagues from the "Great River" and the Frenchmen who had settled there. The French league is about three nautical miles.

Joutel records the Indian method of hunting the antelope, of which "there are many in that country. The Indians have the art of dressing the heads of those creatures, which they put upon their own, and imitate them so exactly, that they can come very near to them, and then seldom fail of killing."

All across southern Arkansas, grass and game were plentiful. "The 23d [June] . . . we cross'd most lovely plains and meadows, border'd with fine groves of beautiful trees, where the grass was so high, that it hinder'd our horses going, and were oblig'd to clear the passage for them.

"When we were within half a league of the village, we saw an Indian, mounted on a large grey mare, coming along with our native, to meet us, and were told that horseman was the chief of the village." When they came near the village, these hospitable Indians met them and carried them into the village on their backs. As Joutel tells it:

> As for my own part, being of a pretty large size and loaded with cloaths, a firelock, a case of pistols, powder and ball, a kettle and other implements, there is no doubt but I made a sufficient burden for him that carry'd me, and because I was taller than he and my feet would have hung upon the ground, two other Indians held them up for me; so that I had three to carry me.
>
> As soon as we were come to the chief's cottage, where we found above two hundred persons, who were come to see us, and our horses were unloaded, the elders gave us to understand, that it was their custom to wash strangers at their first coming; but that we being clad, they would only wash our faces.

All along the route the Frenchmen inquired about the location of the "Great River," the Mississippi, and of other Frenchmen like themselves and of a place called "Cappa," which they knew to be near their destination. The Indians were always helpful and must have had news of the French settlement from De Tonti, as the soldiers were unerringly directed toward the Post.

The continuing hospitality of the Indians is shown by further entries.

> We cross'd . . . the next day, on a sort of float, which we made with much toil and labour, and our horses swam over . . . On the 6th, whilst we halted on the bank of a river to eat, we heard the tingling of some small bells; which making us look about, we spy'd an Indian with a naked sword-blade in his hand, adorned with feathers of several colours, and two large hawks bells, that occasion'd the noise we had heard.
>
> He made signs for us to come to him, and gave us to understand, that he was sent by the Elders of the village whither we were going, to meet us, carressing us after an extraordinary manner. I observ'd that it

was a Spanish blade he had, and that he took pleasure in ringing the hawks bells.

Having travell'd about half a league with him, we discover'd a dozen of other Indians coming towards us, who made very much of and conducted us the village, to the chief's cottage, where we found dry'd bear-skins laid on the ground, and they made us sit on them, where we were treated with eatables, as were the elders after us, and a throng of women came to see us. . . .

The chief and another came again some time after, bringing two loaves, the finest and the best we had yet seen. They look'd as if they had been bak'd in an oven, and yet we had not observ'd that there were ovens among any of them. That chief stay'd with us some hours, he seem'd to be very ingenious and discreet, and easily understood our signs, which were most of the language we had. Having order'd a little boy to bring us all we had occasion for, he withdrew.

These Indians must have been the Quapaw, known as a gentle and hospitable people. According to an incident related soon after, they must have become a little too friendly for Monsieur Cavelier, the priest, whom they took to be the Chief of the French party.

That concert was scarce ended, when the master of the ceremonies brought two maids, the one having in her hand a sort of collar, and the other an otter's skin, which they plac'd on the wooden forks above mention'd, at the ends of the pipe. Then he made them sit down, on each side of Monsieur Cavelier, in such a posture, that they look'd one upon the other, their legs extended and intermix'd, on which the same master of the ceremonies laid Monsieur Cavelier's legs, in such manner, that they lay uppermost and across those of the two maids.

Whilst this action was performing, one of the elders made fast a dy'd feather to the back part of Monsieur Cavelier's head, tying it to his hair. The singing still continu'd all that time, so that Monsieur Cavelier, grown weary of its tediousness, and asham'd to see himself in that posture between two maids, without knowing to what purpose, made signs to us to signify the same to the chief, and having given him to understand, that he was not well, two of the Indians immediately took hold of him under the arms, conducted him back to the cottage and made signs to him to take his rest.

Joutel here records, "This was the first place where we saw the calumet, or pipe of peace," and later at this same village, ". . . we were inform'd by one of the Indians that we were not far from a great river, which he describ'd with a stick on the sand and shew'd it had two branches, at the same time pronouncing the word Cappa, which, as I have said, is a nation near the Mississippi. We then made no longer question, that we were near what we had been so long looking after." He then adds, "we set out on the 11th [of July], to the great sorrow of *those good people*, who had entertain'd us so courteously."

Buffalo and antelope had been plentiful, especially for the last month of their journey. The animals must have been fat and healthy, as there is no mention of grass and forage being in short supply, nor of any difficulty in killing them for food. On one occasion the Indian guides saw buffalo tracks, and after being gone ". . . for two or three hours . . . they return'd loaded with flesh, part whereof we dress'd, and ate it with very good stomachs." And four days later, they killed three bulls and two cows and halted to make jerky.

The description of the country around Arkansas Post leaves little to be desired from a rancher's standpoint. "The plains lying on one side of it, are stor'd with beeves [buffalo], wild goats [antelope], deer, turkeys, bustards [a type of crane or plover], swans, ducks, teal and other game.

"The trees produce plenty of fruit, and very good, as peaches, plumbs, mulberries, grapes, and walnuts."

Far, then, from being a land of somber forest that would discourage future cattlemen and horsemen, as many have portrayed it, what would become Arkansas was a rich—

almost lush—homeland to "those good people," the Quapaw and others. Other writers and travelers agreed that Arkansas was, from the beginning, a land ideal for growing livestock. Repeated reference has been made to the Ozark and Ouachita woodlands in the virgin state as having large trees, widely spaced with grassy areas between, that furnish good cattle range.

Joutel and his four companions left Arkansas Post in early August 1687 to continue on to Canada and eventually back to France. They left their five remaining horses, which, as Joutel said, "were of great use to go a hunting" as gifts to the settlers.

The hospitality of the Indians was still so much in evidence that it held them up a few more days. Joutel writes:

> We would willingly have set out the first of August; but the Chief came and told us, it could not be, because the women had not pounded our corn, which however was done; but they made use of that pretence to oblige us to stay, and to have leisure to give us some diversion, after their manner.
>
> Accordingly, about ten in the morning, the warriors and youth came together to dance. They were dress'd after their best manner, some of them wearing plumes of several colours, wherewith they adorn their heads, others, instead of feathers, had two bullocks [buffalo] horns, and were all besmear'd with clay, of black or of red, so that they really look'd like a company of devils or monsters.

And so, from the trails of De Soto, Joutel, and all the probable Spanish and French adventurers between and following, a large door was opening. European culture was beaming brightly, or looming darkly, through it.

2

Horses Arrive

Imagine this:

The little mare, just under fourteen hands high, for the moment stood listless. She is a light gray with a black mane and tail and stood in the shade of a grove of oak trees on the border of a large prairie.

In the tall prairie grass nearby a dozen or so mares of mixed colors and several newborn foals by their sides are grazing. Off to one side, on a slight rise of ground, a well-muscled mahogany bay stallion grazes fitfully, testing the wind at short intervals. As he raises his head, nostrils flared, the spring breeze tosses his mane and tail in a picture of ruggedness, wildness, and beauty.

The little mare has disappeared now into the deeper wood, where soon a wobbly, leggy, foal will clumsily examine his mother's knees, hocks, brisket, and belly, and any other bump, mound, or knob. But this one will find the source of milk because his sire and dam are wild horses. Years of surviving without man's help have simply eliminated any horses not possessing accurate instincts as well as intelligence, speed, and strength.

All this happened several hundred years ago on what was once called the "Prairie of Wild Horses" in southwestern Arkansas. Now these horses are almost forgotten, but wild horses once roamed in great numbers all across Arkansas, surviving without our help, by instinct, intelligence, and speed. These qualities were honed in each generation as only the best survived.

THE MYSTERY OF DE SOTO'S HUNDRED LOST HORSES

The first Europeans to arrive in Arkansas—Hernando de Soto and his followers—were on horseback. They crossed the Mississippi into Arkansas on June 18, 1541, only forty-nine years after Columbus "discovered" America. After De Soto had landed on the Florida coast about two years earlier with over two hundred horses, there were troubles with the Chickasaw Indians, who drove half the horses into the forests so that the Spaniards entered Arkansas with only around one hundred head.

The exact route of De Soto's wanderings in Arkansas may never be known, but enough is clear to make a generally accurate map. His journey seems to have covered around five hundred miles from east-central to southwestern Arkansas and back out through the southeastern part of the state. He left the state one year after his first sight of Arkansas and around sixty horses short. Here De Soto died. His successor, Moscoso, then attempted to lead the remnant of the party back to Mexico overland but failed. They later returned to the Mississippi to build ships to sail to Mexico.

Some accounts say that De Soto had around two hundred horses at the beginning of his journey. The Inca historian Garcilaso, who evidently interviewed some of the expedition members, speaks of "the three hundred and fifty horses which had entered Florida for its discovery and conquest." This would mean that considerably more than a hundred horses may have entered Arkansas The discrepancy in the number of horses may lie in inaccurate recording, but it may have been that in addition to the two hundred horses furnished by De Soto himself, many of the horses were privately owned by expedition members. Garcilaso, commenting on the quality of those horses, says, "On none of the expeditions which to date have been made in the New World have so many and such fine horses been seen together." Did any of these "fine horses" survive, and was their blood found in the early horses of Arkansas?

Before dealing with this, it may be interesting to consider a few thoughts on wild horses in general: what a wild horse is, whether wild horses are really wild.

Wild horses as we know them in America are domestic horses that have escaped captivity (as some of De Soto's surely did) or have been abandoned. Some say, then, that American wild horses are not really wild, but "feral," domestic animals gone wild. In *Horses of the World*, Pamela Macgregor-Morris says, "No living representatives of this species [*Equus caballas*] can be described as truly wild; those horses which roam free and graze in certain territories are really feral, which is to say that they are merely the descendants of once-domesticated horses that managed to escape." But this is hair splitting. "Feral" means wild, untamed, uncultivated. If a domestic animal gone wild is not really wild, then a wild animal domesticated is not really domestic. The term "naturalized horses" used by the English naturalist, Thomas

Nuttall, to describe these early horses of Arkansas in 1819 is pehaps the most accurate term.

A logger friend of mine described a herd of wild horses that used to range near where I now live in northwest Arkansas. He said that someone asked him if he could get close enough to the stallion to rope him. My friend said, "Rope him!? Man, you can't even get close enough to shoot him!" He described the actions of this wild stallion when, by chance, he would drive his log truck into a woods clearing where the horse happened to be. "He acts just like a buck deer," he said. "He'll snort and jump and maybe give you one flashing view of his sides and won't stop until he's behind a bush or tree, then he'll probably snort another time or two before he gallops away."

Wild horses were a romantic part of Arkansas's western heritage. If you ever jump a domestic horse "gone wild" in a woodland clearing, and he flashes his sides and thunders away through a meadow sprinkled with Deptford pinks and daisies, you're in for a treat that few lucky people have experienced in this day and age.

Now back to the subject of De Soto's expedition and what probably happened to his horses after the remnant of his forces sailed for Mexico, leaving a large number somewhere between the Mississippi River and Caddo Gap.

According to the *National Geographic* magazine of November 1923, De Soto abandoned a few horses on the west bank of the Mississippi, and these, along with others taken to Mexico, comprised "the nucleus from which sprang the wild horse herds of Mexico and Texas, known as mustangs, which later overran the prairies and furnished the mounts of many Indian tribes."

This theory has been attacked by practically every writer since. Hope Ryden in *America's Last Wild Horses* noted that historians have never recorded wild horses in that area of the lower Mississippi Valley and that it was improbable that De Soto's six remaining "wretched animals" could have made it five or six hundred miles to the plains states. In *The Wild*

Horse of the West, Walker D. Wyman acknowledges that two of the six horses liberated by De Soto were stallions, but says that the Indians probably killed them all. Even if some did escape, according to Wyman, it would have been nearly impossible for them to join the wild herds in Mexico because of the great distance through "a fairly well-baked desert" and natural enemies.

Most accounts agree that of the forty or so horses that De Soto had when he left Arkansas, only about six were alive when the Spaniards said "adios" to the Indians. We know from the "Gentleman of Elvias" account that the expedition killed some of the horses and dried the meat for the return voyage.

The Spaniards had pushed the hospitality of "those good people" about as far as it would go, and they were starting to shove back. Whichever route the Spaniards took, they were in danger, in flight, and in a hurry to get afloat.

One account shows that their horses had been unshod for over a year, and that they were getting away. Some may have been abandoned because they were not able to keep up. Some halters may have been broken during the night. An arrow in the night, a squeal of fright or pain, the smell of blood by a horse tied nearby and anything could happen.

Most writers and historians deal only with "these six escapees" on that final day of the expedition's defeat, but from one hundred to possibly two hundred and fifty horses had entered Arkansas with De Soto's expedition. Those opposing the view that some of them survived continually point to the difficulty of reaching the Texas plains from Arkansas, as if the horses' survival depended on getting out of Arkansas.

Those not familiar with horses may not realize how quickly they can return to nature and adapt to natural ways of survival. I have turned horses out on natural woodland range in northwestern Arkansas—purebred and part Arabian, much the same as De Soto's. They ranged old fields and deep woodlands where we had seen both cougar and the big black color phase subspecies of the red wolf. My mares foaled under these conditions, and I never lost one to predators. They did not drift back to the barn, but ranged farther and farther out and always seemed to have gained weight when I found them, even in the winter.

I have always thought that the horse is the king of beasts. Horses have survived in all parts of the earth. Few predators can catch them, and many that have caught them have suffered for it. No Arkansas predator is a match, in speed or power, for a horse, either wild or domestic.

De Soto's horses, then, even though they were domestic, were of strong stock, and within twenty-four hours of being abandoned they would have been contentedly grazing the tall prairie grass. If any did escape, by the first autumn they would have been relishing the date-like persimmons that all horses like, and some would have been pawing the trees to make them fall. Between these sweet fruits and the tons of acorns, grass, and other nutritious plants, these horses would have been enjoying the true fruitcake of nature and putting on fat to survive the first winter.

Why would they leave the prairies and hills of Arkansas? They were surrounded by what La Salle called the finest country in the world. Crossing the area in 1687, Joutel repeatedly mentioned the abundance of feed for grazing animals. He never suggested that the horses suffered for sustenance, or that the Indians ever tried to kill the horses for food. On the contrary, repeated reference is made to the ease of killing wild game, especially antelope and buffalo. Antelope were plentiful all the way to and including the prairie around Arkansas Post. Kirkbride Potts, one of the Arkansas drovers, wrote from Galley Creek in central Arkansas on June 1, 1830, "It costs nothing to raise cattle or horses, they keep fat winter and summer in the woods."

Some writers have assumed that wild horses could not survive in the area, but the record does not support that assumption.

Thomas Nuttall wrote in 1819, while near Arkansas Post, "It is in consequence of this unrestrained liberty, and the advantage of a perpetual supply of food, that the horse has become already naturalized in the southern parts of this territory, and the adjoining province of Spain. . . . The horses of this country are rather small, though very hardy, and capable of subsisting entirely upon cane or grass, even when subjected to the hardest labour."

Walker Wyman mentions the Mendoza-Lopez expedition that moved northwest across Texas in 1683, finding no horses on the Rio Grande, but herds of them as the expedition progressed. Joutel records horses on the east Texas and Arkansas prairies and woodlands in 1687, and they seemed to be easier to trade for as the party moved toward the northeast. He also saw Spanish swords, clothing, and a flat-crowned, broad-brimmed hat somewhere in the Texas-Louisiana-Arkansas triangle. The soldiers traded an axe for a stone horse (stallion) a little farther east, and their records show that they were about forty leagues from Arkansas Post and about two hundred leagues from the Spanish territory at that point. If we compute a league to be three nautical miles, this would place them in southwest Arkansas.

Farther east, probably in south-central Arkansas, an Indian chief riding a large gray mare met the Joutel party, and the Quapaw at Cappa, near the Mississippi-Arkansas river confluence, were using horses' tails in their costumes. Nothing is said to indicate how long these Indians had had horses, but they were clearly not new in 1687. The question naturally arises as to how the Indians learned to care for the horses, and how to ride them. It is fair to assume that De Soto taught them. When he forced the Indians to furnish corn and other forage for his horses, which were kept tied up for ready use, he was unwittingly teaching them. When he defeated them because of the advantage of the horse, they could not help but learn from observing. Sometimes we are inclined to allow too many years for the Indians to learn an art like horsemanship. Most historians like to say that the Indians *ate* horses until it gradually dawned on them that they should be *riding* horses. This might be true of some Indians who lived in desert areas where wild animals for food were scarce, but in the areas under discussion game animals were plentiful the year around.

This might be a typical scene. A Spaniard, though armored, receives an arrow in the neck and tumbles off his horse. Two Indian boys watching from the woods see the horse spook, bolt away through a strip of brush into a hidden meadow, and, being exhausted from battle, start to graze, trailing its reins. One boy watches while the other fetches corn. The tired and hungry horse, having been tied close and ready for action, looks up and nickers softly. The boys approach slowly, and pretty soon the war horse is eating from their hands. Now the big boy says to the little boy, "I'll hold 'im if you'll get on 'im." This old pony has been carrying an armor-clad soldier for the past two years or so; he isn't going to protest this weight.

If this scenario had begun in the early afternoon, then by 3:00 or 3:30 in the afternoon both boys would have had a ride, and sometime before dark they would have led their charger from the shadows of the woods to their village clearing and say: "Please can we keep him?" And the mother might say, "You'll have to ask your daddy."

And the June 1542 romance and wedding of one of De Soto's soldiers is an enchanting scene. This is an early example of Spanish and Indian culture blending. Both the "Gentleman of Elvias" and Garcilaso reported that one of the Spaniards succumbed to a fever over something more precious than gold. This Spaniard, according to Garcilaso, was Diego de Guzman. Guzman had a weakness for gambling and had lost most of his belongings in a card game. The losses included one of his personal horses and an Indian maiden described as "extremely beautiful and . . . eighteen years of age." Rather than give her up he deserted the expedition and joined the tribe with his lady love. This event, which occurred around 1542, was surely the first Spanish-Indian romance west of the Mississippi. It doesn't take much imagination to picture Señor Guzman, a few years down the line, gently placing his sons and daughters on the back of some Spanish steed and teaching them how to ride.

No one can say for sure that the horses of the Arkansas Indians or the early wild "naturalized" horses mentioned by Joutel and Nuttall descended from De Soto's horses, but they came from somewhere, and from De Soto is the simplest and most likely answer. If, indeed, his horses did survive west of the Mississippi, their first wild home would have been in the hills and prairies of Arkansas.

But if they had had horses for as long as this would indicate, we might ask why the Caddo and Quapaw were not known as great horsemen, as the Comanche were reputed to have been. It may be simply a matter of perception. If a Comanche gallops his pony around a wagon train shouting and shooting, and you're in that wagon train and survive, you will surely notice his riding and be inclined to praise it. On the other hand, if you are approached by mounted Indians, as the Caddo and Quapaw might approach, and they extend a friendly greeting, escort you to their village, wash your face, furnish you with food and entertainment, would you bother to record their good horsemanship? However, in *The Quapaw Indians*, W. David Baird says of the Quapaw that in the area of Arkansas Post in the early 1800s, ". . . they provided the trading community with many horses."

THE QUAPAW HORSEMEN

At some time in the distant past a tribe of Siouan Indians wandered down the Mississippi to the mouth of the Arkansas and thus came to be called the "Arkansa" or "Quapaw," meaning the "downstream people." Arkansas is named for them. Old documents show that the Quapaw were horse people. It is altogether possible that they became the breeders of horses lost by De Soto.

Quapaw for horse is "shun-kéh-ä-geh-nee." Their word for dog is "shun-kéh," and for chair, "ä-geh-nee." It was not unusual for early Indians to regard a horse as a large dog. But notice here the addition of "chair." This could mean a large animal to ride like a chair, or one to fit a chair, or saddle, on. Interestingly, the Spanish expression for saddle is "la silla de montar," meaning, "a chair for riding." The first horses the Quapaw would have seen were being ridden by the Spanish explorers, who were likely using the comfortable war saddles that resembled chairs.

The Quapaw were to have a long association with the European conquerors and their culture. But things didn't always work out very well for the Quapaw.

In 1803 the United States bought the Louisiana Territory and a trading post was set up at Arkansas Post called the Indian Factory. The Indian agent was the factor, and a letter book was kept from 1805 to 1810. Agent John Treat in a letter dated November 15, 1805, to Henry Dearborn, secretary of war, writes:

> The Arkansa Indians, or as they are recognis'd and known by the appellation of quapahs, are a people who have never been known to be at variance with the whites, but equally well known for their valor and great bravery display'd when in hostility with other Indian tribes on this side of the Mississippi, however from a residence in the neighborhood of either the French or Spanish and having a general intercourse with those people, they have become reduc'd both in numbers and warlike prowess: . . . Chief Kay-yah-wa-to-me . . . a stout and rather corpulent person who not withstanding he has already seen more than ninety years occasionally rides into the Post. . . .
>
> Those people become less active than formerly they were, or than the Chickasaws or Choctaws now are: the two latter going out on four or six months hunting excursions, whilst the former seldom are out mere weeks, leaving their families at home engaged in raising corn much of which they dispose of in this settlement, and the raising of Horses which they also dispose of both to whites and Indians. . . .

In a later letter dated March 27, 1806, Agent Treat writes in pleading terms for fair treatment of the Quapaw. "And certainly these people present to us the fairest prospect of civilization than any of the Indian tribes I have beheld in all my intercourse among the aborigines of our country. . . . They endeavour to place less dependence upon the chase for a livelihood and become more accustomed to cultivating the soil, as they do it to that extent, as enables a supply to many of the inhabitants here both of corn and horses, they annually resort to their villages for the purpose of procuring the one or the other."

The Quapaw, along with the Caddo, the Osage, and the Cherokee, were forced in the 1830s to move to the "Indian Territory." The Quapaw in particular were peaceful, but so badly abused. It is not likely that they were able to salvage many, if any, of their best horses.

As to the vast herds of horses farther west and north, some believe that these mustangs were spread primarily by Indian theft from Mexico and by early Indian raiders into Mexico. These Comanche tribes were noted for their thievery: Captain Randolph Marcy reported one herd of over two thousand horses and mules being brought to his camp for trading by the Comanche in 1849. Also in those years Jesse Chisholm traded regularly with the Comanche and brought great numbers of horses and mules to Fort Smith to sell to the gold seekers of 1849.

CHICKASAW HORSES

At any rate, another infusion of De Soto's horses may have passed, or attempted to pass, through Arkansas in the 1830s. These may have been descendents of the Spaniards' horses lost in the forest of the Chickasaw in about 1540.

A Cherokee friend of mine told me that during the removal of the Choctaw and Chickasaw Indians to the Indian Territory in the 1830s, the Chickasaw drove a herd of around six or seven thousand horses through Arkansas on their way to Oklahoma, but that most of them were stolen along the way. John Gould Fletcher mentions this event in *Arkansas*; his report was evidently taken from the eyewitness account of Governor Pope's nephew: "'six or seven thousand Choctaw and Chickasaw Indians from North Mississippi and West Tennessee,' mounted on ponies, driving their cattle, the males attired in the usual breech-cloth, leggings, and beaded moccasins, the women with their papooses slung at their backs" passed through the village of Little Rock. The American Indians, like the drovers and others who traveled living off the land, usually drove many horses in addition to the ones they were riding.

During this same period horse thieving was worse than common throughout the Arkansas territory. In *Makers of Arkansas History*, John Hugh Reynolds writes that "our mountains, caves, forests, and cane-brakes afforded secure hiding places for desperate men; and it was difficult to catch them." Reynolds also points out that the penalty for horse stealing then was hanging.

One gang, which was said to be the worst in the state, was headquartered in the Fourche LaFave River Valley. Some of its members were reputed to be fugitives from other states, forming a secret society of horse thieves. Their elected leader turned preacher to cover up their crimes.

The Chickasaw horse was well known at one time and was said to have played an important part in the development of other American breeds, especially the quarterhorse. The Chickasaw must have looked well to their breeding and care. These horses had survived in forested, swampy land, and rugged hill country, and they were said to be prized as backcountry horses. They were sometimes called "forest horses." They were known for their sudden bursts of speed and so made exceptional cow ponies. Being rugged and heavily muscled, they could carry a lot of weight even though they were small, measuring only 13:1 to 14:3 hands at the withers.

The Chickasaw horses that entered Arkansas later possibly, even probably, carried some blood of Thoroughbred strains that had been bred for speed. The Chickasaw had been known as racing enthusiasts from the 1700s or before. They were allies of the English, so it is probable that much Thoroughbred blood was introduced from time to time into the Chickasaw stock. The early colonists in the Carolinas had long favored Chickasaw horses for racing; by the time Arkansas became a territory of the United States, the settlers drifting into it were riding some horses that, as some put it, could pretty much burn a hole in the wind.

Regardless of how or from which explorer the first horses came to Arkansas, these earliest saddle horses were of Spanish origin, and the Spanish horses were partly of Arabian stock. This meant that they would have had very strong, short backs and well-sprung ribs, and that in most cases they would have been rather small and have possessed stamina and endurance, as well as intelligence. These were all traits very much needed in the horses of our pioneer forebears. Indeed, it is doubtful if the West could have been settled by Europeans without such horses.

EARLY BRANDS AND ARKANSAS HORSES

Arkansas Post is today a National Monument located in Arkansas County. In early 1989 I was researching old brands at Dewitt, the county seat, and counted over three thousand marks and brands. These dated from the 1830s until the state brand system took over in 1959. But I knew of an older book there. An elderly historian told me of its existence; it was a book called *Strays and Brands*.

The personnel at the courthouse knew nothing of such a book. They allowed me to search for it, and they searched also. Finally we called the historian, and she said, "Tell them it's in the circuit clerk's office in the back room on top of that old vault among all that stuff that used to be in the Campbell's soup box." We searched again and found it.

I held in my hands an old book of yellowed pages. A sharp bend and the pages would have torn. It contained just thirty-one pages, and we carefully photocopied them. The newest entry is marked "19th day of April A.D. 1844." The oldest is marked "12th of April 1820."

These old records tell an amazing story. We have always been told that the Indians' horses of Spanish stock were small—fourteen hands, more or less. This *Strays and Brands* book, from April 12, 1820, through the remainder of that calendar year, listed twelve strays as being taken in by different individuals. All twelve were horses. The size ranged from ten to fifteen hands high. Three of these were branded. One listing was written in French. The brands shown were "R," an upsidedown "3P," and "DE" on the French entry. Colors shown were sorrel, palomino, iron gray, black with white spots, brown, and black. A stray ad shown in the October 7, 1820, issue of the *Arkansas Gazette*, published at Arkansas Post, lists a mare with an "NV" brand. These four horse brands, then, would comprise the oldest recorded brands in Arkansas, with some possible exceptions shown in old French records and an undated brand in Hempstead County records. Two brands shown were called "Spanish brands," the first described in 1839. I found many Spanish brands in old estray books all across Arkansas.

When I started work on this story I was told that most of the old-timers rode mules. A horse "expert" who had moved into Arkansas several years ago echoed this thought, stating, "with few exceptions the old settlers preferred mules." The oldest estray books do not verify this. Mules were prevalent in Missouri because settlers there kept up a steady trade with Santa Fe, and it was the Spanish who introduced mules. De Soto and other earlier explorers brought horses. Many of the pioneers, including Captain Randolph Marcy, found that for distances over a thousand miles, mules were not as tough as the Spanish horses or oxen. Mules became more common at a later date.

The remainder of that old stray book shows horses at all sizes up to sixteen hands, but the vast majority were in the "Indian Pony" size range. Other colors shown were dun with black mane and tail, dark bay, bright bay, pinto, roan, strawberry roan, clay bank, and flea-bitten gray. The first stray mules showed up on April 9, 1839.

The *Arkansas Gazette*, as the oldest newspaper west of the Mississippi River, dates from the days when these papers carried "stray" ads or "taken up" notices. Descriptions were given of the animals found, their size, color, brand, or earmark, and an estimate of dollar value was provided. Here are some descriptions that I found while "hunting strays." From the *Gazette:*

> January 29, 1820.
> Strayed. $20 reward; Large black horse 15 1/2 hands Lost near the middle of the Big Prairie. Well built, elegantly gaited, racks and trots well. J. Woodson Bates
> June 17, 1820. Taken up one sorrel mare 13 years

old about 14 hands high, stout built, small white blaze in her face, both hind feet white. Branded on near shoulder but not legible. Appraised $40.00. Richard Searcy, J. P.

Strays, One cream coloured mare, white tail and mane, white streak in forehead 13 1/2 hands. One iron gray.

What we see here is the size, range, and the "stout build" of the Spanish horses and the naturalized horses mentioned by Nuttall. Also notice the "large black elegantly gaited" horse with a twenty dollar reward. This reward represented a month's wages at that time and shows that those early settlers were bringing English-type horses into Arkansas at that time or before. Horses that expensive were usually not ranged out and therefore in many cases were not branded.

These "elegantly gaited horses," as this old ad called them, should not be overlooked in the study of early Arkansas horses. These horses were usually tall and graceful and could do gaits called, variously, rack, single foot, running walk, or fox-trot at a pace that would make an ordinary horse gallop to keep up. Yet these gaits were as smooth as a rocking chair. Some modern horsemen have thought that these horses of the Southern gentry "were not tough and were bred only for their elegance." But those who knew them say otherwise. The old-timers tell me that those old gaited horses could hold a rapid pace all day and not tire. And they were bred for distance. Their bloodlines were Thoroughbred plus various outcrosses.

The first stray cattle were described on April 13, 1841, despite the fact that in 1805 an Indian agent had written of large numbers of range cattle on Grand Prairie. Perhaps so few cattle were taken up as strays because, as Thomas Nuttall wrote in 1819, they were "at liberty to roam without limit."

Nuttall's further observations indicate the Spanish background of those horses: "several wild horses were seen and taken in these forests during the preceding year." He said of them, "The horses of this country are rather small, though very hardy, and capable of subsisting entirely upon cane or grass, even when subjected to the hardest labour." This toughness and ability to subsist on grass without grain has been attributed to the Spanish horses' Arabian geneology. As the historian J. Frank Dobie in *Mustangs and Cow Horses* said, "to comprehend stallions that bore conquistadores across the Americas, I had to go back to mares beside black tents in Arabian deserts."

THE AMERICAN QUARTER HORSE

Through the Chickasaw and the Thoroughbred, Arkansas had a significant part in developing the American Quarterhorse. Many horse researchers think that the Chickasaw Indians, since they were allies of the English, had bred some Thoroughbred blood into their horses. When the Chickasaw horses crossed the Mississippi, they were worthy of recognition. At one time they had their own registry. Since the Chickasaw may have had a little English Thoroughbred blood, it may be that some of the early so-called Thoroughbreds may have been tainted (or blessed) by a little Chickasaw blood. It was a case of two good breeds, the Thoroughbred and Chickasaw, coming together to produce a third good breed, the quarterhorse. At the same time, the importance of the neglected Quapaw horse should not be overlooked.

Thoroughbred horses had been brought into Arkansas since the 1820s or before. The following advertisement appeared in the March 29, 1836, *Arkansas Gazette*. "Thoroughbred stallion, Tom Fletcher. $20 stud fee. Dark Chestnut 15.3 hands. Bred by O. Shelby of Tennessee. Sire: Old Stockholder, dam by pacelet, her dam by Bowie. Stockholder sired by Old Sir Archy. At farm twelve miles east of Batesville."

The noted quarterhorse authority, Bob Denhardt, says, "The most important stallion to influence the Quarterhorse after the Colonial Janus [a grandson of the Godolphin Arabian] was that Thoroughbred son of Diomed, Sir Archy.... When he retired he had no equal on the turf."

Denhardt mentions another horse that was described as the "Boss Quarter horse in America." This was the stallion Cold Deck, foaled in 1862 at Carthage, Missouri. He says this was "one of the most popular short-horse bloodlines in Oklahoma and Arkansas." Coke Blake, the pioneer Oklahoma Quarter horse breeder, who himself was born at Cane Hill, Arkansas, the same year as Cold Deck, was the only person Denhardt could find who knew Cold Deck. Blake had seen him at Van Buren, Arkansas, where a sign hung over his stall, "Cold Deck against the World!" and Blake said his idea of "the perfect Quarter horse was formed when he was privileged to see the original Cold Deck at Van Buren." It was said that Cold Deck was never beaten in a race until after he became blind.

It should be mentioned here that the English Thoroughbreds and the Spanish horses were cousins. Both had been built on Arabian horse foundations crossed with their own native stock. America has built many breeds from these types.

THE ENGLISH HORSES AND TENNESSEE STUDS

The English Thoroughbred was developed by crossing Arabian stallions with native English mares. The native mares probably already had some eastern or Arabian blood introduced by the earlier Romans. This background makes the Thoroughbred a cousin to the Spanish Barb or Spanish Moorish cross horses; the differences are due not only to the differences between the native horses of Spain and England but also to their being bred for different purposes. The English horses were bred for speed.

Jimmy Driftwood, the Arkansas folklorist whose song "The Tennessee Stud" was a big hit in the 1950s, tells of one way the herds of Arkansas were important. Jesse Jefferson Goodman, the grandfather (or great-grandfather) of Cleta, Jimmy Driftwood's wife, brought Thoroughbred racehorses to the Mountain View and Timbo area of north-central Arkansas in the 1800s and raced them there, sending back to Tennessee from time to time for stallions, each of which was referred to as "The Tennessee stud." Only a few of the offspring of any breeding program became champions. The rest entered the general population. The horses brought to Arkansas by Jesse Goodman must have had a tremendous influence on the riding horses of Arkansas. Then, as the early settlers continued to come, for the most part, from good horse country, the quality continued to improve.

OUTLAWS AND ARKANSAS HORSES

By the mid to late 1800s, the territory west of Fort Smith, Arkansas, had become the worst outlaw country in the nation. Fort Smith was as far west as the United States went when it was established. The Fort Smith *Western Independent* of August 28, 1873, said, "The length and breadth of the Indian country . . . has been the rendezvous of the vile and wicked from everywhere, an inviting field for murder and robbery because it is the highway between Texas, Missouri, Kansas and Arkansas . . . stealing horses is an everyday occurrence, murder and robbery seem to equal that sin. It is dangerous to travel alone where villains from four quarters of the United States congregate to murder, rob and steal." It was said that there was no Sunday west of St. Louis—no God west of Fort Smith.

In 1875 Isaac Parker took over as Judge for the United States Court for the Western District of Arkansas. The uniqueness of this court was commented on by the booklet, "The Fort Smith Story, 1817–1896," published by the Eastern National Park and Monument Association: "The Federal Court for the Western District of Arkansas was one of the most remarkable courts the world has ever known. This was because of the vast jurisdiction (over 70,000 square miles) and the fact that for 14 years, there was no appeal from Parker's court." That 70,000 square miles stretched from Fort Smith to Texas, Kansas, and Colorado.

Writers have extolled the team work that was required

between the "hanging judge," Parker, and his two hundred marshals. But we must not overlook the part those frontier horses played. As Judge Parker said to one of his marshals, "You'll need a good Winchester rifle and a good horse."

Good horses were certainly available in that Arkansas frontier area back then just as they are now. Some of those marshals undoubtedly rode sons of Cold Deck. Others may have ridden tough Indian ponies that were abundant in the area. There is an old picture, prints of which are sometimes seen around Fort Smith, of the last reunion of Parker's marshals. One of the old prison wagons is in the picture, but the most notable feature of it to me is that the men are mounted on fine-looking horses.

The long miles these men rode through that wild territory can be guessed at by looking at the record. In 21 years 13,490 criminal cases were docketed, 9,454 convictions or guilty pleas were entered, and 79 people were hanged. Sixty-five U.S. marshals were killed in the line of duty. Fort Smith had been a jumping-off point for westward travelers, and it was the jumping-off point at the end of a rope for quite a few criminals. The wildest of the west had been tamed by men riding out from the old fort town on the best of horses.

From the days of the conquistadores over four hundred years ago, to the Quapaw and other Indian horsemen, to our pioneer forefathers, and up to the present, a long trail has stretched. Through these dusty corridors of time have walked, trotted, and galloped the best horses the world could offer. Arkansas has been horse country.

During the California Gold Rush years, Captain Randolph Marcy wrote to advise westward emigrants to wait until they got to Fort Smith and Van Buren to purchase supplies. He wrote, "Horses and cattle are cheap here." By the close of the nineteenth century and for many years into the twentieth, Fort Smith, Arkansas, was known as "the largest horse and mule market in the world."

3

Cattle Arrive

The world's oldest profession, contrary to some sources, is the caring for and raising of livestock. The stories of many cultures tell us so. Genesis, in the first chapter, tells of the creation of livestock before the livestock herder, and in the fourth chapter, the second verse, we read that "Abel came to be a herder of sheep, but Cain became a cultivator of the ground." The early Hebrews soon came to possess large numbers of cattle, and in Genesis, chapter thirteen, verses five through seven, we find a very early written account of a range dispute. "Now Lot, who was going along with Abram also owned sheep and cattle and tents. So the land did not allow for them to dwell all together, because their goods had become many . . . and a quarrel arose between the herders of Abram's livestock and the herders of Lot's livestock."

Over the centuries of man's wandering the earth, cattle had become such an integral part of his wealth that the Latin word *pecus* or cattle became the root for the Latin word *pecunia* or money. Strangely, the word peculiar derives from the same Latin root via the word "peculate" (to embezzle), which probably explains why cattle rustlers (peculators, *pecus*, stealers) and cowboys are usually, down to this day, regarded as "peculiar." Likewise, the word "chattel" derives from the same root as "cattle," and refers to movable property or wealth as distinguished from real property. This meaning adds interest to the account of an early conflict between settlers and rustlers, as recorded by Oren Arnold in his book *Irons in the Fire*. The incident occurred in 1644 on what is today Manhattan Island. To stop the Indians' theft of their cattle, the ranchers built a strong wall of logs, six feet high. "It was a good wall and served its purpose," Arnold writes, "and it determined the name of a modern street of finance which has become famous around the world." Perhaps no other marketing center will ever record the movement of so much of man's "chattel" as Wall Street, U.S.A.

But how and when did cattle, this movable form of wealth, arrive in Arkansas? What breeds were they? What colors? What did they look like? It is strange that we should have to ask. We have documented our wars and political upheavals. Records of mankind's search for wealth in most of its forms are abundant, but references to cattle in the indexes of most history books are either absent, or material is extremely scanty on the subject.

During the wars that we have so carefully dated and documented, the soldiers marched in sandals or boots made in most cases of cowhide. We have documented the horse because it was often an instrument of war, but on its back, held in place by straps of cowhide, was a saddle made of cowhide, and when the battle was joined, its rider withdrew a sword or pistol from a scabbard or holster made from cowhide. When the old wars were won, politicians read the grand announcements and other documents from sheets of vellum, made from calfskin. Before refrigeration, cattle were a walking fresh meat and milk supply. Their horns carried powder for the muskets, were the trumpets for signals, and were made into combs to groom and hold hair. Oxen pulled wagons across continents. Cattle have been our wealth in many ways, and we have taken them for granted.

The first cattle in Arkansas could have been Spanish cattle. Spain brought cattle to North America in the early 1500s, but how they might have drifted or been driven to the Arkansas Territory would be difficult to determine. Arnold reports that the cattle abandoned by Ponce de Leon in 1521 on Florida's west coast were found as far north as Maryland when English settlers arrived there, so it would not seem farfetched to assume that some of the Spanish cattle west of the Mississippi had drifted into what would become Arkansas.

But we are not left totally with assumptions. The records of Arkansas Post are invaluable as perhaps the oldest authentic record of Arkansas's cattle industry.

THE FRENCH CONNECTION

In 1750 one or more ships sailed from France bound for New Orleans. On board were "a large number" of French ladies described in Post records as "worthy but poor girls in charge of suitable agents or guardians, who were instructed to bestow them in marriage, together with a small dowry, upon soldiers who by their good behavior were entitled to an honorable discharge from service." The final destination of these girls was Arkansas Post.

If cattle were not also on board, they had already been shipped, because included in the package deal for each soldier who married one of these girls, in addition to a small tract of land, was "one cow and calf, one cock, five hens, a gun and ammunition, an axe and a hoe, together with a supply of garden seed." All this was provided by the French government to increase the population of the territory.

We cannot be sure what breeds or types of cattle were offered to these adventurous homemakers, but cattle breeders today rank French breeds with the oldest and best the world can offer. Arkansas, as a part of the Louisiana Territory, was off to a good start, and if some of the earlier Spanish cattle from Texas had drifted or been driven into the area, they would undoubtedly have been improved by the French cattle.

How did these early families and their cattle fare? Again, records of Arkansas Post provide an answer. In the *Letter Book of the Arkansas Trading House* [Arkansas Post] *1805-1810* we find a letter from the factor, or Indian agent, John B. Treat to "The Honorable Henry Dearborn, Secretary of War," dated November 15,1805, and reading, in part:

> The population here is between sixty and seventy families nine or ten of which are from the three states, Virginia, Maryland, and Pennsylvania; the others, one or two Spaniards excepted, are all French, either natives, or those who imigrated from Illinois, N.Orleans and two or three from Europe, all of whom either reside in the village, or within a circuit of between three and four miles, there are also scattered up the River, seven or eight families, the nearest of them not residing within fifty miles and the furthest double that distance, by land, which by the River is perhaps forty leagues. . . . Horn-cattle sheep and hogs, the two first particularly, if they are to be boasted of throughout the Union, certainly those inhabitating this country will not readily yield the palm to any, and the having them to boast of, does not entitle them to much credit; for nature having made such ample provision, that man takes no trouble about them, the winters, which are so mild affording a bountiful supply of cane, and the prairies, equally abundant support throughout the other seasons of the year. Those praries one of which commencing within

two and a half miles of this village affords, when in yellow plums, a scene not to be excelled in nature, at its commencement its width is about three English miles varying from that rather increasing for the first few leagues, to eight, and ten; which is said to be the greatest breath throughout its extension to the distance of forty leagues to the north west, there we behold nature in her most varied and beautiful attire notwithstanding, not only the summer months had pass'd but the first of the atumnal; and till the coming of the frost other flowers had the appearance of shooting forth to change the scene; though, not possible to add an additional beauty to the enchanting one which had preceded through-out the season, till late in autum, large numbers of cattle are to be seen grazing here.

These were, in all probability, Arkansas's first range cattle, and tracing them back to 1750 would place their origin forty years before the ratification of the Constitution of the United States. We can only assume that those early range cattle were French breeds. French cattle today are ranked among the best and are being used to produce superior beef all across the West. Cattlemen who, in modern times, drive them to and from summer and winter ranges tell me they are good movers, but take skill in handling. This quality could account for the success Arkansas drovers had in moving herds long distances. They were tough range cattle that could endure the long trail and bring top prices at the other end.

A few cattle had existed around Arkansas Post prior to 1750. An estate settlement for a "Widow Lepine," dated 1743, lists "twelve horned cattle" plus receipts and money for around ten thousand pounds of tallow. The tallow could have been from bear or buffalo as well as domestic cattle.

The free roaming of these early herds would necessitate brands and earmarks. According to Manfred R. Wolfenstine in *The Manual of Brands and Marks*, the first Louisiana brand of record was registered in 1738. These earliest brands were probably French, as this was still French country. Branding was a very old art in France, especially in the southern Camargue region, where horses ran wild and cattle brands were ornate, much like certain old Spanish brands. Wolfenstine goes on to say that "in the Southwest, the first recorded brand was that of Richard H. Chisholn, registered with the county of Gonzales, Texas in 1832." In various editions of the *Arkansas Gazette* from the 1820s, several brands are listed on strayed stock notices. Branded horses and cattle evidently ranged the eastern Arkansas prairies and woodlands over half a century before Lewis and Clark made their famous journey.

SPANISH LAND GRANTS

In 1763 Arkansas came under Spanish control and several large Spanish land grants were awarded. These ranged in size from a few thousand acres to over a million acres. One of the most important of these grants, for this discussion, was mentioned in the *National Geographic* magazine of September 1946: "The pioneer Stillwell family ancestors of Miss Caro Stillwell of the National Geographic Society staff, settled there in 1798. Stillwell Point, on the river, is named for them, and they still run a plantation hereabouts. The Spanish gave all the land from Arkansas Post up to what is now Little Rock to the Stillwell and Winters families, provided they colonized it."

Thomas Nuttall in 1819 mentioned this land grant and the cattle that ranged there:

> The horned cattle increase and fatten without any labour or attention, more than the trouble of occasionally ascertaining their existence in the wilderness through which they are at liberty to roam without limit. . . . The cattle throughout this country are generally left to provide for themselves, and suffered to range at large, excepting such as are in domestic use. . . . No hay is provided for fodder, nor does it indeed appear necessary, except to assist in fattening for the stall, but this piece of economy, like almost everything

else which might promise comfort is neglected, and the cattle are killed just as they are hunted up from the prairies or the cane-brake. It is from the prevalence of the cane, and the shave-rush (*Equisetum hiemale*), that the cattle are kept in tolerable condition, and often even fat, through the severest part of the winter.

Spanish cattle could have been brought in during the period of Spanish control, but evidently they were not; Nuttall notes that "as to the breeds of domestic animals, no selection of those commonly raised has yet been attended to, nor any foreign ones introduced."

OUR CHEROKEE HERITAGE—WITH A LITTLE SCOTCH

As far back as the late 1770s the Cherokee Indians were beginning to settle in Arkansas bringing horses and cattle with them. They were later assigned specific territory, and part of Arkansas came to be the Cherokee Nation west until their forced removal to Oklahoma in the 1830s. As to the Cherokees' cattle, Nuttall notes on his 1819 tour through the Cherokee territory that the land was well fenced and well stocked with cattle.

A point not to be overlooked in the study of the Cherokee heritage of Arkansas is the Scotch connection. The famous Indian scout and trailblazer, Jesse Chisholm, is often referred to as half-Cherokee, half-Scotch. The story of the Scotch and Scotch-Irish migration to America—why they came, and where they settled—helps us to see the Scotch-Cherokee connection.

The Scotch and Scotch-Irish had come to America, as James W. Raine says in *Land of Saddle-Bags*, to escape what was called "tyrannical legislation" of the English. They had been prohibited from exporting horses, cattle, or dairy products to England, causing the value of their animals to drop to practically nothing. Also, high duties were placed on other export items such as wool and linen.

The fierce independence of these people caused them to seek wilderness areas where they would be unmolested as they farmed and raised livestock. So they were attracted to the American frontier. As Raine points out, the Northern Indians were not very friendly toward the new immigrants: "But in the early days the Southern Indians, especially the Cherokees, were friendly. They traded with the settlers, sold land to them, and made honorable treaties." So to this favorable wilderness came families like the Chisholms. And when the early Cherokee moved west of the Mississippi, some Scotch blood moved with them. One of the descendents of this migration was Jesse Chisholm.

WHITE SETTLERS AFTER 1803

The 1803 Louisiana Purchase, which made Arkansas a part of the United States, sparked afresh the western movement, and large numbers of cattle were involved. Four to six head of oxen were hitched to each pioneer wagon, and many more were driven along as replacements and as a walking milk and meat supply. These formed the nucleus for cattle herds in the newfound homelands.

Kirkbride Potts, who came to Arkansas from Pennsylvania in 1828, wrote these words to his sister Ann in New Jersey in 1830: "I live in the Arkansas territory . . . our land is of good quality and the country new it cost nothing to raise cattle or horses they keep fat winter and summer in the woods." Some of the old brands of Arkansas came across the Mississippi burned on the hides of cattle in the early 1800s. One of the respondents to my brands questionnaire reported that his grandfather left his enemies in Tennessee where they fell and fled to Arkansas in the mid-1800s. The brand his cattle bore, with some modifications, is still registered in Arkansas's Carroll County.

One of the old breeds that might well have been included in the herds of the pioneers was the English Longhorn, which we seldom hear of today. Discussing them in his *Cattle of the World*, John B. Friend notes that:

> . . . in medieval times the cows of this breed were milked, and the steers used to pull ploughs. At the end of their working life they were fattened and driven many miles to the meat market at Smithfield in London. This triple purpose breed became one of the most popular types in Britain prior to 1800. It was known in different parts of the country as the Lancashire, Leicestershire, Warwickshire, or Dishley breed. . . . Longhorn cattle have a dense, silky coat of long hair that varies in colour from roan to dark red and brindle. In all animals a white line runs along the back and down the tail. . . . There is also a white patch on each thigh, and the lower parts of the leg and brisket are often white.

Texas Longhorn

English Longhorn

The characteristic large horns are then described as having "a forward sweep or curve downwards and inward towards the mouth." The *National Geographic* magazine of December

1925 says further, "ordinarily, however, the horns start laterally from their base, taking various twists as they develop." Their description seems identical to that of our own southwestern Longhorns of Spanish descent. These cattle, except for being fatter and smoother, were apparently dead ringers for the famous Texas longhorn. The horns were graceful and long and carried beautiful curves. *National Geographic* notes further that ". . . specimens [of the English longhorn] were imported into the United States . . . into Virginia and Kentucky more than a century ago [a century before 1925]." Perhaps this triple-purpose breed, mixed or pure, pulled many of our pioneer forebears as they headed west into the Arkansas Territory. In any case, the story of the English Longhorn adds interest to the study of a breed that some writers have suggest originated in Texas.

Before Arkansas became a state in 1836, breeds that we recognize today had been prospering in the East and had begun showing up west of the Mississippi. Durham, or shorthorns, were among the first. Old-timers I have talked with have often mentioned Durhams or shorthorns as being prevalent here in olden times. These were cattle that were crossed with the Brahman to produce the Santa Gertrudis of Texas fame. These shorthorns, when crossed with earlier Arkansas stock, made good range cattle, and many fine herds were driven west to improve other stock.

The Hereford breed was slow in coming to America. Harold Oppenheimer says in *Cowboy Arithmetic* that Henry Clay, the prominent statesman from Kentucky, imported the first recorded Herefords in 1816. Oppenheimer agrees with most others that the breed was not known in substantial numbers in the West until the late 1800s, but I have some testimony to the contrary. As I was going through the brand books at Ozark, in Franklin County, Arkansas, the County Clerk told me that I should talk to a Mrs. Shirley Demere of that community. When I hesitated and kept turning pages, the clerk dialed Mrs. Demere and handed me the phone. I described the nature of my research, and a firm clear voice on the other end said, "My great-grandfather, William Ewin Armstrong, drove a herd of Hereford cattle to California in 1851 or '52."

"You said, 'Hereford cattle?'" "Well, my grandmother said they were red with white faces. They left here and went through Oklahoma. It was a regular cattle drive with a chuck wagon and cowboys."

Black Angus cattle did not make an appearance until after the Civil War. There were black cattle in Arkansas in very early times, and, as mentioned previously, they may have been related to the Scotch breed, but Aberdeen Black Angus, as such, were one of the later breeds to enter the state.

A few old issues of the *Arkansas Gazette* and some estray books should help us spot some favorite breeds from years gone by.

> *Arkansas Gazette*, July 29, 1820. Taken up near Big Rock. One cow and calf. Cow a red color marked with a slope on the under side of the left ear and an underbit from the right ear appraised $15.00. One black heifer with a motley face, 3 years old, marked the same as the cow, appraised $12.00. One black heifer, a motley face, and a young calf. The heifer 3 years old, marked with a swallow fork in the left ear appraised to $15.00. Edmund Hogan J.P.
>
> *Franklin County Estray Book*, Ozark, Arkansas, June 4, 1866. Black ox 6 or 7 years old. Branded left horn "F" and () left hip. Some white in forehead and some white on his belly. Appraised $20.00.
>
> Dec. 31, 1866. 10 year old steer, blueish white. Cropped left ear, slit in right. Appraised $20.00.
>
> Dec. 31, 1866. Small red cow with white belly and tail and white spot on top of the hips. Swallow fork in left ear. Red and white heifer calf. Appraised $15.00 the pair.
>
> Feb. 9, 1867. A frosty collour cow. Sharped right ear, slit in left. Appraised $16.00.
>
> Jan. 14, 1868. Heifer Calf, a red brindle with some white hides about her hips and flanks. Overbit in left ear and slit in right.

These entries were typical of estray book entries from 1820 on, all across the state.

For well over two hundred years now, since before the United States was an independent nation, Arkansas's cattle herds have been prospering and increasing. In 1850, according to the *Arkansas Historical Quarterly*, Arkansas had 292,710 head of cattle. Captain Randolph Marcy had advised those forming westward bound wagon trains to wait until they got to Arkansas to buy horses and cattle for the California trek, as they were plentiful and cheap at Fort Smith. Thousands of head of cattle had pulled wagons and been driven in beef herds from Arkansas to California from 1850 to 1860; even so, the 1860 census showed the count within the state had nearly doubled. The total in 1860 was 567,799.

The Civil War hurt, lowering the count drastically, as beef was needed for Southern troops until Arkansas was occupied. Then it was needed for the Northern forces. By 1880, however, Arkansas's cattle numbered 708,000.

That count may be a little shy, as it was taken for tax purposes and stockmen claimed they didn't know how many head of cattle they had. In *The Voices of Moccasin Creek*, Tate Page tells us, writing of cattle carrying the Scott Page brand, that "the herds were never actually totaled. . . . When the cattle-buyers came, and most of the cattle were driven in out of the woods, the numbers were astounding."

In recent years, the count fluctuates between one and two million head. Many millions of cattle have been produced in Arkansas since the French government gave to each ex-soldier of "good behavior" a "worthy but poor" French girl and "one cow and one calf."

4

Lost Trails West

THE ARKANSAS RIVER: TRAILWAY TO THE SUNSET

Hernando de Soto was determined to cross the wide river to its western shore as he and his men shoved across the Mississippi into what is now Arkansas. After an initial period of wandering around in the new territory, they headed their one hundred or more horses west, following the course of the Arkansas River. And so, just forty-nine years after America's discovery by Columbus, this land of the peaceful Quapaw, who for thousands of years had known the gentle glide of the canoe and the soft tread of moccasined feet, felt the thundering of horses' hooves. Hard steel, gunpowder, lead, fiery horses, and pale, bearded men—five things totally new to the Indian—the West was being invaded along the banks of the Arkansas River.

Over a hundred years later, Marquette entered the mouth of the Arkansas. A few years later, La Salle also brought the friendly French touch to the shores of the river, leading to Henri de Tonti's establishment of the village of Arkansas Post. It would to be the first European settlement west of the Mississippi to hold a key position in the vast western trade.

In 1687, Joutel, still chronicler for the remnant of the Gulf Coast-to-Arkansas Post expedition, reports finding such Spanish items as horses, swords, and broad-brimmed Spanish hats all across the southern and southwestern territory of what is today Arkansas; according to the Indians, most of these items had been obtained from Spaniards in the New Mexico territory. La Salle's party bargained for horses and packhorse equipment and left them in turn at Arkansas Post, thus setting up trade between Santa Fe and French settlers on the Mississippi River 144 years before Josiah Gregg established his famous trade route between Independence, Missouri, and Santa Fe in 1831. La Salle's purpose had been to establish trade with the Indians and possibly the Spanish. This trade was significant in the development and settlement of the West, especially the Southwest. (Joutel also mentions well-marked trails, and that several of the party deserted to follow those trails and live with the Indians.)

In 1740 Pierre and Paul Mallet, after reaching Santa Fe by way of the Platte River, returned along the Canadian and Arkansas rivers to Arkansas Post, convinced that this was a shorter and better route. In 1749, three deserters from Arkansas Post reached Santa Fe, and undoubtedly others followed. We are led to wonder, then, why more trade did not develop. The answer seems to lie in the fact that France and Spain used the Quapaw warriors to restrict others from using the Arkansas River as a trade route to the areas west of the Mississippi. So, it was not because the Arkansas was not as good as a trade route to the West but because it was a better route that it was held back. A look at a map of the American West shows the Arkansas River pointing like a giant finger straight towards the central Rocky Mountains, and a branch of it, the Canadian River, pointing directly towards the historically important trade area of Spanish Santa Fe.

The Quapaw blockade was not to last forever. History seems to indicate that their loyalty to France caused the Quapaw to fall when the French fell. (Even the Spanish, during the years that Arkansas Post was Fort Carlos, found it best to use Frenchmen to deal with the Quapaw.) So, over the years, settlement continued to progress upstream along the banks of the Arkansas.

From 1775 into the early nineteenth century the Cherokee, spelled "Cheraquis" by the Spanish, also moved west and settled along the banks of the Arkansas. On a warm spring evening in 1819, Thomas Nuttall described a walk near the Dardanelle, where bluffs overlook the river:

> In the evening, we crossed to the right-hand cliff of the Dardanelle, where Mr. D. again renewed his trade with the Indians and their retailors. I embraced this opportunity to make one of my usual rambles, and found an extraordinary difference in the progress of vegetation here, exposed to the south and sheltered from the northwestern wind. Proceeding leisurely towards the summit of the hill, I was amused by the gentle murmers of a rill and pellucid water, which broke from rock to rock. The acclivity, through a scanty thicket, rather than the usual sombre forest, was already adorned with violets, and occasional clusters of parti-coloured Collinsia. The groves and thickets were whitened with blossoms of the Dogwood (*Cornus florida*). The lugubrious vociferations of the whip-poor-will; the croaking frogs, chirping crickets, and whoops and hallos of the Indians, broke not disagreeably the silence of a calm

and fine evening, in which the thermometer still remained at 70 degrees.

These Arkansas Cherokee had moved west willingly, some bringing cattle and horses with them. This was a migration that in its first phases predated the Trail of Tears by as much as half a century. A few miles up river from where Mr. Nuttall made his evening walk, Spadra Creek enters the Arkansas. Here lived a half-Cherokee, half-Scotch lad named Jesse Chisholm; in the year 1819, young Jesse was thirteen. He will make his appearance in a later chapter of this story.

Following the days of the well-made dugout canoes of some of the native Arkansas Indians and the occasional visits of the birchbark canoes from the north, the flatboats and keelboats were instrumental in pushing the western frontier up the Arkansas. Buffalo hides and meat were items of trade. An early settler wrote (as recorded in the volume XI, 1952, issue of the *Arkansas Historical Quarterly*): "Then we moved to Big Mulberry [downriver from Fort Smith]. In 1816 we made up about thirty families and lived there two years in all the luxuries of life that a new country could afford, such as buffalo, bear, deer, and elk and fish and honey. . . . About that time Major Bradford came to Fort Smith and set up that post and we furnished him buffalo meat for the soldiers."

From the initial opening of the Arkansas to westward expansion, travel had not been limited to watercraft. Old invoices from Arkansas Post indicate the extensive use of the trails that ran alongside the rivers. An 1805 invoice lists:

2 women's saddles	$20.
6 men's saddles	$48.
6 saddle bags @ 3.12 1/2 pr.	$18.75
2 1/2 doz. curb bridles	$27.50
6 snaffle bridles	$4.25

A more extensive invoice of 1806 lists, among other things,

50 heavy rifles @ $11.00	550.00
25 kegs FF gunpowder, 25 lbs each @ 40	250.00

5000 gun flints	*27.00*
24 gun locks @ 2.00	*48.00*
120 blankets	*210.00*
50 blankets	*100.00*
12 men's saddles @ $7.00	*84.00*
6 men's saddles @ $8.00	*48.00*
4 doz. double rein curb bridles @ 15.00	*60.00*
6 pr. saddle bags @ 3.12 1/2	*18.75*
6 doz. spurs @ 9.00	*54.00*

An advertisement in the *Arkansas Gazette* of March 25, 1820, mentions a shipment unloaded at Arkansas Post that tells a lot about the population at that time. "Just received, 2 cases Ladies Beaver hats, 2 do. Gentleman's broad brims. . . . and 1000 pounds treble F Gunpowder." We note, among other things, that this merchant expected to sell over forty pounds of gunpowder for each man's hat. Clearly this was an outfitting post for the western frontier.

A few years earlier a key player in the frontier drama may have outfitted here. This was William Lewis, a buffalo hunter who built the first structure erected by a white man on the present site of Little Rock. This was in July 1812. The cabin was described as being about "ten feet by eight, the top covered by clap-boards." In October of that year Lewis was said to have gone "up the river hunting buffalo," as if he were Arkansas's own Buffalo Bill.

A historic item appeared in the *Arkansas Gazette* of April 1, 1820. "We are highly gratified in announcing the arrival at this place, about 10 o'clock last night, of the new elegant steamboat COMET. Captain Byrne, from New Orleans, in eight days from port to port, and 149 running hours. The COMET is the first steamboat that has ever ascended the Arkansas." Two years later the *Robert Thompson* was the first steamboat to reach Fort Smith.

By the time of the 1849 California gold rush, the following steamboats were arriving at Fort Smith on a regular basis, some from New Orleans, but many of them making regular runs to and from Cincinnati: the *Penny Wit, Ponteac, J. L.*

Webb, Alert No. 2, Kate Kirkwood, Medium Armstrong, P. H. White, Cashier, Duroc, Swallow, Oella No. 2, Cotton Plant, Sallie Anderson, Robert Morris, Hudson, Lucy Wing, and *Cora.* From 1820 until 1868 there were over two hundred steamboats that operated on the Arkansas. These went upstream as far as Fort Gibson, thereby linking the Indian Territory with Pittsburgh, Pennsylvania.

Most maps of the western movement show Independence, Missouri, to be not only the most important jumping-off point, but in many cases the only one, not even showing a dot or a line in Arkansas. One is inclined to say that this is due to dishonesty or laziness on the part of such historians, as documentation is easy to find, but there are other contributing causes for the failure to give the Arkansas River its due.

The Missouri River is navigable for a much greater distance than the Arkansas, and the Missouri angles to the northwest, reaching to fewer than one hundred miles of the Canadian border. Most writers on the subject see the fur industry and the trapper as the all-important factors in opening the West. From this standpoint, the importance of the Missouri would easily eclipse the Arkansas, since the colder northern climate produced better pelts. However, we are following the opening up and development of the West from the cattleman's viewpoint. The trapper is not the hero here, but the cowboy is.

To the west and southwest of Fort Smith the steel jaws of a trap were not nearly as much a symbol of the western movement as they were farther north. In the Southwest, it was the cowboy with his cow pony, his stock saddle, and his *reata*, or lariat, who opened the West. The miners and the trappers came to take from the land, rather than to give to it. They blazed many trails, but drovers and cowboys have always been able to blaze their own way when the time came, and besides, the buffalo and wild horses had already done that. As a friend of mine, who raises longhorns in west Texas, said recently, "It was not the gambler, or the miner, or the trapper, it was the cattlemen and the cowboys that ultimately tamed and settled the West." And while I have always been a cowboy at heart, I would add sheepherders, too, and other livestockmen, and even farmers, where they didn't plow under too much of the range land. This should be a more complete list of those who founded the West.

This is not to say that trade in animal hides was not big business along the Arkansas. We have seen that it was, but in the Southwest the cattle industry was growing rapidly in the form of range cattle. Farther north, in the Grain Belt, feed lots would flourish, but the cow-calf operations would supply them with their stock. Precisely because the Arkansas was not navigable as far as the Missouri was, the horse was forced to play a larger role, and the culture of horse and horseman developed early. It was the horseman, in glamorous fiction and in fact, that was a key figure in developing and taming the West.

OTHER RIVER TRAILS

All of Arkansas's navigable streams flow into the Mississippi or its tributaries from the territory to the west. This fact means that all those waterways were important highways to the settlement of the west.

According to Mattie Brown's M.A. thesis, "A History of River Transportation in Arkansas from 1819–1880," "It would be difficult indeed to find another state whose entire surface is so well supplied with natural highways as is that of Arkansas . . . fifty-one of its seventy-five counties are watered by navigable streams."

These streams, whether from the Ozarks or the Ouachitas, flow down from sandstone and limestone hills that were excellent livestock range. The river trailways were shipping lanes for animal hides as well as bear's bacon and buffalo beef and other items of wilderness trade. All these items mentioned were received at the "Indian factory" at Arkansas Post as early as 1805–10.

The following is from an 1806 letter from the Indian factory letterbook, p. 61: "975 pack of deerskins . . . weighing about 100 lbs each 1000 Bear skins," numerous other small animal skins including beaver, "100 buffalo Beeves, salted up the river," and "a quantity of Bears oil."

These items were said to be coming from the White, St. Francis, and Black rivers, as well as the Arkansas.

In 1818–19 Henry Schoolcraft journeyed through northern Arkansas and mentioned this continuing trade. He also revealed that at least by those years, beef from domestic cattle was being shipped along with the wild animal products. While descending the White River and passing the mouth of the Buffalo, Mr. Schoolcraft observed:

> There is now a keel-boat lying here, which ascended a few weeks ago on a trading voyage among the hunters and farmers. It is a boat of thirty tons burthen, built at Pittsburgh, and decked and painted off in the neat and convenient style of the generality of Ohio and Mississippi boats of her class, but is prevented from going higher by the Buffalo shoals. The articles brought up in it, for the purpose of exchange, were chiefly flour, salt, and whiskey, with some coffee,

calico, and a few smaller articles, In return, beaver, deer, otter, bear, and raccoon skins, bear's bacon, fresh pork, and beef, in the gross, venison, bees'-wax, honey, and buffalo beef are taken.

This was in the general vicinity of the area where one of the respondents to my 1988 brands questionnaire commented that "the Cherokee owned black cattle." So while these other river routes were not as important to the expansion of the West in general, they were important "market roads" to the expanding livestock industry of Arkansas.

The vigorous trading going on along these river routes had another side too. In many western states, the killing off of the buffalo was a drama that the curtain was drawn on before the opening of the equally dramatic saga of the cattle industry could be enacted. This was no less true in Arkansas. However, another drama blazed across the Arkansas frontier that never had the limelight focused on it: the killing off of the great numbers of bear in what was then called the "Bear State."

The old stories about the abundance of bears in Arkansas told around the campfires are verified by invoices at Arkansas Post and other written records of the Bear State. In the letter quoted earlier showing a thousand bear skins being shipped, five hundred others were later mentioned as having been brought in by the Osage Indians for shipment. A letter by Indian agent Treat claims that after paying one hunter "upwards of three thousand dollars," that hunter returned within three months with "upwards of nine thousand skins." He went out again with around one hundred and fifteen other hunters.

Most of these skins were probably deer skins, but the bear was the most sought after. Schoolcraft was told by one hunter that deer were so plentiful that they were hardly worth shooting. The village of Oil Trough, a few miles up the White River from Newport, got its name from the great quantity of bear oil gathered and shipped from that point.

One happy note among all this killing was that at least a part of the meat of these animals was used for food, and some of the surplus shipped out to other settlements. From repeated references by early writers, and from records of Arkansas Post, one might even say that Arkansas's livestock industry, as far as exporting meat was concerned, had its start with "bear's bacon, and buffalo beef."

Horseback and foot trails existed along the banks of most of Arkansas's rivers and streams. One of the White River trails was called the Bear Hunters Trail. This great network of trails and streams was invaluable in opening up the remote areas to farming and livestock ranching. Domestic cattle and horses were brought in over the same trails that had been shipping lanes for the bear's bacon and buffalo beef.

Schoolcraft observed the abundance of good grass and water. He also noticed that several of the hunter families were building more permanent dwellings and bringing in domestic livestock, especially cattle. While leading his horse down Spring River in northeastern Arkansas he stopped by a large spring that he described as rushing "out an aperture in a lime-stone rock, at least fifty yards across . . . the waters possessing the purity of crystal." Here he "discovered an elk's horn of most astonishing size, which I afterwards hung upon a limb of a contiguous oak, to advertise [to] the future traveller that he had been preceded by human footsteps in his visit to the Elkhorn Spring."

Schoolcraft said this spring "deserves to be ranked among the natural phenomena of this region." He then describes an amusing situation where he mistook the extremely clear water to be "two, or at most three feet deep," and his pack horse plunged in "below his depth, and was compelled to swim across, by which our baggage got completely wetted." I myself have observed instances of these "phenomena" in northern Arkansas and southern Missouri, where the water is so clear as to be almost invisible. This area today is in Fulton County, Arkansas, and is contained in Mammoth Spring

State Park. Mammoth Spring, among the world's largest, is said to flow at an average rate of nine million gallons per hour.

From this brief consideration we can see how important the rivers and other wilderness trails were to the developing cattle industry in Arkansas. Before 1880 the old Bear State was said to be a "commonwealth of trails," which "were used not only by travelers but by heroic cattlemen and trail drivers in marketing their cattle and hogs." The trails were used extensively all across the state. It is noteworthy to consider that by 1850, or just thirty-one years after Schoolcraft's observation of bear's bacon and buffalo beef being shipped down the White River, Arkansas's statewide census showed well over two hundred thousand head of cattle. This was long before the Bear State had become the "Land of Opportunity," with a system of modern highways. Those old rivers and trails had served well.

CHISHOLM'S TRAILS

Spadra Creek tumbles down from the Ozarks and enters the Arkansas River about twenty miles up stream from Dardanelle, the place where Thomas Nuttall took his walk one warm spring evening in 1819 and reported hearing the pleasant sound of the halloing of Indians. Here, C. W. Dub West tells us in *Among the Cherokees*, young Jesse Chisholm, his mother, and his aunt, Tiana (also called Diana and Talihina), had settled some time after 1817. They evidently lived here until Jesse was about twenty, so he spent all his growing-up years in an area where in 1830 Kirkbride Potts wrote, "I . . . think no more of killing buffaloe, bear or deer here, than I would [in New Jersey] of killing rabbit."

Here was where the Osage territory touched, and sometimes chafed against, the Arkansas or Quapaw Indian territory. Into this zone of clashes the Cherokee had come to reside, farming and raising cattle. Some say that the word

"Ozark" is a combination word from "Osage-Arkansas," though some say it is derived from "Aux Arkansas," and there are other theories.

Jesse Chisholm came to know the tragedy of war early in life. His Aunt Tiana was widowed in one of the battles between the Osage and the Cherokee, and, perhaps due to this and other such events, he came to dislike war to such an extent that he became a skilled peacemaker. I have found no indication that Jesse Chisholm ever showed fear of or hatred for the "wild plains Indians," or that they ever feared or hated him.

Jesse Chisholm was born in Tennessee in 1806. His father, Ignatius Chisholm, was of Scotch descent, and his mother, Martha Rogers, was a sister of Tiana Rogers. Her father was Captain John "Hell-Fire-Jack" Rogers. *Among the Cherokees* traces the family relationships through which Will Rogers was related to Jesse Chisholm.

Growing up in the Ozark foothills and along the Arkansas River bottoms and prairies must have taught valuable lessons to the young trailblazer and scout. He was to become recognized as one of the most colorful frontiersmen of his day. Chisholm was an excellent interpreter able to converse in fourteen Indian dialects. He was in constant demand for his services, as well as for his skills as a scout and wilderness guide in and around Fort Smith.

As early as 1839, ten years before the gold rush, when Jesse was thirty-three, he guided an expedition to California. Apparently his party took the southern route, as Grant Foreman reports in *Marcy and the Gold Seekers* that they traded with the Comanche on the return trip, purchasing several Mexican children.

To most of us, the name Jesse Chisholm evokes images of the Old Chisholm Trail, and our mind conjures up pictures of Texas longhorns. It is true that Chisholm laid out a part of that trail, though most modern researchers discount his role in this by pointing out that Jesse Chisholm was not a cattle drover and probably never set foot in Texas. This observation unfairly shrugs off the man's stature and accomplishments. The *Fort Smith Herald* of May 2, 1849, reports that "During the winter Jesse Chisholm was trading with the Mescaleros Indians on the Brazos and Red rivers when he met with a band of Southern Comanches headed by 'Oh-he-we-kee.'" The various accounts of this meeting show Chisholm describing the coming influx of whites, and he very probably pointed out the opportunities that this would offer for trading. At any rate, he talked the Indians into coming with him to the settlements, offering to be their guide and interpreter. Later, at the Seminole agency in the presence of Chisholm, these Comanche met with agent Du Val, Lieut. F. F. Flint, and others, including one person called "the sagacious Seminole Wild Cat." On this occasion important peace agreements were made, and all evidence is that as long as Jesse Chisholm lived, the Comanche were easier to deal with.

In *Marcy and the Gold Seekers*, we read that

> The merchants of Fort Smith stocked their stores with large quantities of merchandise to supply the great demand of the gold seekers and traders. One of these was Abel Warren, an old and experienced Comanche trader, who, early in July, 1850, purchased several thousand dollars worth of goods. He outfitted a trading expedition in which he was assisted by Jesse Chisholm and Black Beaver. His object was to purchase mules from the Comanche and Apache Indians and he expected to bring back 500 or 600 the next fall or winter, prepared to sell them to California emigrants in the spring.
>
> These goods filled three large ox-drawn wagons; Chisholm commanding a convoy in charge of this precious cargo, took his departure from Fort Smith for Cache Creek to trade with the Comanche Indians.

Grant Foreman goes on to include the following eyewitness account from one of a party of gold seekers who, arriving at Fort Smith by river boat, reported seeing a line of black dots in the Arkansas River.

> At first I thought the black dots to be ducks, but now I saw that they were forty or fifty of the faithful mules. As they emerged from the water I saw all of them were very small and thin in flesh. As they struck dry ground they dropped down and commenced rolling in the dirt and grunting. After a little they would get on their feet, shake themselves and bray with seeming joy....
>
> These animals belonged to one Chisholm an Indian trader with the wild Indians of the great plains and the Mexicans.

These mules and horses brought in from the Comanche and Apache would quite often, according to Captain Marcy, have a Mexican or Spanish brand. An American brand, from north of the border, can usually be "called" or "named"; for instance, a lazy "J" or circle "R" or a simple letter or combination letter brand. But Mexican or Spanish brands are sometimes so purely visual and complicated that they cannot easily be read. I was reminded of this while going through an old estray book, in the courthouse at Ozark. On page three I found this notice: "Following description and valuation of said beast and we do value the said mule to be worth forty dollars description of said mule is a black horse [male] mule 9 years old branded . . . with the Spanish Brand. Dec. 22, 1866." This might well have been one of the thousands of mules stolen from Mexico by the Comanches, and possibly even brought to Fort Smith by Jesse Chisholm.

When we study the history of the Comanche and the Apache, we cannot help but marvel at the courage, diplomacy, and skill Jesse Chisholm must have possessed to be able to trade among these tribes all his life. An example of Chisholm's good influence among the Comanche is recorded in *Cherokee Cavaliers*, by Edward Everett Dale. At a council in which some Northern army officers during the Civil War attempted to persuade the Comanche to massacre Southern whites, and in which Jesse Chisholm served as interpreter, a Northern officer offered the Comanche a large amount of goods, including many guns and much ammunition, if they would make war on the South, kill all the men and boys, take the women and children prisoner, and steal the cattle and horses. The Northerners promised to take the white women and children and buy the livestock, but said the Comanche could keep the Southern Indian women and children.

Chisholm advised the Comanche (in Comanche, not understood by the officer) not to listen to "the Northern men's bad talk." The Comanche Chief told the officer in turn that he had friends and brothers in the South and would not make war on them. He would, instead, stick to a treaty he had signed with Albert Pike. The officer replied that in that case he could not have the guns and goods. To this the Chief said that he would do without the guns, that he could still kill the buffalo with his bow and arrows.

In 1989 at Medicine Lodge, Kansas, I was told of a history-making peace council held there in 1867, when thousands of Indians of several warring tribes were gathered to join in a treaty of peace. The infamous Sand Creek, Colorado, massacre of peaceful Indians had made the tribes hard to placate. I was not surprised to learn that Jesse Chisholm, along with his friend, Delaware Chief Black Beaver, were there, helping to coordinate the event and serving as interpreters. The council is recorded in volume II of *Chronicles of Oklahoma* published by the Oklahoma Historical Society.

It was said of Jesse Chisholm by those that knew him, Indian or white, that he was "a square shooter, a square dealer, and a man with a straight tongue." It is doubtful that any of the rough, tough element that rode the trail that bore Chisholm's name could compare with him. This remarkable scout, trailblazer, and peacemaker, who spent his teen years around Spadra Creek, Arkansas, left an indelible mark on the West.

Jesse Chisholm died on March 4, 1868, less than a year

after the Medicine Lodge Peace Council. Some say he died from eating bear meat cooked in a galvanized bucket, but whatever the cause, the frontier had lost a good man. His creed reminds us of the creed of early Arkansas Indians who were called "those good people" by the Frenchman, Joutel. "No man ever came to my camp hungry, and went away unfed, or naked and departed unclad. All my life I have tried to live at peace with my fellowman and be a brother to him. The rest, I leave with the Great Spirit, who placed me here and whom I trust to do all things well."

THE BUTTERFIELD STAGE: "KEEP THE WHEELS ROLLING, OR THEY'LL SLIDE"

> Most drivers would have been content to drive slowly over this spot.... But our Jehu was in a hurry with the "first States' mail" and he was bound to put us through in good time. I suggested to him that a bad man riding on this road was on the very brink of the bad place and likely to depart thence at almost any moment if anything should break. He said, "yes, but they didn't expect anything to break," and whipped up his horses just as we started down a steep hill. I expected to see him put down the brakes with all his might but he merely rested his foot on them, saying, "It's best to keep the wheels rolling, or they'll slide"; so he did keep the wheels rolling ... down the steepest hills at the rate of fifteen—yes, twenty— miles an hour, now turning an abrupt curve with a whip and crack and "round the corner, Sally," scattering the loose stones ... and nearly taking away the breath of all.

These words were written in October 1858 by Waterman L. Ormsby, special correspondent for the *New York Herald,* and the only through passenger on the history-making, record-breaking first run of the Butterfield overland stage.

On September 16, 1858, Mr. Ormsby had written:

Today the first overland mail to San Francisco from St. Louis and Memphis, started from this city, under the direction of Mr. John Butterfield, the president of the company.... Thus is inaugurated, under the administration of Mr Buchanan [U.S. president], a second great event of the age. The first linked two nations together [completion of the laying of the Atlantic Cable in August 1858], the second cements a union of the extremes of a nation separated heretofore by time and distance, but now to be united by the facilities of rapid communication; . . . and I think I may safely pronounce it another great event of the age.

That first run of "the Butterfield overland mail," the first transcontinental stage line, broke several records. The total distance from Memphis or St. Louis to San Francisco of approximately 2,800 miles set a distance record surpassing that of any American stage line, and the time of twenty-three days and twenty-three-and-a-half hours broke all previous time records across the vast western territories. In addition it was the largest mail contract ever given up until that time, and it shut a record number of mouths by proving that the southern route to California via Fort Smith was a good and practical route. Indeed the merits of that route were proven by the fact that for the three years that the overland stage ran, it was late only three times. Modern transit systems, even airlines, can hardly equal that record.

The northern route had many advocates. The political and commercial interests of the areas involved pointed out the advantages of the more direct route via Independence, Missouri, by the North Fork of the Platte, through the South Pass of the Rocky Mountains, via Forts Laramie and Bridger, to Salt Lake City, thence to the branch of the Oregon Trail, at latitude 42 degrees, and thence almost directly to San Francisco. But, for Butterfield's stage, the route was impractical. Waterman Ormsby reports in *The Butterfield Overland Mail*:

This route can hardly be said to have entered into competition with the others in the selection of the great overland mail route . . . the temperature is almost universally conceded to be too cold to admit of the possibility of running stage coaches semi-weekly the year around, as provided in the present contract. Gen. Burr, the Surveyor General of Utah, found snow from twenty to forty feet deep during the middle of April, in the Rocky Mountain passes. . . . Though the route was partially advocated by a certain ignorant journal in your city, which takes pains to imitate your typographical appearance, it was never seriously thought of by any one at all posted on the subject. the recent success of the new mail arrangements have, however, rather enhanced its reputation as a summer route.

The value of a similar northern route as a summer cattle drover's trail had already been demonstrated by Arkansas cattlemen, but it was rejected as a suitable year-round stagecoach route.

The road from Fort Smith, Arkansas, to El Paso, Texas, was the same, except in minor details, as the wagon road discovered and recommended by Captain Randolph Marcy in 1849 for California-bound travelers. Marcy deserves the credit for this road and other roads that never bore his name. He employed Indian guides and located the only practical route in those years for skirting and crossing parts of the staked plains of Texas. Marcy measured the road with tape, made marks and notations where water could be found, and wrote for future travelers a wealth of information that could and undoubtedly did save the lives of many westward-bound pioneers.

In *Marcy and the Gold Seekers*, Grant Foreman points out:

Captain Marcy's road became part of the great highway over which emigrants traveled from the East through the Indian Territory to El Paso and California. In 1858, when the overland mail service to California was established on the southern route,

John Butterfield carried the mail over the principal part of Marcy's road. Butterfield employed more than 100 Concord coaches, 1,000 horses and 500 mules, and nearly 800 men. The stages traveled from Fort Smith to Boggy Depot and crossed the Red River just below the mouth of Washita River on Colbert's ferry. They passed Sherman, Gainesville, Fort Belknap and on to the Horsehead Crossing of the Pecos River a short distance below where Marcy crossed; and then on to El Paso, and beyond to California.

Some who opposed the southern route called it "Butterfield's oxbow route," referring to the southern curve the route made for geographic reasons. Marcy was told by some of the Comanche that even they didn't cross certain parts of the Texas staked plains except following good rains. However, it should be noted that more areas than St. Louis, Independence, and San Francisco were to be served by the new stage line. Important developing settlements all across Arkansas, the Indian Territory, Texas, New Mexico, Arizona, and southern California stood to benefit by that much-criticized "oxbow" route. It was not so much an oxbow if you lived in the South or were arriving by steamship from New Orleans.

Arkansas was the only state that had two branches of this historic stage route within its boundaries. The following quotation is special correspondent Ormsby's impression of a part of the Arkansas route from the north.

> Fayetteville is in Franklin County [actually Washington County], Arkansas, among the hills of the Ozark range of mountains. We left there on Saturday, the 18th inst., at two minutes before noon—just twenty-two hours and thirteen minutes ahead of the time required of us by the time table. Even among these hills you do not lose sight of the prairie nature of the West; for just after leaving Fayetteville you see a fine plain, surrounded with hills—in fact, a prairie in the mountains. After a rather rough ride of fourteen miles, which we accomplished with our excellent

team in one hour and three-quarters, we took a team of four mules to cross the much dreaded Ozark range, including the Boston Mountain. . . .

I might say our road was steep, rugged, jagged, rough, and mountainous—and then wish for some more expressive words in the language. . . . I can only say that our mountain views in the Highlands of the Hudson are but children's toys in comparison with these vast works of nature.

The term "Boston Mountain" is, I believe, derived from a prevailing western fashion of applying that name to anything which is considered very difficult. But Connecticut hills and roads are mere pimples and sandpaper compared with the Ozark ranges. By hard tugging we got up, and with the aid of brakes and drags we got down; and I can assure you we were by no means sorry when the herculean feat was accomplished. The mules which took us over the mountains carried us, in all, about nineteen miles, when we took another team of horses to carry us to Fort Smith.

We crossed the Arkansas, in a flatboat much resembling a raft, at Van Buren, a flourishing little town on its banks. Our course through the soft bed of the flats (which were not covered, owing to the low state of the river) was somewhat hazardous, as our heavy load was liable to be sunk on the quicksands which abound here. But by the aid of a guide on horseback, with a lantern (for it was night), we crossed the flats, and up the steep sandy bank in safety. Picking our way cautiously for five or six miles, we reached Fort Smith on the Arkansas River, just on the border of Arkansas and the Indian Territory, at five minutes after two o'clock A.M., having made the sixty-five miles from Fayetteville in fourteen hours and seven minutes, or three hours and seven minutes less than schedule time. We had anticipated beating the mail which left Memphis, Tenn., on the 16th to meet us at Fort Smith, several hours; but as soon as we entered the town, though at so unseasonable an hour, we found it in a great state of excitement on account of the arrival of the Memphis mail just fifteen minutes before us.

But, though they had 700 miles to travel, five hundred of them were by steamboat, from Memphis to Little Rock, and it was said that they got their mails before we did.

On the Memphis branch of Mr. Butterfield's route stood the then new stagecoach station built by Mr. Kirkbride Potts. This to my knowledge is the only stagecoach station on the entire route paid for with the proceeds from long-distance cattle drives. Mr. Potts had sold the last of two herds near Red Bluffs, California, in the fall of 1857, and Mr. Butterfield had made his historic first transcontinental run in the fall of 1858. Potts had taken the northern route. But nine years before, in 1849, Mary Conway had made even a bigger splash by riding a tall black horse, and setting hearts awhirl, all along the route taken by the Butterfield stage. Records and hearts had been broken for 2,800 miles of trail in the great American Southwest.

THE CHEROKEE TRAIL: COWBOYS AND INDIANS UNITE

On February 3, 1849, a group of Cherokee Indians met in Tahlequah, Indian Territory (now Oklahoma). In a time when cholera and other white settlers' diseases were rampant, these Indians had succumbed to another serious white ailment, gold fever.

This preliminary meeting was to lay the groundwork for the Cherokee mining company. The purpose of this company was to provide the strength and organization necessary for an overland trek to the California gold fields. The trail used by this adventurous party would become one of the most used routes to the West, and it would possibly see more cattle driven over it to feed hungry miners and to stock more ranches than most of the famous cattle trails known today. Yet, this venerable old trail is one of the most unknown, the most forgotten, and least publicized of any of our pioneer routes. It is truly one of those old lost trails.

Most historians never mention this trail, and their maps

showing pioneer routes show not a dot or a line where it went. Descendants of the emigrants and drovers who traveled it list the Oregon Trail, the Mormon Trail, or the Independence Trail as the route their forebears followed, never knowing that the Cherokee Trail even existed.

Among the provisions set at that first meeting was one that there were to be no fewer than a hundred fighting men in the company. Each was to be armed with a rifle and three pounds of powder and nine pounds of lead. Other details such as wagons, teams, and tools were discussed, and the Indians' white neighbors from Arkansas and Missouri were invited to attend succeeding meetings. Since Arkansas had been the home of many of the Cherokee prior to the 1830s, they had many friends there.

On Monday, April 24, the 130-member party, including some whites, met. Lewis Evans of Evansville, Arkansas, was elected captain of the company. Other officers were: Thomas Tyner of Washington County, Arkansas, first lieutenant; Peter Mankins, second lieutenant; James S. Vann, secretary; and Martin Matthew Schrimsher, commissary. The last two were members of the Cherokee Nation.

Old records indicate that their company was referred to not only as the "Cherokee Company" but also sometimes as the "Lewis Evans Company" or the "Fayetteville Gold Mining Company and Cherokees."

A look at the list of names in the company shows that a number of those who later drove commercial herds of cattle to California were along on that initial trip. These included John Carter and William Shores, owners of the herd and outfit mentioned in the Columbus Seay letter describing an 1853 cattle drive. Also on the roster were the Holmes brothers, who later drove several herds, the first in 1852, from Rogers, Arkansas, to California.

According to records in old copies of the *Cherokee Advocate* and noted in *Marcy and the Gold Seekers*, the company, at its departure on April 24 and 25, 1849, consisted of forty wagons and about four hundred head of horses, mules, and oxen.

The record says that they camped just northwest of the site of present-day Claremore, Oklahoma, on April 27. (By coincidence, one hundred and forty years later, on April 27, I saddled my horse just west of Claremore and continued my ride from Arkansas to California, following the same old Cherokee Trail.)

The Prairie Traveler, by Captain Randolph Marcy, describes the route of the trail as it was used later by cattle drovers and other westward travelers. The trail progressed from Fort Smith, Arkansas, to Fort Gibson, Indian Territory, and there crossed the Grand River. Drovers and emigrants, leaving from Fayetteville and adjacent points, would strike the Cherokee Trail north of Fort Gibson, the exact point depending on their points of departure. Further progress according to Marcy was "thence up the valley [of the Verdigris River] . . . for 80 miles, when it crosses the river, and, taking a northwest course, strikes the Arkansas River near old Fort Mann [just west of present-day Dodge City, Kansas], on the Santa Fe trace; thence it passes near the base of Pike's Peak, and follows down Cherry Creek [near present-day Denver, Colorado] . . . to its confluence with the South Platte, and from thence over the mountains into Utah, and on to California via Fort Bridger and Salt Lake City." When *The Prairie Traveler* was published in 1859, Utah contained part of what is today Wyoming and Colorado.

Some earlier writers referred to that part of the trail that ran over the already existing Santa Fe route as the Cherokee and Santa Fe Trails. However, the original Cherokee Trail proper was the part of the route that left the Santa Fe Trail to the point where it connected with the California Trail at Fort Bridger, near present-day Mountainview, Wyoming. The Cherokee Company was said to have been the first to travel that route in its entirety.

One naturally wonders why the Cherokee Company and the later drovers would go so far north through Wyoming. The answer seems to be that they wanted to avoid the highest and most rugged parts of the Rockies and skirted around them to the more favorable terrain of southern Wyoming. However, there was no need for them to go as far north as the Oregon Trail, or the other South Pass routes, as some historians may have thought.

There were many advantages to avoiding those overused emigrant trails. The Cherokee Company and the drovers undoubtedly found more grass for their cattle by staying away from those trails, and the trek through southern Wyoming was shorter for those coming from Arkansas. Later cattle drovers may have varied their route from year to year to adjust to available grass and other varying conditions, but they still generally followed the Cherokee Trail. Southern Wyoming, incidentally, has a greater consciousness of the Cherokee Trail than any place I visited along the historic old route. At Encampment, Wyoming, I researched old documents relating to the trail that to my knowledge are to be found in no other libraries or museums, anywhere in our nation.

There seem to be some differences of opinion as to where the trail went through Wyoming. My research and my ride across the entire distance on horseback indicate that the Cherokee may have taken several different routes. At times they may have split up to explore the best route, as Elva Evans points out in a paper, "the Cherokee Trail," in the Grande Encampment Museum. "For those explorers and travelers coming west across the Laramie Plains suddenly a little range of mountains stood firmly in the way, the Snowy Range. Some of the Cherokees went south around it through North Park, across the Platte River near the state line, across the Encampment River at Riverside, across Cow Creek at the old Al Huston Ranch, and thence northwest to Twin Groves."

The main body of the Cherokees, according to Kleber Hadsell, "traveling in wagons from the present site of Laramie, paralleled the Overland Trail, crossed the Medicine Bow River about eight miles south of Elk Mountain, then southwest through pass Creek Basin and over Oberg Pass, down Lake creek and to the North Platte River. After crossing the river they went west to Twin Groves where the two trails merged."

Another part of the Elva Evans's paper clarifies another side of the trip through Wyoming: ". . . it is evident that they had little fear of the Ute or Mountain Indians but desired if possible to avoid the plains or Arapahoe and Cheyenne Indians which were powerful tribes at that time. They probably also considered that the nearer they could keep to the mountains, the better, purer and more frequent would be a good water supply, timber and game." Further west, according to this paper, "the Overland went through Bridger's Pass, while the Cherokee Trail went south by way of Savery."

From Fort Bridger west, the Cherokee and later cattle drovers would follow the California trail on any of its several variations. Records indicate that the original Cherokee went through or by Salt Lake City and down the Humboldt River across Nevada and on to California.

The Cherokee Trail proved to be a good route for cattle drovers. Material published by the Kansas State Historical Society in the book *The Beginning of the West* indicates that the number of cattle driven over that trail may have been much greater than historians are aware of. A contemporary newspaper, the *Fort Smith Herald*, cited in *The Beginning of the West*, reported: "Droves of Cattle may be seen every day, in our city, for California. . . . The road to California will be filled with cattle from Arkansas for many miles, we have no doubt but 100,000 head will go from our state."

Of course many of these may have been driven over the Southern route, via El Paso, Texas, and the Gila trail. But another item from *The Beginning of the West* quotes an 1854 observer as saying that he had seen "large droves of Cattle . . . from Texas and Arkansas" along the trail between Bridger's Pass and Salt Lake City. He also reported that "the number of cattle taken over that road the past summer was about 25,000." There may very well have been many other herds taking branches of the trail that observers didn't see. Moreover, if the head counts of various drives were taken in Salt Lake City, we may have a very underestimated number. Many drovers, according to actual letters, bypassed Salt Lake City after leaving Fort Bridger and went through Idaho and on to California.

Information at The Grande Encampment Museum, at Encampment, Wyoming, paid fitting tribute to that old trail by commenting on the trails of southern Wyoming:

> Perhaps the earliest known trail was the Cherokee. . . . When the Cherokees returned they journeyed down to the South through Carbon County to Cherokee Pass, La Porte and back to Arkansas. This first migration over the trail discovered and made by them was long before the days of any Wyoming organization.
>
> The real significance of this old thoroughfare is not so much in the story of its origin as it is in the use made of it by the emigrants in the ensuing years. In endless procession, in every type of vehicle, through all the summer months for a period of years, men and women wended their westward way from Arkansas, Oklahoma, and Missouri and even from parts of Texas, seeking new lands, new homes, and fresh adventures.

JUSTICE ON THE TRAIL

The cattle trains and mining companies from Arkansas were in most cases well organized. This was an important factor as it helped to insure that problems would be handled that might otherwise hinder the successful completion of the drive or emigration. The Clarksville and California Mining Association was a good example of practical organization for such a company. The articles of association for that company help us to realize that our pioneer forefathers in many cases were men of strength and character, foresight and determination. The articles specify everything from how much weight each wagon in the train will bear to the officers that will be in charge of the wagon train to the amount of liquor the train will carry.

This train departed Fort Smith around the middle of April 1849, and Foreman points out in *Marcy and the Gold Seekers* that the Clarksville company was "composed of a large number of men with 100 yoke of oxen hauling twenty wagons." they traveled part of the time with or near the Little Rock mining company. Robert Brownlee, who traveled with the Little Rock company, recorded in his journal that "the Clarksville, which was an ox train, had, say 600 oxen," and "200 saddle horses." The Clarksville company was evidently driving along a sizable herd of cattle in addition to the work oxen. These were probably some of the first cattle driven to California during the gold rush years. Driving along extras would allow members of the team to be replaced, and provide a walking food supply and an extra cash income, in the event all were not needed along the way.

This train took the southern route and traveled for some distance south of the Mexican border. Brownlee reveals in his journal that the Sonoran governor had proposed to "levy a $40. tax on each of the company's wagons." He said that Captain McVicar of the Little Rock Company "showed that he was a no-nonsense man" by announcing that if the governor insisted on a tax they would "pay it in powder and lead." I did not discover whether either train paid the tax (in lead or gold), but on re-entering the American territory the train followed the Santa Cruz River to join the Gila River Trail. It was along this stretch that a tragedy happened that caused the previsions of their articles of association having to do with the government of the train to be enforced, and future travelers would read the following statement found attached to a stake by the road: "This spot is made memorable by the tragic fate of two young men from Arkansas: the two, one by the name of Davis, the other Hickey, quarrelled and fought. Davis proved the stronger and was taken off, whereupon the other rose and stabbed Davis through the heart, causing his instant death. The following day Hickey was tried by his company, condemned and shot for murder."

The two evidently were drovers, or were working as such

when the quarrel started. George Hickey said Elijah Davis had threatened him while they were watering the cattle. A witness said Davis was not along when they drove the herd to water, but was hunting for a missing steer. Davis showed up later, and the quarrel seems to have developed over Hickey's threats to whip a younger member of the company. At any rate the fight developed, and according to testimony at the trial Hickey yelled, "Take him off," and while two men pulled Davis off, Hickey rose and stabbed him with a knife. Davis lived only about ten minutes after the stabbing.

The murder happened on September 5, 1849, and the council was called together that same day. The horn was sounded and Captain Redmond Rogers served as judge. The facts of the case were brought out, and a death penalty was handed down by the jury.

The encampment assembled again the following day. The execution verdict was sustained by a forty-six to eleven vote. Hickey was said to have made light of the proceedings, as though he didn't really believe he would be executed.

The place for the execution was chosen about a mile from camp, and a military-style firing squad was used. Twelve riflemen were selected by drawn lots. Six rifles were loaded with powder and balls and six with powder only. No rifleman was to know if he had a rifle loaded with powder and balls or just powder. The rifles were stacked and a blindfolded member (Dave Logan) was selected to hand out the rifles.

A. D. King, a second captain of the train, recorded the final scene. "When the place of the execution was reached Hickey was placed on his knees near the open grave and blindfolded. A white piece of paper was pinned directly over his heart. The firing squad then took their positions and at the signal of the 'Ready, Aim, fire,' the 12 rifles were discharged and Hickey fell back dead. Four of the rifle balls had penetrated his breast."

The Clarksville Mining Company continued onward to California.

5

The Cattle Drives

THE DROVERS

The days of the cowboy have not ended and may never end, but the days of the drovers are past. Once also called a cowherd, or a herder, he drove herds of cattle two thousand, even three thousand miles. The days of the big Texas longhorn drives came after the Civil War, from the late 1860s until farming and homesteading closed the trails near the turn of the century.

The drives described in subsequent chapters, however, occurred in the decade before the Civil War, from 1849 to

1857, and while they didn't involve the millions of cattle that moved across the land after the war, they did involve many thousands and were generally over twice as long as the later drives. And while the movies, T.V., and novels have endlessly romanticized the post–Civil War drives, the earlier smaller, but longer drives have been all but forgotten. Not only is truth stranger than fiction, it is often more exciting, more tragic, more exhilarating, more shocking, and in many cases even more romantic and more unbelievable.

The romantic heritage of the drover and cowboy is generally considered to be entirely of Spanish origin, and in truth many of the things we consider western and associate with the cowboy culture did come from Spain by way of Mexico. In fact they came from the Arabs by way of Spain and through Mexico. The deepest roots of the hot-blooded horse, braided leather, the guitar, and many other facets of the cowboy's arts and way of life were really of Arab origin. But remember, the same horses of the Arabs had also influenced the horses of England, and that ultimately the horse culture of the world was perhaps affected more by England than by Spain. Certainly nobody's horses ever consistently outran the British horses. Speed is not everything, and I myself prefer the Spanish and the pure Arabian horse, but this is not an uncontested view. As one western rancher put it, "No speed no horse," and in the words of another, "The only time the [English] Thoroughbred hurts is when you ain't got it."

Just west of the Mississippi River, Mr. Kipling's assertion notwithstanding, East and West met as these two cultures came together. Here is where the Spanish saddle improved the English saddle, where *la reata* became the lariat, where "naturalized" horses or wild horses—perhaps descended from De Soto's and other Spaniards' horses—blended with the English Thoroughbred to produce the world's best cow horses, the long-distance horses of the drover. Here is where the Spanish cattle interbred with the English white-faced cattle and other breeds, and here is where the bronze-skinned *Homo sapiens* who had crossed the Bering Strait or the Pacific from the Far East met, fought, and intermarried with the pale-faced *Homo sapiens* from Europe. Here is where the American cowboy was born.

We are accustomed to thinking of the *vaquero* tradition south of the Rio Grande, but not so much of a cowboy tradition in the United States before the western movement. There was, however, a strong tradition of horsemanship in the Old South, from which many of the cowboys came. Clement Eaton writes in *History of the Southern Confederacy* that "Southern planters were trained to ride horses from their youth, and a love of fine horses was characteristic of the plantation gentry," and in his recent book, *Cowboy Culture*, David Dary points out that Southern colonists had, from the start, herded and rounded up cattle on horseback.

A Civil War cattle raid and drive headed by Wade Hampton, a famous Civil War cavalryman from South Carolina, bears on this subject. On September 14, 1864, Hampton led a cavalry troop of between 2,500 and 3,000 some 50 miles and to encircle over 50,000 Union soldiers. About 5 o'clock the next morning they attacked the Union troops and within two hours had started back toward their own lines with the object of the raid: around 2,400 head of beef cattle to relieve hunger in the Southern ranks. Many of these ex-rebel cavalrymen from the Southern states, including Arkansas, drifted over into Texas following the Civil War and had a part in the postwar drives north. Quite a number of Southern horsemen had preceded them, some ending up at San Jacinto and at the Alamo.

So western horsemanship came to be as a convergence of two paths: the path of Southern culture as well as that of Spanish culture. Clearly few of the cowboys who drove herds all the way to California were tenderfeet. They had grown up on the frontier; most or all were probably familiar with the Indians' inter-tribal sign language. Many knew from childhood how to handle range cattle, and most were mounted on horses that would have been a credit to cattle drovers anywhere in the world.

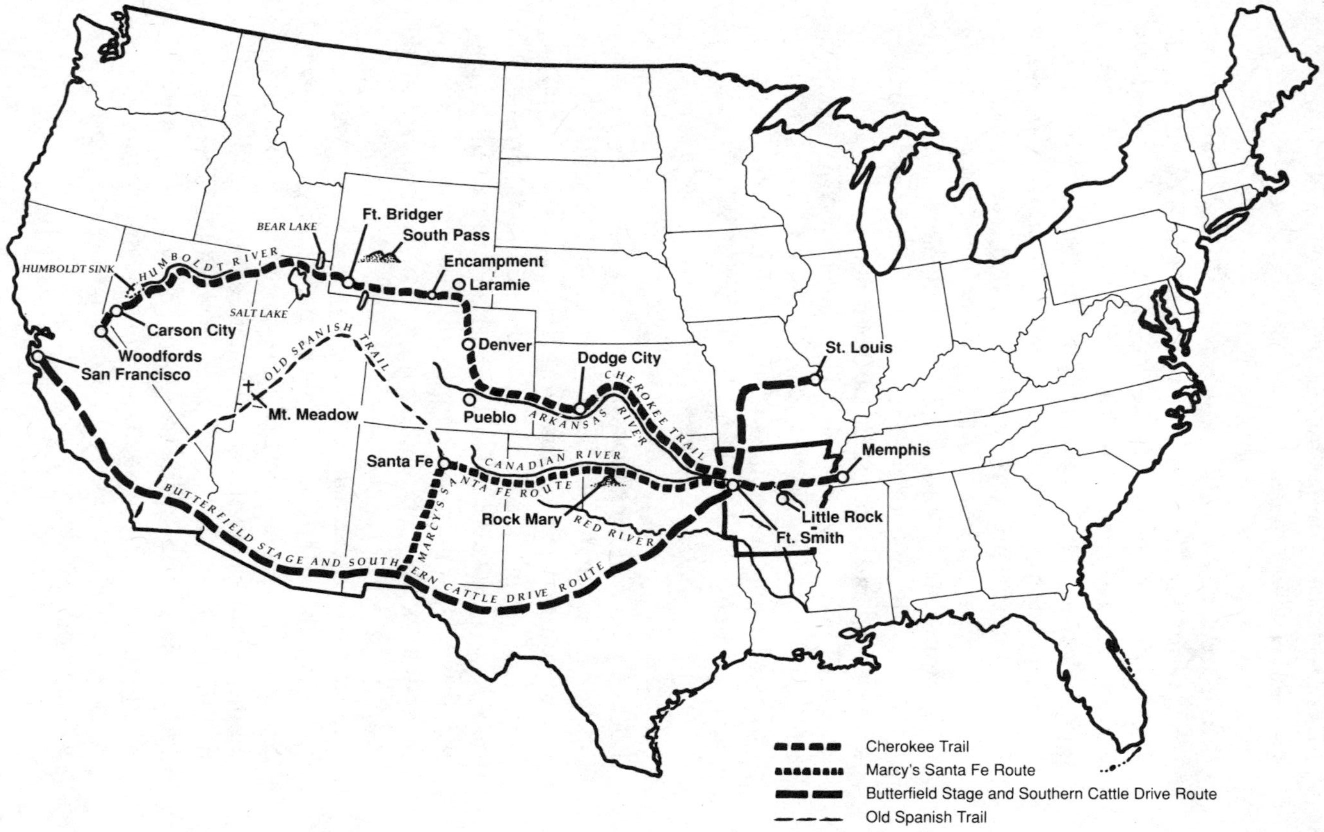
Ft. Bridger
South Pass
Encampment
Laramie
Denver
Pueblo
Dodge City
St. Louis
Memphis
Little Rock
Ft. Smith
Santa Fe
Rock Mary
Mt. Meadow
Carson City
Woodfords
San Francisco
HUMBOLDT SINK
HUMBOLDT RIVER
BEAR LAKE
SALT LAKE
OLD SPANISH TRAIL
CHEROKEE TRAIL
ARKANSAS RIVER
CANADIAN RIVER
MARCY'S SANTA FE ROUTE
RED RIVER
BUTTERFIELD STAGE AND SOUTHERN CATTLE DRIVE ROUTE
Cherokee Trail
Marcy's Santa Fe Route
Butterfield Stage and Southern Cattle Drive Route
Old Spanish Trail

But why California? The state had a surplus of cattle in the early 1800s. Around 1810, though, and afterwards, a series of droughts caused the California ranches to suffer badly as cattle starved and disease followed. Also, conflicts with Indians led to the loss of thousands of head. All this took place just a decade or so before the great influx of immigrants, thousands each day, by the 1850s. The supply of beef was lowest just when it was needed most.

Many of the Arkansas drovers had been to California earlier and, not finding gold, had seen richer opportunities. Back in Arkansas there was an oversupply of good range cattle that in California would sell for fifty dollars or more a head and in Arkansas would cost ten dollars or less. The stage was set for the saga of the long-distance drovers.

JAMES MILES MOOSE: THE BIG JUMP

Imagine this:

A herd is grazing the early summer grass along Cherry Creek in the foothills of the Colorado Rockies where Denver will one day stand. The night air is pleasantly cool, and the Arkansas drovers are using their cow horses to drag up a good supply of firewood for the evening's entertainment. As large dead logs are thrown on the fire, the flames leap and crackle, sending sparks spiraling upward where they seem to blend with the stars until they burn out.

There is a keg of whiskey and to decide who would pay to tap it, they come up with the idea of a broad-jumping contest.

"Okay Moose, it's your turn," yells one of the drovers, as young James Miles Moose, barely twenty-six, stands back from the starting line, eyes sparkling with the challenge. A few days before, he had climbed Pikes Peak, farther south, and later had killed a deer for camp meat. His herd of Arkansas range cattle grazes nearby. His dream is to drive the herd all the way to the California gold fields and to make a small fortune doing it.

Moose makes his run for the starting line, the fringe on his buckskins flying. At the line he makes a tremendous leap, to the shout of the other drovers; when the distance is measured, he has jumped twenty-one feet. James Miles Moose doesn't have to pay for the drinks. "A pretty good jump for a Moose!" someone shouts, as the handsome young man waits to be offered his reward.

James Miles Moose was born in Tennessee in 1827 and came to Arkansas with his parents when he was eleven years old. His father, John Lewis Moose, had come from North Carolina, and, with two sons, James and his brother, had been among the first to reach the California gold fields in 1848. James Miles had returned to Conway County, Arkansas, in 1851 and had purchased the herd of cattle he drove to the then-fabulous California market. With the proceeds from this venture he invested in rich farmland in and around where Morrilton, the present-day county seat of Conway County, stands. By the time he returned to Conway County he had traveled on horseback at least five thousand miles, or roughly one-fifth the distance of Magellan's voyage around the world (if Magellan had traveled a straight line, that is).

In 1987, while researching this story, I was eating breakfast in a small cafe on the north side of Morrilton, the place where the Moose drive had started. I asked the cafe owner if he had grown up around there, and when he answered yes, I asked, "Ever hear of a man named Moose and a cattle drive from here to California?" He said, "No," and as I finished my last cup of coffee I could see Moose Street in my mind's eye, running north and south alongside Division Street, dividing Morrilton east from west. It is said that once a coin had been flipped to see if the little town would be named after the Morril farm to the west and become "Morrilton" or the Moose place to the east and become "Mooseville."

On the west side of Moose Street is the Kordsmeier Western World and Furniture Store. Mrs. Kordsmeier is a great-granddaughter of James Miles Moose.

The Kordsmeiers raise quarterhorses and rodeo stock on

their Rocking K ranch, and both Mrs. Kordsmeier and her daughter, Tracy, rodeo frequently, roping calves and riding steers and broncs.

On the south side of the little town of around seven thousand, on the road to Petit Jean Mountain, stands the elegant James Moose residence, built by the drover himself in 1866. A little to the west, back toward Moose Street, stands the home of Charles Reed Moose, grandson of James Miles, where I learned from James Moose's granddaughter-in-law of the climb up Pikes Peak, the killing of the deer, and the jumping contest.

That day I had been invited to photograph a branding on the Winrock ranch, on Petit Jean Mountain just south of the Arkansas River, near Morrilton. As I drove up on Petit Jean I could see below me miles of the great river as it stretched its winding course to the West, pointing out the trail of the long-distance drovers a century ago, west along the Arkansas almost to Pikes Peak, then north, to where Denver and Fort Collins now stand, on north to the Medicine Bow range, then bending westward, ever westward, and on to California.

WILLIAM EWIN ARMSTRONG AND THE TRAIL DUST OF TIME

"My great-grandfather set out to drive a herd of Hereford cattle to California in 1852 or '53."

"You say *Hereford cattle?*"

"Well, my grandmother said they were red with white faces."

I had this conversation with Shirley Demere of near Ozark, Arkansas, in the summer of 1988, as I mentioned before. I was not aware, at that time, that enough Hereford cattle could have been found to justify a western drive of such distance in the mid-1850s. Harold Oppenheimer reports in *Cowboy Arithmetic* that Henry Clay from Kentucky was the first importer of Herefords, but that they were interbred with

77

his shorthorns and "their identity was lost." Oppenheimer says, incidentally, that "Colonel Charles Goodnight . . . was probably the principal pioneer in introducing Herefords to Texas and the Southwest." The foundation of his herds came from finch, Lord, and Nelson of Burlingame, Kansas, in 1883, long after the drive Shirley Demere spoke of.

Mrs. Demere went on to share some interesting details of her great-grandfather, William Ewin Armstrong. In 1838, he had one horse, and his personal property tax was 12.5 cents. The following year he had a horse and a cow and his tax was 25 cents. The cattle drive story came to Mrs. Demere through her grandmother who said "it was a regular western cattle drive, with cowboys and a chuck wagon." The drovers left Carroll County with the herd several days ahead of Armstrong, and he planned to catch up later. The herd was probably into Indian Territory when Armstrong died, of unknown causes, and so he never rejoined the drovers.

He had sold forty acres of land and all his belongings to purchase the herd. Some time earlier, he had gone back to Kentucky for his bride; possibly he had also brought cattle back to Arkansas, in which case the herd he started toward California may very well have been Herefords.

This is all that is known of the drive. At the same time that William Ewin Armstrong rode into the sunset, his herd of cattle disappeared into the trail dust of time.

CARTER-SHORES: THE COLUMBUS SEAY LETTER

Owners of the fifteen hundred brands currently registered in Arkansas were recently asked to respond to a number of questions, one of which was the following: "Do you have any information on cattle drives (a) through Arkansas from Texas (1860)? (b) from Arkansas to California (1850–1860)?" The space was usually either left blank, or drew a response such as, "Never heard of any such a thing."

However, a few had heard of these drives, and one respondent put me in touch with a treasure: a letter describing an entire trip, written by one of the drovers of an 1853 drive. It began near Fayetteville, evidently with the purpose of stocking two separate ranches in northern California, one owned by a Mr. John W. Carter and the other owned by a Mr. William D. Shores. It is reprinted here from the *Cincinnati, Arkansas, 1836-1986*, a publication compiled by Juanita Wilson and published by Siloam Springs Printing, in Siloam Springs, Arkansas.

Editor, "Argus";—

At your solicitation I will give you a sketch of my trip over the plains to California in the year 1853. I and five other boys, viz: L. Hill, D. Crumley, Sam Kelley, F.. A. Licklyter and John A. Tennant made arrangements with John W. Carter of Cane Hill to drive stock for him to California. Mr. Carter and William Shores had gone to California in 1849, and returned the winter of 1852 to purchase a drove of cattle and drive them to California in 1853.

I was then 19 years old, and Mr. Carter agreed to pay me $8 per month. I started with two small mules of my own. We left Cane Hill on the Morning of April 9th and went to Mr. Shores who lived near Fayetteville, where we remained four days. On the fourth day we loaded our six wagons hitched four yoke of cattle to each wagon and moved out about 150 yards from the house and struck camps. This was done in order to see that everything was in readiness to make an early start the next morning.

All things being ready, we drove our heard [herd] of cattle, consisting of 550 head, and made good days travel, camping that night on the Lindsley Prairie. [Lindsey's Prairie was near Siloam Springs, Arkansas, which was not yet a settlement in 1853.] Then we crossed to the Indian Territory, crossing [Grand?] River at the Salt works, thence to Verdigres. There were no settlements after crossing Grand River. At the Verdigres we lay over for a few days so that we might get better grassing for our stock. Here we got 150 more head of cattle. We then had 700 head of cattle and about 50 head of horses and mules. After renewing our journey, in a few days had many sore-footed cattle caused by walking over the fresh burned stubs.

When we left the Verdigres we took what was then known as the Lewis-Evans trail. (Evans crossed the plains in '49.) [We] traveled a few days passing through skirts of timber. One evening we camped on the open prairie and found no wood for fuel. Timber was in sight, so some of the boys said they would get on their mules and go bring some wood. Mr. Shores said "Boys it is at least ten miles to that timber." Then they concluded not to go. We just walked out on the plains and gathered "Buffalo" chips for fuel, and in order to keep the wind from blowing our fire away we dug pits in which to make the fires.

About this time some emigrants fell in with us and it was amusing to see the ladies gathering buffalo chips in their aprons to cook their meals with. In a few days we came to Walnut Creek. Here we had plenty of wood. The next night we camped on Cottonwood Creek and next morning struck out on the open plains in good earnest, occasionally we could find a little willow brush for fuel. So far plenty of good water and grass. Then we came to an Alkali pond once in a while, occasionally losing a cow from drinking too freely of the water. In a few days we came to a U.S. fort, then called Fort Man, and in a short time after leaving him there came to the Buffalo range.

They seemed to have a line of trail drawn extending north, and I couldn't see a track 50 yards east of the trail. They would consume all the grass west of the line and then move further east. We were among them 2 or 3 days and as far as the eye could see the whole plain was black with them. In some herds there look as if there were thousands. The first evening after we came to the buffalo and horses, about twenty head, ran away with the buffaloes and we had to run in ahead of them and circle them back to the train. They must have ran 12 or 15 miles. When we stopped to camp that evening Mr. Shores got off his fine mule which he had purchased at a high price to ride across the plains, when it broke loose from him and ran away with the bridle and saddle, and the last we saw of the mule he was tearing across the prairie with a heard [herd] of buffaloes. We had a pretty bad time keeping the buffaloes from stampeding our cattle, and were glad when we got out of their range.

I killed only one buffalo as we had but little time to fool with them. Just as we were camping the day after we had passed the buffaloes we saw a band of wild Indians coming in a line of battle, all in a sweeping gallop over the plain. I will here say; that there was [a] scared boy for a little while. I heard someone say something to Mr. Shores about them and he said he thought them to be a hunting party after the buffaloes, and so they were. They came in 150 yards of us and halted, and the leader rode out in front of them and made some signs. Mr. Shores motioned him to come up, when he said they were after the buffaloes and wanted something for his men to eat. Shores told him to bring up his men which he did and ordered them to dismount. Mr. Shores then brought out some Sugar and Hardtack, and the leader issued it to them. They all got on their knees in a straight line and in this position ate their bread and sugar. I judge there were fifty of them. When it began to get good dusk they mounted and left for their own camp.

The next morning, as we were leaving they passed us, all mounted on good ponies. About this time we struck the Santa Fe trail, or rather roads, as there were two broad well beaten roads about 30 feet apart. Here we found the finest mosquete grass [mesquite] that we saw on the plains. On the night before two of our horses got loose and started back for Arkansas. We found where they had come into the road about two miles from camp, and four of us started to follow them, while the train moved on. We found them about 2 o'clock about a quarter of a mile from the road, and when we left the road to go to them they jumped up and ran like wild antelopes. I suppose we ran them five miles before catching them, and if it hadn't been for the long ropes with iron stake pins which they had tied around their necks, we would not have got them at all. We then had to go to the train that night, as there was no chance of anything to eat until we did. We caught up with it between 11 and 12 o'clock hungry and nearly worn out.

In a few days we struck the Arkansas River and traveled up this stream to the Rocky Mountains. I have carried wood many evening across the river on my mule. We left the mountains to our left and came to a very cold swift stream, called the Cash la Tudy [probably the Cache la Poudre River in Colorado] and had to make a raft to cross it. Here a little incident occurred that was amusing to all of us save one; Uncle Cal Shores pretended to be sick. He didn't want to get wet, he said. So as we had to wade in about three feet of water, Uncle wanted some one to carry him across. About 20 of us proposed to do this, but he was afraid to risk any of us, so a man by the name of Fritz proposed to carry him out dry. Uncle Cal thought he could be trusted so he got on his shoulders with many an admonition to walk carefully. Fritz started out but his feet became tangled and down he went carrying Uncle to the bottom. Then there was some nice apologies made by Fritz.

We had hard work getting our cattle across the river, and had to croud [crowd] some of them into the water before we could get them started, and then four steers broke away and ran off and we never could get them back into the river. We heard of several trains trying later to make them cross but they failed. Right here I will speak of another hard ride I and four other boys had to make while on the Arkansas. (When there was any hard riding to be done among us who owned our own horses or mules had to do it.) We were ordered back and looked among droves of cattle that were behind us for any stock that we might have lost, as we would lose some occasionally, and any drover coming across lost stock would bring them along until the drover called for them.

We started after an early breakfast, passing trains

every few miles until about noon we came to no more trains that day, but about dusk we thought we heard bells and travelled on till about 8 o'clock, still hearing those bells, But no train could we find, so we turned off the road into the prairie and camped, but had to go to sleep without supper. At daybreak the next morning, we mounted and started down the river again after those bells which we could still imagine we heard. We travelled until 8 o'clock then having sighted no train we turned back and reached the last train we had passed the day before, at dark. We spent the night with them and were treated like brothers. We reached our own train after dark the next night.

After we got across the Cash la Tuty, another train came up, but they had no cable rope so the boss wanted to borrow ours promising to bring it on after getting his train across the river. The boss of the train was a Baptist preacher and when he got across he just sold the rope to another train for $25.00 and pocketed the money. Then he rode around hunting cattle we had lost, and found several head, so we heard. Shores sent some men back to find them but they failed to come across him.

In a few days after leaving the Cash la Tudy the Indians stole some horses and mules from us. One night a severe storm came up and water ran into our tent so we had to set up most of the night but one of the boys kept us in good spirits preaching Baptist sermons. When day came there was not a cow to be seen, but we found them about five miles from camp behind a large mountain.

I will just say that driving cattle over the plains is the laziest work I ever did. I would go to sleep every day after noon, on my mule and very often when I would wake up would be near the front of the heard [herd] of cattle. The next stream that was of any size was the South Platte river, which we forded but when we came to the North Platte we spent nearly two weeks making a ferry and getting across it. Several head of our cattle were drowned in crossing. After leaving this stream we would find only very bad water, and used sage brush for fuel. When we came to a patch we loaded it in our wagons for fear we could not find any at night. Good grass so far.

The next stream of size was called Medicine Bow Butte, and when we crossed it was fordable but heard three days later that it was one half a mile wide. Along here we came to some snow drifts and one cow ran into one of these drifts and bogged down. This was on the 4th of July. flowers were in bloom within two feet of snow. The next place of importance was Green River which was wide, deep and very swift. We were detained several days at this stream and finally crossed by lashing two wagon beds together. They made a very good boat and we got across dry and alright. In a few days we struck the head waters of Bitter Creek. It certainly has the right name, for the water is very bitter. Traveled down this stream over 100 miles and then passed a U.S. Fort, the name of which I have forgotten. It was about 50 miles from Salt Lake City.

We struck Salt Lake Valley about the 20th of July. Lay over one day and went to the city. The prettiest town I think I ever saw. Here some of my comrades got mad at Mr. Shores and left the train. They were intending to walk to California, but I could not stand to see them start afoot so I turned my mules over to them, telling them if we ever met in California they could pay for them. I then drove a wagon on to California.

We passed through the city leaving the lake to our left, thence through the settlement for about 40 miles, when we came to Bear River. Here a Mormon had a ferryboat for the accommodation of immigrants. We got there at noon and had to wait until 1 o'clock next day before our turn came. His charge for ferrying a wagon across was from $5 to $8, owing to the weight of the wagon. He would lift one wheel of each wagon then make his charge, receive the money, go to his tent and sit down and we did the work.

In a few days we struck the Humboldt River. At first the water was clear and cool, but it did not remain so as we traveled further down it became impure from so much dead stock in the river. When we camped at night and went to the river for a bucket of water to drink and cook with there was no use to go above a carcass to get water for you could look up the river and see more of them. All there was to do was to dip up the water as quickly as possible and hurry away.

After traveling down this river we came to the trail that led to Oregon, known as Lossom Trail. As we were going to Northern California we took this trail, which we had to cross. The first day we traveled 25 miles when we came to a small spring. Found water enough to cook with and by working till late at night and getting at it early the next morning, [we got] enough to fill our water kegs, but none for our stock. The next water was 50 miles further on. We traveled all day and until 8 o'clock in the night when we stopped to rest our teams. There wasn't 50 head of loose stock with the train. They must have scented the water and deserted the train in their haste to get to it.

Mr. Carter rode on and reached the spring at daybreak. Most of the stock was already there. At daybreak the train moved on and got to the water about 10 or 11 o'clock. Here we found plenty of grass and water, but the water was boiling hot and stock had to go a mile or so down the brench [branch] before they could drink the water. The spring was the largest I ever saw. It must have been 40 or 50 feet across and the water would boil up every little bit 3 or 4 feet high. Don't know how deep it was. We tied two 40 foot ropes together and let them down but found no bottom. The next day we traveled about 3 miles passing many springs, though not so large as the first one. Neither were they so hot, and stopping to rest our men and cattle.

Renewing our journey the next morning we came to a small creek which we traveled up to its head. Before we came to the head of this creek, we passed through a narrow rough canon [canyon] about two miles in length. The canon [canyon] was not over

100 yards wide at any place, with almost solid rock walls about 100 feet high. Then we came out on the high plains.

The next important place was the Great Sierra Nevada Mountains. It took us one whole day to get over the mountains and we had to hitch eight yoke of cattle to each wagon, to get up, and the wagons were nearly empty, too. It was nearly two miles up the mountain and about three down. We then struck a fine level timbered country and came to a lake called Goose Lake. Here a company of U.S. Calvary was stationed to protect emigrants from hostile Indians. These Indians had masacreed a train of emigrants the year before. Some of the soldiers went with us for three days as guards. After leaving Goose Lake we passed many smaller lakes. One day we had some cattle give out on us near one of these lakes and the next morning [we] could see smoke where the stock was left. The Indians had come from their hiding place, killed the stock, and were cooking them. Some of out boys and the soldiers went back with determination to kill some of the Indians, but they failed, as the Indians hid in the lake. I think these lakes are in Oregon.

We then came to Lost River. It was about 50 yards wide, the water cold and clear. We crossed this river on a natural bridge as the river was somewhat swollen. The bridge was under about two feet of water. After passing over some rough country we arrived at Yreka City in the Northern part of California. We then crossed the Scotts Mountain into Scotts Valley. On the western slope of these mountains was the tallest and mot beautiful timber I ever beheld. Scotts Valley was Mr. Shores' journeys end and Mr. Carter lived about 100 miles further south. So Shores and Carter settled, Shores kept all the wagons as there was no wagon road through the mountains to Carter's. Nothing but a pack trail. five of us boys accompanied Mr. Carter on. After taking our departure we went up Scotts River to its head, going up the mountain. Right on top of the mountain there are two springs not more than ten feet apart. One is the head of Scotts River, the other the Trinity River. We started down the Trinity.

We were ten to fifteen days making the trip and had to live on salt meat and slap jacks till we got near Weaverville, when Mr. Carter went to the town and brought some provisions back to camp. We were tired of living on what we had been eating and we got away with that grub in short order. The next day we passed through Weaverville and across [the] Trinity Mountains to Mr. Carter's Ranch which was located in a small valley on Trinity River.

We reached our journeys end on the 10th day of November 1853, having been on [the] road five months and twenty-seven days. I will just say that such a trip as that is enough to try any man. I must say that Mr. Carter came nearer being the same all the way from Arkansas to California than any of us. He was a wholesome man.

KIRKBRIDE POTTS: THE CATTLE DROVER WHO PAID THE TAVERN BILL

Galley Creek July 1, 1830

Dear Sister

I received your letter yesterday and was mutch pleased to hear from you. . . . I live in the Arkansas Territory four hundred miles from any of my connections. . . . The land which I live on belongs to the general government, and I hold a preemtion wright to the land that when it comes into market I have prefference to it. I have bin living here near two years and raise more corn and wheat than we consume but live on a public road where I can sell all the surplus. . . . Our land is of good quality and the country new it costs nothing to raise cattle or horses they keep fat winter and summer in the woods. . . . I married Pamela Logan February the 10, 1828.

. . . My sister, I must tell you that I see more pleasure and happiness now than I ever did in my life living with a fine and agreeable woman. . . . I am doing well I have a very good start in the world more cattle and horses than we use hogs and beef are always fat without corn. Therefore we have the corn to sell, nothing could induce me to live in jersey now for I can make more in one year here than I can there in five with the same labour. . . . I do not think I should tell you a lie if I should say that two hundred families moved by us last fall and winter principally from Kentucky and Tennessee some few Missouri. I am now pretty much reconsiled to the back woods and think no more of killing buffaloe bear or deer here than I would there of killing rabbit. . . . I write in a hurry but do not fail to answer this as soon as you get it and direct it to me Pope County Gally Creek Arkansas Territory, give my love to aunt Lydia and uncle Samuel all my cousins and inquiring friends I shall now conclude by subscribing myself your affectionate Brother

Kirkbride Potts

This letter, carrying the imprint of the original old wax seal, is in the Potts family letters collection of the Arkansas History Commission at Little Rock.

Kirkbride Potts, according to family records, came to Arkansas from Pennsylvania sometime in the 1820s and was then a young bachelor. Pamela Logan, his wife, was a member of the pioneer family that gave its name to Logan County. Potts had homesteaded one-hundred-sixty acres of land in adjoining Pope County following the 1828 treaty with the Cherokee Indians.

Open-range grazing was plentiful in those years, and by the 1840s Potts was well established in stock raising, farming, and building. John L. Ferguson and J. H. Atkinson tell us in *Historic Arkansas* that by 1841 Thoroughbred horses and Durham cattle were being raised in Arkansas, and Potts was in on the ground floor.

According to a letter written to his sister Ann, dated 1852, he had been to California two years earlier. In his words:

> I went by land across the plains the distance from here is about twenty five hundred miles. We were

five months making the trip. We took wagons as far as the great Salt Lake where the Mormons live and from there on pack mules. We saw a great many Indians on the route and a great deal of wild game. Such as Buffalow Elk Antilope and deer and occasionly a grisly bear we killed quite a quantity of game so that we had fresh meat the most of the time but it is a long and fateagueing trip and well calculated to wear out the patience of almost any one though I saw many families on the road who appeared to enjoy themselves very well indeed. As I returned I came by water that is mutch the shortest trip making it in about six weeks.

Following this adventure, Potts, who may have had a degree of success in mining, started building a home that still stands today and according to "Potts Tavern-Historic Stagecoach Station," a leaflet published by the Pope County Historical Foundation, was lived in by the Potts family and descendents from 1858 until it became a museum in 1970.

This still-sturdy structure is described as one of the best preserved stagecoach stations on the Butterfield Overland mail route between Memphis and Fort Smith. Standing in the town of Pottsville, the building has two-and-a-half stories, modeled after the great houses in Potts' home state of Pennsylvania. Almost all the wood was cut on the homestead and hauled by oxen to a local sawmill. The boards were hand-planed; some of the marks from the plane bit can still be seen. The brick used for the nine fireplaces was made on the place, and the molds and racks are on display. It is, as it was, a plain and functional frontier home and stage depot.

When money for the project ran low, Potts turned to one of the surrounding country's most abundant forms of wealth, cattle, and during the next few years drove two herds to California. Here is a letter from one of those drives, printed at the time as an open letter.

Ark. Gazette and Democrat
Sat. morn. July 25, 1857

Letter from Kirkbride Potts, Esq.

Red Bluffs, California, June 15, 1857

Dear Captain: I have no doubt you will be somewhat surprised at receiving a letter from me, situated as I am, at this time almost on the confines of the state of California, herding a little over three hundred head of cattle. I left my home, in Pope County, on the 22nd of April, 1856, expecting to have returned last winter; but not getting an offer for any stock that I thought would justify for the time, trouble, and expense, I concluded to stay one summer with them and bring them into market this coming fall or winter. They are now in fine order, and will be very fat by November, at which time I hope to meet a good market for them, and return to Arkansas by January, if possible.

The crops are very light here this year, owing to the drought in some portions of the Sacramento Valley. The wheat and barley have been dead and dry for a month. In other places, more favord by Providence, a good half crops will be made. In the extreme North, about Humbolt Bay, they have had plenty of rain and have fine crops. I suppose taking California all over, good half crops will be made—sufficient probably for the present population. I see an occasional number of the Gazette and Democrat in this country.

Beef is down to ten cents on foot, owing to the quantity of Mexican cattle pushed into market. Last winter American beef was 12.5 to 13.5 on foot, and I think will bear that price again the coming winter. There is not much large American Beef in the country; a few thousand head have been driven in from Oregon this spring; but it is doubtful if they get to be good beef by fall. They come in as poor as cattle driven from the States across the plains; and the grass being very short, and pretty much dried up, but few of them will be fit for the market the coming fall. I should be pleased, Captain, to hear from you. My post office is Red Bluffs. Hoping this may meet your eyes fully restored. I remain yours.

Kirkbride Potts

So we know that Arkansas cattle were not only classed as "large American beef," but were tough enough to stand the 2,500-mile drive to arrive in as good a condition as those driven in from neighboring territories. We know, too, that the drover period would not last indefinitely as a "quantity of Mexican cattle" were being moved in.

Kirkbride Potts evidently sold everything, including teams and wagons, and returned by water, making the return trip "in about six weeks."

The following information is provided at the Potts museum.

> fourteen buildings were on the home acreage, according to old documents, providing barns for stagecoach horses and the Potts' animals, a chicken house, tack rooms for stage and family leather goods, carriage houses for Potts' wagons and buggies, house or barn for overnight stagecoaches, a smokehouse, a well house, two servant houses, a six-hole privy, and the main house. The well house and the smokehouse are the only remaining auxiliary buildings. A doctor's office and a milk house are additional buildings also restored.
>
> The guest room downstairs was used by distinguished guests many times on their way up and down the Arkansas River Valley. Besides the stage passengers it was used by river people who tied up at Galla Rock. . . . Governors, military officers, and Cherokee chiefs shared the hospitality and delicious fare assured by Mrs. Potts.

To my knowledge this is the only existing stagecoach station that was paid for with the proceeds from long-distance cattle drives.

Potts Tavern today is as imposing as ever, a landmark that gave the little town its name and gives reality to the past and to a pioneer cattle drover who, not counting return trips, rode five thousand miles behind two herds of cattle to pay the tavern bill.

THEY TOOK THE SOUTHERN ROUTE:
MAYES AND HACKETT

Historians still wonder why more drovers did not choose the southern route. It was known to have had a longer snow-free season. It was a much shorter route, especially if the drive originated in Arkansas, Oklahoma, or Texas. One might assume that the northern route was favored because it avoided the deserts of the Southwest. If this was originally the reason, they would certainly have been very disappointed when they crossed northern Nevada and watched the Humboldt River gradually diminish in the desert, to disappear completely at the Humboldt sink. Captain Randolph Marcy reported in 1858 that while traveling the Humboldt route, "I seldom found myself out of sight of dead cattle for 500 miles along the road." This was in August, and, as he said, "large numbers of cattle pass over the road annually," soon to "consume all the grass in these barren localities."

Clearly, hardships could not be avoided over either route. The high altitudes would bring snow, rain, and bone-chilling cold, and the deserts would wring a drover out, dry him up, and feed his horses and cattle to the buzzards. However, some did choose the southern route.

One drive, possibly one of the first by a mining company intent on a supply of beef for its own operations, was the Clarksville Company, which according to Robert Brownlee cited in Patricia Etter's *An American Odyssey*, had around six hundred oxen and two hundred saddle horses when it left Fort Smith in the early spring of 1849.

Two other drovers who used the southern route were Samuel Mayes and John Hackett. Both had been to California earlier with mining expeditions. The Cherokee Indians, who had previously been among Arkansas's first cattlemen and had transferred their herds to Oklahoma, were then living in the Indian Territory, and it was from the Cherokee that Mayes obtained both financing and cattle. In about 1852, Mayes mortgaged a slave to a son-in-law of Cherokee Chief John Ross for $1500 and bought a herd of around three hundred head of cattle. These were driven over the southern route to be sold near Sacramento, and evidently a small fortune of around $6,000 was realized, equal to perhaps $150,000 today. However, intrigue and murder on the trail prevented the return of the money to the Indian Territory with its rightful owner.

Still another drover to choose the southern route was John Hackett, who had also been to California before. He was with Captain Dillard's company in 1849, traveling in close proximity to the Clarksville Company's six hundred head of cattle. Hackett had been in position to observe and learn on the first trip.

In 1853 John Hackett returned to Arkansas where he gathered a herd of between nine hundred and one thousand head of cattle and headed up his own long-distance drive. No chronicle of this drive has come to my attention, but it would surely be worth reading. Hackett was reported to have arrived in Stanislaus County, California, with only 182 head, and he settled there to farm and raise livestock. If the survival of the fittest was at work on these drives, California received some good cattle.

JOHNSTON AND JOHNSTON: TWELVE HUNDRED
HEAD OF CATTLE THAT LEFT NO TRACKS

Emigrants to the Far West were usually accompanied by their families. This increased the likelihood that a journal would be kept. Sometimes emigrants would travel in company with cattle drovers for mutual protection, so that any journal became also a record of the drive. Cattle drovers themselves rarely kept journals.

In April 1854, John I. Johnston and his son, James, started a herd of around 1,200 head of cattle to California. The herd must have left from the vicinity of fort Smith, as it was mentioned by Priscilla McArthur in *Arkansas in the Gold Rush* as being outfitted by Johnson and Grimes, a Fort Smith outfitter of the day. An ad in the March 14, 1848, *Fort Smith Herald* reads, "10,000-lbs. first quality bacon for sale by Johnson and Grimes," and a later ad (March 7, 1849) advises, "Mules! Mules! Mules! Twenty or thirty good mules for sale for very low for cash. Johnson and Grimes." The ad was dated at the bottom, Dec. 6, 1848.

The only additional detail known about this drive is that with them were "a number of emigrants."

Perhaps, in this case, no news is good news. Almost certainly, if there had been, say, a massacre, it would have been documented in some way. I like to think that this was a team of experienced drovers who simply "drifted 'em on through" without fanfare, and so the pages of history took little note.

J. H. SPARKS: A DROVER'S DIARY

The small diary was well made and covered with brown leather. It measured seven and one-half by five inches. The drover flipped back the flap that protected the edges of the closed pages, opened the book, and wrote: "Commenced crossing my cattle Tuesday 18th of April 1854, and on Sunday the 24th camped at Sam Lattimores 3 miles out. Remained there Monday and Tuesday. On Wednesday started, and the route from there to Fort Gibson can better be imagined than described. Suffice it to say that it is the meanest road in the world, both for wagons and cattle. Hind axel of Singletons wagon broke 2-1/2 miles out and fore axel of same wagon at Salisaw, and fore axel again 2-1/2 miles from Salisaw—the weather very broken, hail and rain."

This train of seven hundred head, over fifty horses and mules, and seven wagons belonging to J. H. Sparks crossed the Arkansas River at Fort Smith in the spring of 1854. The diary kept by Sparks is of great historical value, even though—aside from the expense and inventory pages—only twenty three entries were penned. The first entry is quoted above. On May 27, he wrote "Wolf Creek, rain all day. Good campground here. Rain all night." Then the diary ends.

The record is mostly of rain and hail and broken axles and broken wagon wheels. Interestingly, the inventory included "40 spokes and bows . . . $160" indicating that this problem had been anticipated. On the bright side, frequent entries mention "water plenty and good, good grass." Or "good grass, W & W [water and wood] plenty." These commodities would decrease, however, as the drovers moved westward.

On May 12, Sparks reports simply that "On same creek [not named] 1 mile below, broke a wheel, stopped + fixed. Heavy thunder and hail storm at 10 OC at night. Cattle broke, got all back." Those five words, "cattle broke, got all back" undoubtedly represented several miles of hard, muddy riding, claps of thunder, flashes of lighting, and rain and sweat running together.

A look at the expense account and inventory brings the drive into still clearer focus. The captain of the train is listed as "Capt. Rogers," probably the O. F. Rogers listed later on the general roster as having two personal horses, "Kib & Ajax." Each rider's personal horses were listed and named in addition to twenty-four company horses. J. Wheeler is shown to have had "Jimmie Mules," (two or more mules are evidently indicated here), and one animal is listed in the company's remuda as "sorrel mule."

The horses' names are a little different from some we hear today. In addition to such common names as Nelly, Red, Big Red, and Button, we find such names as Smith, Coodz, Preacher, Puss, Warhorse, Wolf, Dick Jumper, Doctor, Swendt, Boston, Jenney Lynde, Hoouber, Hooper, and Blucker.

Several entries on wages are of some interest: 6 months herding—$48 (or eight dollars per month, the same as nineteen-year-old Columbus Seay was paid the year before with the Carter-Shores drive over the same route). 1 month $22.50 (so by the time we add the "free room and board," we could calculate for easy figuring around a dollar a day).

Arms and ammunition—$150 (translating in today's terms to around $4,500); cooking utensils—$75 (or $2,250 on today's scale); saddles, bridles and blankets—$75; 6 Buffalo robes—$30; 4 wall tents—$100. The seven wagons were valued at $525, "1 pr. leggins" or chaps at $5. Buckskin pants were $5 and a pair of boots were $10. One buckskin coat was listed at $12.

Among items bought at "Gib" (presumably Fort Gibson) was listed "one violin string—fifty cents." This may have been for an instrument brought along for the entertainment of the drovers or for the purpose of soothing the herd at night. Probably for both.

The riders whose primary assignment was with the herd were listed as "herders," and the total number of twelve was divided into three groups or shifts of four each. Herders 1: M. Jones, I. (or J.) P. Williams, Bob Plunket, and W. Henry. Herders 2: Adam Ross, John Wheeler, C. Azrhandt, and L. Ball. Herders 3: T. Wheeler (evidently Theodore, mentioned in a later incident), P. (illegible), H. Bell, and T. Costello.

The wagon master was named as R. Plunket, and four guards were named: I. (or J.) A. Smith, I. [or J.] H. Taylor, W. Hecket, and A. Euper. Three men were listed as cooks or a cook and two helpers. The other names on the roster were probably fortune seekers working their way to the gold fields.

The herd followed the Cherokee Trail past Pikes Peak and later bedded down near Cherry Creek, near the present site of Denver where the James M. Moose drive had staged its jumping contest to decide who would pay for the keg of whiskey two years earlier. Here an argument arose between one of the drovers, Theodore Wheeler, and a man named Brown from Cincinnati, Ohio. Two shots rang out, one immediately after the other. Wheeler fell dead and Brown followed. The second shot had been fired by Tuge Rector who, being from Fort Smith, was probably a friend of Wheeler's. Brown's name was not on the roster; he may have joined the train later. Wheeler and Brown were buried side by side in the same grave.

J. H. Sparks and his herd and caravan were reported to have wintered about ten miles out of Salt Lake City and to have pushed on to California the following spring of 1855. An additional entry in the expense column, "improvements, hay + cane—$200" was probably to winter the herd and repair equipment for a fresh start in the spring. The worst was still to come, with the Nevada desert ahead of them. I like to think the violin strings held out. I'm sure they would have appreciated a little music for the celebration at trail's end.

From: *Fort Smith Historical Society Journal*, vol. VI, no. 2, Sept. 1982, pp. 60–63.

THE FANCHER TRAIN: THEY PUT THEIR GUNS AWAY

"Here comes the train!" And a beautiful train it was. It had begun its flow over hills and across plains at a place called Caravan Springs, south of Harrison, in north Arkansas. It would come to stop at another spring in a mountain meadow over fifteen hundred miles away, where superstitious people would report hearing the screams of children for the rest of their lives, and some would say the grass never grew because of a curse from God.

Captain Alexander Fancher was in charge of the caravan, which was said to be the finest that ever crossed the plains. There were forty wagons, along with fancy carriages for the ladies, as the train consisted of many families—altogether about 140 men, women, and children—migrating to California, some to search for gold and others to establish ranching operations there. About one thousand head of cattle were being driven along, and a hundred or more horses and mules were included in the remuda. One outstanding stallion belonging to the Fanchers was said to be valued at two thousand dollars. In today's terms that would equal the value of some of today's syndicated Thoroughbreds.

An ordinary horse in those years would be valued from

$20 to $65 in Arkansas, but the Fanchers were horsemen, and it is not surprising that the stallion was included in the remuda. Horse racing had become popular in many areas of Arkansas, and the stallion was very probably a Thoroughbred of the finest Kentucky or Tennessee bloodlines.

Alexander Fancher was born in 1812 in Overton County, Tennessee, and in the 1840s had settled with his family in the Osage community, along Osage Creek in Carroll County, Arkansas. The caravan and cattle herd, according to some reports, assembled at Caravan Springs, in what is today Boone County, in late April or early May 1857. The total value of the train was estimated at around $70,000, over $2,000,000 in today's currency.

I asked a descendent of Captain Fancher what color she thought the expensive stallion was and with a broad smile she answered enthusiastically, "It was probably a bay, because it was an old saying that you could always tell if you were at a Fancher's house, there would be a lean bay horse saddled and tied out front, ready to go. They seemed to have a liking for bays." Then she showed me an old-black-and-white photo of a cowboy roping off a tall lean horse that looked as if it might have been a bay. She said, "Their horses were usually lean because they rode a lot." The picture was of Denton Fancher, a grandson of Alexander's. We sat in the living room of the Auburn Fry home and discussed the Fancher stockmen, their brands, and the drive of 1857. I was shown the hand-forged "F" branding iron that stood not for Fancher but for Auburn Fry. It was the one that Fry had brought from Tennessee in 1867 in haste after he had left the bushwhackers, who had molested his family "where they lay," and settled west of the Mississippi in Arkansas. I was told that some of the Fanchers also branded an "F" on the left hip, and that it may have been used as a road brand, as the Fanchers were noted as cattle drovers in the old times. The present Fry brand is a backward L connected into an F, a Carroll County brand registered at Little Rock.

We looked out over a beautiful valley and a swinging foot

bridge over Osage Creek. We were a few miles downstream from Osage community, and it was impossible not to fantasize about a day gone by.

The tall covers on the wagons rippled in the spring breeze, children waved good-bye to their grandparents as the wagons rumbled past and out of sight. The large herd and the drovers followed. On wet days, the mud, churned by the forty wagons and over four thousand hooves, was all but unbearable, and on dry days the dust cloud drifted for miles. The cow ponies pranced around as they always do in the early days of a drive and the drovers flirted with and tipped their hats to the young ladies on the wagons or waved good-bye to the ones they were leaving behind. The manes and tails of the drovers' horses were whipped about in the wind as they headed and turned back stubborn cattle that had little interest in heading for California, and the mane and tail of a magnificent stallion waved for the last time above the lush grass and clear creeks that flowed alongside the limestone bluffs of Carroll County.

This combination cattle drive and wagon train headed across the prairies and may have followed the Cherokee Trail, or, if Captain Fancher thought he could find better going for the ladies' carriages, the train may have gone farther north and taken the South Pass route. In either case, they reached Salt Lake City by late summer and there turned south with the intention of connecting with the Old Spanish Trail to southern California.

Captain Fancher was undoubtedly familiar with his route, as he had been over it twice before. He would have been familiar also with the religious and political unrest among the Mormon population of Utah at that time, but he had no way of knowing what awaited him at a spring in southwest Utah, at a place called Mountain Meadows.

A red dot on the map of Utah, Mountain Meadows lies a little over thirty miles southwest of Cedar City. This had long been a stopover campsite for emigrants taking that route, and it was here that Captain Fancher called a halt to rest and "recruit the stock" on Sunday, September 6, 1857. Unknown to the peaceful group camped by the spring, Mormon Church leaders and some Paiute Indians had slipped in under cover of darkness and were waiting for sunrise. Sallie Baker Mitchell, one of the small children of the train, wrote her memoirs in 1940. Here is part of her story.

> On the morning of September 7, our party was just sitting down to a breakfast of quail and cottontail rabbits when a shot rang out from a nearby gully, and one of the children toppled over, hit by the bullet.
> Right away, the men saw they were being attacked by an Indian war-party. In the first few minutes of fighting twenty-two of our men were shot down, seven of them killed outright. Everybody was half scared to death and I reckon the whole crowd would have been wiped out right then and there if Captain Fancher hadn't been such a cool-headed man.
> He had things organized in next to no time. All the women and children were rounded up in the corral, formed by the wagons, and the men divided into two groups, one to throw up breastworks with picks and shovels and the other to fire back at the Indians.

Jim Lair points out in *Mountain Meadows Massacre* that Alex Fancher had had some military experience to draw upon, and the defenders may well have won the battle if they had not run out of water and nearly out of ammunition. Even under these conditions they held out from Monday until Friday, September 11. The attack had come not only from the hills overlooking the campsite, but from Indians who had stationed themselves in the ravine in which the spring was located, shutting off the water supply.

One can imagine the deadly effect of the defenders' rifle fire when we realize that many or most of the boys had learned to shoot while squirrel hunting back in Arkansas. In the face of this defense the Indians had backed off, and the Mormon leaders held a special council of war at Parowan, a town to the north of Mountain Meadows, to decide the fate of the wagon train and how best to draw out the defenders from their wagon corral fortress. The cattle had already been run off, and the Arkansans were now fighting for their lives.

The quotations that follow are from Juanita Brooks's *The Mountain Meadows Massacre*. Juanita Brooks is a Mormon who earned my respect by stating that she was "born into the church and raised in it," and was telling this story because of her assurance "that nothing but the truth can be good enough for the church to which I belong." Mrs. Brooks writes that her grandfather, also a Mormon, was in the vicinity of Mountain Meadows at the time of the massacre. She believes that one John D. Lee was the scapegoat for the crime and quotes from Lee's confessions and his reaction to the decision of the Latter-day Saints as they returned from the Parowan meeting to notify him that he had been chosen for the special detail.

> As soon as these persons gathered around the camp, I demanded of Major Higbee what orders he had brought. I then stated fully all that had happened at the Meadows, so that every person might understand the situation.
>
> Major Higbee reported as follows: "It is the orders of the President, that all the emigrants must be put out of the way. President Haight has counseled with Colonel Dame or had had orders from him to put all of the emigrants out of the way; none who are old enough to talk are to be spared."
>
> After prayer, Major Higbee said, "Here are the orders," and handed me a paper from Haight. It was in substance that it was the orders of Haight to decoy the emigrants from their position, and kill all of them that could talk. This order was in writing. Higbee handed it to me and I read it, and then dropped it on the ground, saying,
>
> "I cannot do this."
>
> The order was signed by Haight, as commander of the troops at Cedar City.
>
> Haight told me the next day after the massacre, while on the Meadows, that he got his orders from Colonel Dame.

> I then left the council, and went away to myself, and bowed myself in prayer before God, and asked him to overrule the decision of that Council. I shed many bitter tears, and my tortured soul was wrung nearly from the body by my great suffering. I will here say, calling upon Heaven, angels, and the spirits of just men to witness what I say, that if I could then have had a thousand words to command, I would have given them freely to save that company from death.

Jim Lair quotes Lee from his *Mormonism Unveiled* as follows:

> Soon after breakfast [on Friday morning] Major Higbee ordered the two Indian interpreters, Carl Shirts and Nephi Johnson, to inform the Indians of the plan of operations, and to place the Indians in ambush, so that they could not be seen by the emigrants until the work of death should commence.
>
> This was done in order to make the emigrants believe that we had sent the Indians away, and that we were acting honestly and in good faith, when we agreed to protect them from the savages.
>
> The orders were obeyed, and in five minutes not an Indian could be seen on the whole Meadows. They secreted themselves and lay still as logs of wood, until the order was given for them to rush out and kill the women. . . .
>
> The Indians were to kill the women and large children, so that it would be certain that no Mormon would be guilty of shedding *innocent blood* [the emphasis is Lee's] if it should happen that there was any innocent blood in the company that were to die. Our leading men had said there was no innocent blood in the whole company.

The stage had been set, and John D. Lee, who testified that he feared for his life if he disobeyed, along with one William Bateman, approached the wagon corral carrying a white flag. Here again, it would be best to let Lee himself tell the story.

> When I entered the corral, I found the emigrants engaged in burying two men of note among them,

who had died but a short time before from the effect of wounds received by them from the Indians at the time of the first attack on Tuesday morning. They wrapped the bodies up in buffalo robes, and buried them in a grave inside the corral. I was then told by some of the men that seven men were killed and seventeen others were wounded at the first attack made by the Indians, and that three of the wounded men had since died, making ten of their number killed during the siege. As I entered the fortifications, men, women and children gathered around me in wild consternation. Some felt that the time of their happy deliverance had come, while others, though in deep distress, and all in tears, looked upon me with doubt, distrust and terror. My feelings at this time may be imagined (but I doubt the power of man being equal to even imagine how wretched I felt.) No language can describe my feelings. My position was painful, trying and awful; my brain seemed to be on fire; my nerves were for a moment unstrung; humanity was overpowered, as I thought of the cruel, unmanly part that I was acting. Tears of bitter anguish fell in streams from my eyes; my tongue refused its office; my faculties were dormant stupefied and deadened by grief. I wished that the earth would open and swallow me where I stood. God knows my suffering was great. I cannot describe my feelings. I knew that I was acting a cruel part and doing a damnable deed. Yet my faith in the godliness of my leaders was such that it forced me to think that I was not sufficiently spiritual to act the important part I was commanded to perform. My hesitation was only momentary. Then feeling that duty compelled obedience to orders, I laid aside my weakness and my humanity, and became an instrument in the hands of my superiors and my leaders. I delivered my message and told the people that they must put their arms in the wagon, so as not to arouse the animosity of the Indians. I ordered the children and wounded, some clothing and the arms, to be put into the wagons. Their guns were mostly Kentucky rifles of the muzzle-loading style. Their ammunition was about all gone—I do not think there were twenty loads left in their whole camp. If the emigrants had had a good supply of ammunition they never would have surrendered, and I do not think we could have captured them without great loss, for they were brave men and very resolute and determined.

Just as the wagons were loaded, Dan. McFarland came riding into the corral and said that Major Higbee had ordered great haste to be made, for he was afraid that the Indians would return and renew the attack before he could get the emigrants to a place of safety.

I hurried up the people and started the wagons off towards Cedar City. As we went out of the corral I ordered the wagons to turn to the left, so as to leave the troops to the right of us. Dan. McFarland rode before the women and led them right up to the troops, where they still stood in open order as I left them. The women and larger children were walking ahead, as directed, and the men following them. The foremost man was about fifty yards behind the hindmost woman.

The women and children were hurried right on by the troops. When the men came up they cheered the soldiers as if they believed that they were acting honestly. Higbee then gave the orders for his men to form in single file and take their places as ordered before, that is, at the right of the emigrants.

I saw this much, but about this time our wagons passed out of sight of the troops, over the hill. I had disobeyed orders in part by turning off as I did, for I was anxious to be out of sight of the bloody deed that I knew was to follow. I knew that I had much to do yet that was of a cruel and unnatural character. It was my duty, with the two drivers, to kill the sick and wounded who were in the wagons, and to do so when we heard the guns of the troops fire. I was walking between the wagons; the horses were going in a fast walk, and we were fully half a mile from Major Higbee and his men, when we heard the firing. As we heard the guns, I ordered a halt and we proceeded to do our part.

I here pause in the recital of this horrid story of man's inhumanity, and ask myself the question, Is it honest in me, and can I clear my conscience before my God, if I screen myself while I accuse others? No, never! Heaven forbid that I should put a burden upon others' shoulders, that I am unwilling to bear my just portion of. I am not a traitor to my people, nor to my former friends and comrades who were with me on that dark day when the work of death was carried on in God's name, by a lot of deluded and religious fanatics. It is my duty to tell facts as they exist, and I will do so.

I have said that all of the small children were put into the wagons; that was wrong for one little child, about six months old, was carried in its father's arms, and it was killed by the same bullet that entered its father's breast; it was shot through the head. I was told by Haight afterwards, that the child was killed by accident, but I cannot say whether that is a fact or not. I saw it lying dead when I returned to the place of slaughter.

When we had got out of sight, as I said before and just as we were coming into the main road, I heard a volley of guns at the place where I knew the troops and emigrants were. Our teams were then going at a fast walk. I first heard one gun, then a volley at once followed.

McMurdy and Knight stopped their teams at once, for they were ordered by Higbee, the same as I was, to help kill all the sick and wounded who were in the wagons, and to do it as soon as they heard the guns of the troops. McMurdy was in front; his wagon was mostly loaded with the arms and small children. McMurdy and Knight got out of their wagons; each one had a rifle. McMurdy went up to Knight's wagon, where the sick and wounded were, and raising his rifle to his shoulder, said: "O Lord, my God, receive their spirits, it is for thy Kingdom that I do this." He then shot a man who was lying with his head on another man's breast; the ball killed both men.

I also went up to the wagon, intending to do my

105

part of the killing. I drew my pistol and cocked it, but somehow it went off prematurely, and I shot McMurdy across the thigh, my pistol ball cutting his buck-skin pants. McMurdy turned to me and said: "Brother Lee, keep cool, you are excited; you came very near killing me. Keep cool, there is no reason for being excited."

Knight then shot a man with his rifle; he shot the man in the head. Knight also brained a boy that was about fourteen years old. The boy came running up to our wagons, and Knight struck him on the head with the butt end of his gun, and crushed his skull. By this time many Indians reached our wagons, and all of the sick and wounded were killed almost instantly. I saw an Indian from Cedar City, called Joe, run up to the wagon and catch a man by the hair, and raise his head up and look into his face; the man shut his eyes, and Joe shot him in the head. The Indians then examined all of the wounded in the wagons, and all of the bodies, to see if any were alive, and all that showed signs of life were at once shot through the head. I did not kill any one there, but it was an accident that kept me from it, for I fully intended to do my part of the killing, but by the time I got over the excitement of coming so near killing McMurdy, the whole of the killing of the wounded was done. There is no truth in the statement of Nephi Johnson, where he says I cut a man's throat.

Just after the wounded were all killed I saw a girl some ten or eleven years old, running towards us, from the direction where the troops had attacked the main body of emigrants; she was covered with blood. An Indian shot her before she got within sixty yards of us. That was the last person that I saw killed on that occasion.

And from the perspective of a few of the survivors who were "too young to tell," Jim Lair records the following, from one survivor:

> The Indians opened fire and then charged down with their tomahawks. Each Mormon walking along

with our men wheeled around suddenly and shot the men next to him, killing most of them on the spot.

The women and older children screamed at the top of their lungs and scattered every which way, but the Indians ran them down. They poked guns into the wagon, too, and killed all of the wounded. . . .

I was sitting on my daddy's [George Baker's] lap in one of the wagons. The same bullet that snuffed out his life took a nick out of my left ear, leaving a scar that you can see to this day [1940].

I wasn't quite three years old. But even when you're that young, you don't forget the horror of having your father gasp for breath and grow limp, while you have your arms around his neck, screaming with terror. You don't forget the blood-curdling war-whoops and the banging guns all around you. You don't forget the screaming of the other children and the agonized shrieks of women being hacked to death with tomahawks. And you wouldn't forget it either if you saw your mother topple over in the wagon beside you, with a big red splotch getting bigger and bigger on the front of her calico dress.

When the massacre started, Mother had my baby brother, Billy, in her lap and my two sisters, Betty and Mary Levina, were sitting in the back of the wagon. Billy wasn't quite two, Betty was about five and Vina was eight.

We never knew what became of Vina. Betty saw some Mormons leading her over the hill, while the killing was going on. Maybe they treated her the way the Dunlap girls were treated—later on I'm going to tell about the horrible thing that happened to them. And maybe they raised her up to be a Mormon. We never could find out.

A 14-year old boy came running up toward our wagon, and the driver, who was Mormon, hit him over the head with the butt end of his gun, crushing the boy's skull. A young girl about 11 years old, all covered with blood, was running toward our wagon when an Indian fired at her point blank.

107

From another survivor:

> Bewildered we stood there. The Indians, shrieking, shooting, yelling, tumbled down the slope triumphantly. For a moment the entire wagon train was frozen into immobility.
> I started to follow my mother and stumbled. The last I saw of her, she was running toward our carriage with little Billy in her arms. And the Indians were upon us.
> Now I could see they weren't all Indians. Whites had painted themselves to resemble their savage companions. With bloodcurdling yells they leaped on the defenseless pioneers. I sought shelter under a wagon and peered out between the spokes.
> I saw my father fall to the ground.
> The Indians and their white companions killed and killed. The sight of blood sent them into a fanatical frenzy. One huge white kept shouting, "For Jehovah!"
> The fiends slackened their butchering only when there were no more victims. Dripping paint and blood they stood panting, searching for any signs of life among the hacked and clubbed bodies.
> A white man took me by the hand and led me to a wagon where several other children had been placed.
> I found my sister, Sarah Frances, there.

And another vivid memory:

> Captain John T. Baker had me in his arms when he was shot down and fell dead. I saw my mother shot in the forehead and fall dead. The women and children screamed and clung together. Some of the young women begged the assassins after they had run out on us not to kill them, but they had no mercy on them, clubbing with their guns and beating out their brains.

After the massacre, all the valuables of the train were divided among the Indians and the whites. The clothing, according to William Wise in *Massacre of Mountain Meadows*, was taken to Cedar City and stored for a future sale in the church's tithing office.

Eighteen children considered too young to testify were allowed to live and taken into Mormon homes in the area. A congressional investigation led to seventeen of these being brought back to Arkansas two years after the massacre. One, a girl, was reported to have remained in Utah and later to have married a Mormon.

Christopher "Kit" Carson Fancher was one of the survivors and must have had the nickname of "Charley," according to the following account by Lee from *Mormonism Unveiled*:

> About this time an Indian rushed to the front wagon, and grabbed a little boy, and was going to kill him. The lad got away from the Indian and ran to me, and caught me by the knees; and begged me to save him, and not let the Indian kill him. The Indian had hurt the little fellow's chin on the wagon bed, when he first caught hold of him. I told the Indian to let the boy alone. I took the child up in my arms, and put him back in the wagon and saved his life. This little boy said his name was Charley Fancher, and that his father was the Captain of the train. He was a bright boy. I afterwards adopted him, and gave him to Carolne [*sic*] [Sarah Caroline (Williams) Lee, John D. Lee's fourth wife]. She kept him until Dr. Forney took all the children East. I believe that William Sloan, alias Idaho Bill, is the same boy.

Lair's account also records that "Kit Carson Fancher saw his father murdered and after the massacre, while herding sheep, found one of the wives of a Mormon wearing his murdered mother's cape or mantle." In those days, before the Civil War, many Arkansas farmers and stockmen were quite prosperous, and, according to old invoices, the river steamboats brought in much fancy women's apparel, including French lace, so the clothing from the massacre could have been well worth preserving.

I visited the Mountain Meadows Massacre site in 1988 and found myself standing on a broad mound stretching for some distance in a straight line from the hill near the spring.

I realized that it was in all probability the grave mentioned in the May 6, 1859, report by Charles Brewer, an assistant surgeon of the United States Army and recorded in Lair's account:

CAMP AT MOUNTAIN MEADOWS
UTAH TERRITORY, MAY 6, 1859

CAPTAIN: I have the honor to report, that this morning, accompanied by the detachment of men furnished by your orders, I proceeded to inter the remains of the men, women, and children of the Arkansas emigrant train massacred by the Mormons at the Mountain Meadows, Utah Territory, in the month of September, 1857.

At the scene of the first attack, in the immediate vicinity of our present camp, marked by a small defensive trench made by the emigrants, a number of human skulls and bones and hair were found scattered about, bearing the appearance of never having been buried; also remnants of bedding and wearing apparel.

On examining the trenches or excavations, which appear to have been within the corral, and within which is was supposed some written account of the massacre might have been concealed, some few human bones, human hair, and what seemed to be feathers of bedding, only were discerned.

Proceeding twenty-five hundred yards in a direction N 15° W., I reached a ravine fifty yards [sic] distant from the road, bordered by a few brushes of scrub oak, in which I found portions of the skeletons of many bodies—skulls, bones, and matted hair—most of which, on examination, I concluded to be those of men. Three hundred and fifty yards further on, and in the same direction, another assembly of human remains were found, which, by all appearance, had been left to decay on the surface. Skulls and bones, most of which I believe to be those of women, some also of children, probably ranging in age from six to twelve years of age. Here, too, were found masses of women's hair, children's bonnets, such as are generally used upon the plains, and pieces of lace, muslin, calicoes, and other material, part of the women's and children's apparel. I have buried thirteen skulls, and many more scattered fragments.

Some of the remains above referred to were found upon the surface of the ground, with a little earth partially covering them, and at the place where the men were massacred: some lightly buried, but the majority were scattered about on the plain. Many of the skulls bore marks of violence, being pierced with bullet holes, or shattered by heavy blows, or cleft with some sharp-edged instrument. The bones were bleached and worn by long exposure to the elements and bore the impress of the teeth of wolves or other wild animals.

The skulls found upon the ground near the spring, or position of the first attack, and adjoining our camp, were eight in number. They, with the other remains there found, were buried, under my supervision, at the base of the hill, upon the hill-side of the valley.

As I stood there at the Massacre site I realized, too, that I was near where in 1877 John D. Lee was executed, as a scapegoat after all the others who participated in the crime were unable to remember anything except that John D. Lee did it. The following are Lee's final words before he was shot. They are a part of the Lee confessions as quoted by Juanita Brooks.

> I have but little to say this morning. Of course I feel that I am upon the brink of eternity; and the solemnities of eternity should rest upon my mind at the present. I have made out—or have endeavored to do so—a manuscript, abridging the history of my life. This is to be published. In it I have given my views and feelings with regard to these things.
>
> I feel resigned to my fate. I feel as calm as a summer morn, and I have done nothing intentionally wrong. My conscience is clear before God and man. I am ready to meet my Redeemer and those that have gone before me, behind the veil.
>
> I am not an infidel. I have not denied God and his mercies.

111

I am a strong believer in these things. Most I regret is parting with my family; many of them are unprotected and will be left fatherless. When I speak of these things they touch a tender chord within me. I declare my innocence of ever doing anything designedly wrong in all this affair. I used my utmost endeavors to save those people.

I would have given worlds, were they at my command, if I could have averted that calamity, but I could not do it. It went on.

It seems I have to be made a victim—a victim must be had, and I am the victim. I am sacrificed to satisfy the feelings—the vindictive feelings—or in other words, am used to gratify parties.

I am ready to die. I trust in God. I have no fear. Death has no terror.

Not a particle of mercy have I asked of the court, the world, or officials to spare my life.

I do not fear death, I shall never go to a worse place than I am now in.

I have said to my family, and I will say it today, that the Government of the United States sacrifices their best friend. That is saying a great deal, but it is true—it is so.

I am a true believer in the gospel of Jesus Christ. I do not believe everything that is now being taught and practiced by Brigham Young. I do not care who hears it. It is my last word—it is so. I believe he is leading the people astray, downward to destruction. But I believe in the gospel that was taught in its purity by Joseph Smith, in former days. I have my reasons for it.

I studied to make this man's will my pleasure for thirty years. See, now, what I have come to this day!

I have been sacrificed in a cowardly, dastardly manner. I cannot help it. It is my last word—it is so. Evidence has been brought against me which is as false as the hinges of hell, and this evidence was wanted to sacrifice me. Sacrifice a man that has waited upon them, that has wandered and endured with them in the days of adversity, true from the beginnings of the Church! And I am now singled out and am sacrificed in this manner! What confidence can I have in such a man! I have none, and I don't think my Father in heaven has any.

Still, there are thousands of people in this Church that are honorable and good-hearted friends, and some of whom are near to my heart. There is a kind of living, magnetic influence which has come over the people, and I cannot compare it to anything else than the reptile that enamors its prey, till it captivates it, paralyzes it, and rushes it into the jaws of death. I cannot compare it to anything else. It is so, I know it, I am satisfied of it.

I regret leaving my family; they are near and dear to me. These are things which touch my sympathy, even when I think of those poor orphaned children.

I declare I did nothing designedly wrong in this unfortunate affair. I did everything in my power to save that people, but I am the one that must suffer.

Having said this, I feel resigned. I ask the Lord, my God, if my labors are done, to receive my spirit.

After the cattle, wagons, and clothing were divided among the spoilers, there remained the question of the stallion worth two thousand dollars. Did some local rancher get him and stand him at stud? Did he race away, broken lead rein trailing to one side, to join wild horse bands in those rugged and beautiful hills and cedar breaks in southern Utah? If he did escape, there were very probably some mustang colts born in the next few years that would have been hard to catch, but worth catching.

On the courthouse lawn in Harrison, Arkansas, stands a tall memorial stone that briefly tells the story of the Mountain Meadow Massacre. One side lists those, as far as names were known, who were killed. The other side lists the survivors.

THE DOW HIGH DRIVE: THOSE OLD CATTLE DRIVES COULD DRIVE YOU CRAZY

In July of 1981 I was breaking horses in northwestern Nebraska for a rancher who owned part interest in a stallion kept near Lusk, Wyoming. One day, as I went with him to take a mare to be bred to the stallion, he pointed out Rawhide Butte and told me the story of how the formation got its name. Back in the 1800s, a young man passing through with a wagon train bragged that he would kill the first Indian he saw. The first he saw turned out to be a maiden, and he killed her, which led to an Indian attack on the train. The Indians said they only wanted the man who had done it; when he was delivered over to them they staked him and skinned him alive, close to the wagon train, where the travelers could hear his screams. His skin later dried on the butte, thus the name "Rawhide Butte."

I have no way of verifying the story, but in 1988 while doing research in Carroll County, Arkansas, I ran into a similar story that bears the earmarks of being true. The original story was related by Catherine (for Kitty) Russell, who was with Dow High Drive. The story begins with several meetings held in the Antioch Church in Carroll County in the early spring of 1857. The meetings were arranged by Mr. Dow High, who planned to drive five hundred head of Arkansas cattle to California for resale. One Isaac Standlee was going along with thirty select heifers, as he was planning to stock a two-thousand-acre ranch in the area of Goose Lake, near Alturas in Modoc County.

This drive was only a few weeks, or maybe days, behind the Alexander Fancher party, and would have been with it except that Isaac Standlee's brother, John, was sick with typhoid and the party waited until he was able to travel. When he had recovered enough to ride in a wagon, his horse was tied behind it and the train got under way. Later he recovered enough to ride his horse.

A young man, described as "reckless," threatened to kill

the first Indian he saw to avenge suffering his people had received at the hands of some Indians. When word of the threat came to the wagon master, who was evidently Dow High, he took the young man aside and impressed upon him the danger such an act would bring to the entire party, saying that if the young man persisted in his threats he would be sent back.

The drovers were warned of the usual dangers as they approached Indian territory, but Kitty Russell said that it was a long time before they saw any Indians. Then, one day, the young man saw "an Indian woman sitting on a log in the shade of a small tree, nursing her baby," and he shot and killed her. The angry wagon master informed the killer that his action could result in the death of all in the train, and that they would not protect him. Here is where the story differs slightly from the others.

Later that day, the account says, a mounted Indian war party overtook the drovers. The wagon master formed the wagons into a circle, but according to Kitty Russell's version, he did not wait for the Indians to make demands. Instead, he went out alone to meet them and agreed to turn the guilty man over to them.

The Indians, however, did make demands. They ordered all the women and children to come out and watch as they staked the man face down on the prairie. Kitty Russell said that she told her children to watch and that "she didn't want to hear them cry or say one word." The young man was left for drovers and emigrants to bury.

This drama would make a deep impressions on those watching, and for John Standlee, perhaps because he was still weak from the typhoid fever, it evidently went deeper than anyone knew, as we will see. While it seemed that he was recovering, Kitty Russell, who had helped look after him, felt that he was far from well, and had "gained too much weight and had little endurance."

As if the fate of the rebellious young man wasn't enough to bear, later in the summer or early fall they reached Mountain

Meadows, before the full truth of the massacre was known. A description of the site as reported by later visitors is recorded by Lair in *Mountain Meadows Massacre*. This was evidently in the fall of 1857.

> . . . the bodies were still well preserved and most of them lay just as they had fallen, each wound that caused death being immediately above the corresponding pool of coagulated blood on the ground. The eyes of all who had fallen upon side or back had been pecked out by the crows, but otherwise none of the bodies had been mutilated or disfigured by decay, the weather being cold with a few patches of snow on the ground. . . .
>
> At this point a pit had been dug and a number of bodies thrown into it, but as it had not been covered over the wolves had pulled some of the bodies from the surface, and in doing so had mutilated them to some extent. Most of the bodies in this group, however, were still lying just as they fell, many of them (especially the men) having been stripped of clothing by the Indians after the Mormons had killed them . . .

The spring at Mountain Meadows was the last good water hole and grazing ground before a long desert, so the party stopped for a while. According to Mrs. Russell's report the sight and smell could hardly be endured. They stopped long enough to cover the dead, and "John Standlee labored with the rest." About this time it began to be noticed that he wasn't talking much.

The first night after the party had reached California, they felt relieved and sat up late around the campfire telling stories and jokes and singing songs. John didn't join in. The next morning, with the final goal in sight, everyone got up early. Standlee slept in late, and when he did rise he didn't roll his bed but headed off on his horse, with a rope for a bridle and no saddle, moving east at a fast gallop.

One of the men was said to have taken food and to have tried to catch him but found only his dead horse. Later, when the Russells moved back to Arkansas they found John

Standlee there. He had gone completely mad and never lived in a house again, but under trees and in caves.

Back in California Dow High evidently sold his herd, and Isaac Standlee had cut out his heifers and had drifted them on north where he started his ranch, with over a hundred acres of alfalfa and over two thousand acres of grazing land. The drive for him was successful; it had driven his brother mad.

How did John Standlee make his way back to Arkansas alone? Perhaps the ancient Indian superstition that insane people are demonized had protected him from being attacked, as they wanted no contact with him. But the season was late. Did he winter over in some protected valley, canyon, or cave? I can only theorize that, even though the human qualities of his mind were gone, he still had the animal part of his brain intact and may have found his way back to Arkansas by pure instinct, the way a dog or wolf would have.

I found further confirmation of the John Standlee story while researching marks and brands in Sevier County, Arkansas. In the county clerk's office at DeQueen, I was shown an old book entitled *An Index of Cattle Growers Who Registered Their Brands 1839-1882 as Found in Record of Marks and Brands in Sevier County—Book "B"*. The handmade cover with this imposing title had been carefully attached to a partially deteriorated old book. On page 33, dated December 9, 1852, I found the name of John Standlee. He was surely the same person as the John Standlee in our story. He had registered an earmark, an under half crop in the left ear and a swallow fork in the right. I had found the proverbial needle in a haystack. Out of over sixty thousand old marks and brands, this one had caught my eye.

Thomas Jefferson Linton: The Romantic Drover

Walnut Creek
June 19, 1857

Elizabeth, dear Wife,

I take this opportunity of dropping you a few lines thinking that I may get them conveyed or handed to the mail running from Independence, Missouri, to Santifee, which will pass this place next month.

I hope that you get these lines, though I have nothing new to write. We are getting along tolerable and are all well. We have lost but four cattle; we have 625 head; yet we are about five hundred miles from home and are a few days behind the other drovers. I think we will get through with six-hundred head and but a little behind the rest.

We are now in the Buffalo regions. I think that I would not enlarge to say that I saw one hundred thousand on yesterday in sight of the road. Bill, Mack, and me had to go ahead of the wagons and drive them from the road to keep the cattle from running off with them. John Hale and Ance Verdon killed the first one that was killed in our company....

We traveled seventy-five miles and hauled wood to cook with all the time and it is with difficulty that we get wood for cooking yet. We travel fifteen to twenty miles a day.

Our cattle stampeded the other night and run off and Dunn and me standing in as hard a storm of rain as you ever saw. We could not see a cow only when it would lighten. It was early in the night and some of the boys followed the bell until day, and next morning we come up short one hundred and fifty head. We hunted that day and got all but two.

I will add no more at present and if I write to you again before I get to California it will be a chance like this. Yours affectionately.

Thomas J. Linton

From *Arkansas Historical Quarterly*, vol. 28 (1969), pp. 278–79.

Thomas Jefferson Linton was born September 4, 1826, in Tennessee. Thomas Jefferson, the third president of the United States, had died July 4 of that same year in Virginia. Linton's father, Alson, was from North Carolina, and some of his folks were from Virginia. Thomas Linton was described as "a fine stockman" and owner of some prize horses.

The family historian's writings I consulted for this work was a granddaughter of drover Linton. She modestly states that "he had taken the herd of cattle to California and sold them, profitably. It would take a man of experience to make such a trip." The phrase "a man of experience" becomes especially meaningful when we realize that he crossed the same area where Captain Marcy said that for five hundred miles he was never out of sight of dead cattle, and where the drovers he mentions in his letter as being only a few days ahead may have included the Fancher and Dow High trains, at least until their trails branched. Still, Linton mentions no unusual problems or losses.

He does say, in another letter to his wife, that "I lost a brindle cow (that I bought off of J.W. Linton) in crossing the mountain. She died with the bloody meron. She left a fine heifer calf worth $20, though, when she died I counted a $50 slug lost."

It is worth remembering here that the drovers of Linton's day were not government subsidized. They took the risks on their own shoulders, whether those risks included Indians on the plains or the deserts of Nevada. When they saddled those "fine horses" they were looking between those horses' ears at around 2,500 miles of risks. This was free enterprise at its roughest. Those thousands of miles of mountains, deserts, and Indians were like a huge sieve, separating out the strongest in horses, people, and cattle, though happenstance sometimes caused even the best to perish. Linton himself said on the prospects of his return trip: "I may fail anyhow as hundreds of better men have done before."

It has been said that the Arkansas cattle driven to California were not tough range cattle like the longhorns, but were barnyard cattle. Still, they made the trip, with no Purina feed stores along the way, and they brought top prices when they got there. In 1987 I visited Bill Linton of Scottsville, Arkansas, just six miles from Dover and near where drover Linton began his drive. A most hospitable host, he gave me a tour of the area in his pickup truck and pointed out where the old open-range areas began.

Like most of the open-range country of Arkansas, this area is composed of sandstone and limestone hills and narrow fertile valleys. The timber is mostly hardwoods and pine interspersed with a natural variety of grasses and herbage that produced not only good-looking, heavy cattle but the bone and stamina that enabled them to cross over two-thirds of the continent, living off the land, and to arrive in good health. In many cases, these herds would winter in some grassy California valley and be marketed the following fall, fat and in good condition. Linton's herd had wintered near Carson City, Nevada.

From Russellville, Arkansas, you can look north into the Ozarks and south into the Ouachitas. If at this point on the map of Arkansas you set a divider compass at ten miles you can draw a circle around an area filled with enough tourist and historical interest to fill a fair-sized book. When I had finished reviewing material at Bill Linton's, he took me to the bank in the small town of Dover where he made photocopies of the documents I needed and asked me if I had noticed the large cast-iron kettle in the town square. It was an awesome experience to view this monster kettle used at nearby Salt Springs by the Cherokee Indian, Sequoyah. Most know him as the only person ever to originate an alphabet by himself, but few know of his locally famous salt works near Scottsville, Arkansas.

The circle on the map would include the site. It would also include Pottsville, the old tavern and the stagecoach station paid for by Kirkbride Potts's drives to California. Just south of the Arkansas River at Russellville you would have encircled the "Counsel Oaks" where in 1820 chief Black Fox signed away all the Cherokee land south of the Arkansas River. Those old oaks are still standing. I counted eleven steps, walking around the base of the larger of the two. These venerable witnesses to that ancient treaty stand just downstream from Dardanelle bluff, mentioned by Thomas Nuttall in his scientific expedition up the Arkansas River in 1819. The Butterfield stage route passed through here, and through this circle would have drifted the herd driven by James M. Moose in 1852. Just a few miles upstream from this area was the boyhood home of Jesse Chisholm.

Thomas Linton, like so many adventurers, was a hopeless romantic. If it had not been for his love for and devotion to his wife Elizabeth, and the many letters he wrote to her, we would know little or nothing of the details of his 1857 adventure. It would seem that he, and many like him, were often motivated by the romance of the undertaking as much as by the possible profits to be realized. But his love and loneliness for Elizabeth caused him to fill her in on so many details that his letters are of interest to us today.

From some of the comments in Thomas Linton's letters to his wife, it is apparent that the cattle on his drive included the herds of several drovers. In a letter dated June 13, 1858, he writes, "The 34 head that I have sold amount to $1810. I have 34 head left and 7 calves besides those I left in Carson. They ought to sell for a good deal more than the others, and would in the same market, I think." Earlier, he had written, "I will go on to state to you the sales of some of my cattle and my luck in Carson. I only found 68 head of my cattle in Carson, though I think I will get more of them, yet. I gave my friend (Brittern) the description of those and he said that he would find them for me if they were in the valley. . . .

"My Jo Reed oxen sold at $135.00. I then sold to Jamieson 7 heifers at $50 each. To Peter Davis and Orell Muley, I sold a red headed heifer and a little black motley faced heifer that I raised. I sold one heifer and calf for $75."

In another letter we find, "I guess I will have to haul down my calculations considerably below five thousand." It seems, from amounts variously mentioned, that he probably realized around four thousand dollars total. Considering that good wages then were about a dollar a day, four thousand dollars would equal a sizable fortune today.

Linton was not too proud to mention his follies, writing at one point, "I can say to you that I have taken a few days in hunting gold and silver, and as two of us, in one day's panning, paid out about one cent, I have no idea that I will spend any more time that way."

He shares with his "dear Elizabeth" his impressions of California's big trees:

> I can say to you that I saw the big tree, the mother of the forest. I found it to be 33 steps around, 327 feet high and the bark was pealed off 116 feet high. I then went on the stump of the big tree that was converted into a ballroom, very neat at that. Also on the log they have built a double line ten pin alley and barroom. This tree is said to be 32 feet through at the base. The bark is 18 inches thick....
>
> I told Jamieson that I would freely give the remaining of my possessions in Arkansas to have you and the children to take a walk with me in the ballroom on the stump of the big tree, as ten years would be as much time as I would want to make an independent fortune off of 30 cows, for all the children we have or ever will have.

A letter of April 18, 1858, speaks of the drover's loneliness, his frustration at the few letters he has received, his saving sense of humor, his poetic tendencies, and his thoughts of the long road home.

> Elizabeth my dear,
> I again take my pen in hand to bother you with another letter, though I confess it is an ungrateful act, for I have not often been bothered with a letter from you (though I think I might have gotten later news than the 30th of January). However, if you should not write anymore I will avenge myself by

> writing every two weeks and if you are too busy to read them just lay them to one side. . . .
> I stayed with Walter Scott night before last, alls well. He sold 12 cows and calves the other day for $70 round. Some of them were two year old heifers. Cattle are rising here. They are all rising in the south, that is Spanish cattle. Consequently, there will not be very many driven here.

This is evidently to say that by "rising," the cattle are increasing to the point that future drives will not be profitable. If "rising" meant prices going up, it would have meant more droves coming in; however, the drover period to California was nearing its end.

The letter continues:

> If you should conclude to come over some Saturday evening, please bring your knitting and the children with you. When you get to Stockton take up Main Street until you come to the blacksmith shop. There take the right which leads out about ten miles to Hitchcock Ranch, where I am located. Wind up your business, though, before you start, for I am certain if I had you and the children here I would never travel the road again. I may fail anyhow as hundreds of better men have done before. . . .
> In the following lines I will endeavor to explain to you the reason why I so often bother you with my letters. I hope you will excuse me for so doing and answer as many as you can, conveniently.
> I am bound to think of the bosom
> that have rendered these temples repose.
> Though life may toss me as the sea
> does the moss on the rock where it grows.
> Yet never the rush of its battle,
> its surf or its ceaseless storm
> shall sever the link that connects me,
> with life to thy guardian for me.
> Until death have caused us to sever
> and time upon earth is no more,
> and we've left the green forest forever
> and at rest on a glorious bright shore.

> ... Ere you get this 12 months will have rolled around since I left you, six more, I think, will bring us together again. That is if you don't conclude you can do better than to wait so long.
>
> Without idleness and nonsense my letter would have been short. In this you'll see I remember thee, though many miles apart we be.
>
> Thomas J. Linton

During his stay in California, allowing his cattle to fatten, Linton had not been idle. He mentioned working "a month or two" in the grain harvest, and that "Meart and me ... got 150 cords of wood cut. ... We have hauled some in and are getting $6 per cord as fast as we can haul. Meart is fitting out a horse team and will start them next week."

The 1857 cattle drive of Thomas Jefferson Linton was a grand success, from which he returned safely to Arkansas and his beloved Elizabeth.

HOLMES AND HOLMES: CATTLE BARONS FROM ARKANSAS

When I finished my cross-country ride from Arkansas to California in September 1989, I was contacted by Jack Woods of Sebastopol, California. He said he was a grandson of one of the Arkansas cattle drovers and had considerable information on a drive. I visited him and got this story.

His grandfather was John Riley Woods, who helped his uncles, Calvin and Henderson Holmes, drive a herd of six hundred cattle from Rogers, Arkansas, to the Sacramento Valley in 1852. In checking the roster of the Cherokee Mining Company under the leadership of Lewis Evans, I noticed that both Calvin and H. P. (undoubtedly Henderson) Holmes, along with Cuthbert Holmes, were listed. That trek had taken place in 1849, so the Holmes brothers were experienced and knew the route.

The pioneer Woods and Holmes families had moved to Arkansas from North Carolina and Tennessee. They were partly of Scotch-Irish descent, which was typical of so many livestock men that moved west in those history-making years. John Riley Woods had been sheriff of Benton County, Arkansas, before making the cattle drive.

Jack Woods, a grandson of John Riley Woods, was then as close as I had been to one of the 1850s drovers.

Jack gave me a copy of a letter that his grandfather had written to his wife Margaret Ann, back in Arkansas, after they had finished the drive. The letter was dated Sept. 27, 1852. In the letter, John Riley Woods comments on the "almost endless journey," and that they were "five months to a day on the plains. . . . While I came through in good health, thousands have fallen to the sand. I got both of my horses here. Twig is in good plite considering. Since we got in I have been offered for him $300 [roughly three years' drover's wages]. Noah is tolerable thin. I did not ride him for 700 miles on the latter part of the journey. I have been for 5 months a stradle of a horse or mule and I feel like a forked log. Henderson and Calvin make a lucky trip. I think they only lost about 25 head of stock on the plains [Jack said he though some of these were given to the Indians to keep peace]. . . . The dreaded Humbolt has been a celebrated place for grass this year, which was greatly in favor of the migration."

The trials of the trail were sometimes spoken of as a blessing in disguise. It was mentioned about a certain youth that must have been a little overly rambunctious, "The wagon run over John and skined his a head a little which helpt him a good deal." For others, however, the trail's trials meant little. "Henry Mises got in good health without any difficulty, tho Sarah's under lip would sometimes get limber." Those men and women were certainly of strong and courageous stock. Any problems, dangers, or losses were not emphasized, but a generous sprinkling of humor and good news dominated the letter. Stock prices, for instance, were good: "Horses of good size is worth from $100 to $300. Cattle are better than the [gold] dust itself." Similarly, one of Thomas Linton's letters to his wife had mentioned that selling cattle, rather than seeking gold dust, was a way to make enough money to retire.

The Holmes brothers drove several herds of cattle from Arkansas to California. The first, as already stated, was from Rogers, Arkansas. Others may have been from combination Texas and Arkansas herds.

Material from the Sonoma County area, copied and sent to me by Jack Woods states:

> Beef cattle became a factor in Sonoma County agriculture as soon as the first of many Missouri [actually Arkansas] cattle drives brought replacements for the short-legged, shaggy Mexican cattle that yielded meat as tough as the hides for which they were raised. . . . The Holmes brothers . . . , Calvin and Henderson, were among the early cattle "barons," bringing droves across the plains in 1852. . . . The Holmes' first ranch was part of the old San Miquel Ranch north of Santa Rosa. Henderson retained this property in 1861 when Calvin settled 2,500 acres in Knight's Valley on the Napa County line.

Jack Woods told me an amusing story from old family records of Calvin Holmes' wife, Elvira. Calvin had offered to send her around the Horn by ship and pick her up in San Francisco. She said, "No, if you can face that long drive and Indians I guess I can." So she rode her mule from Rogers to Santa Rosa. While I was in California in 1989, Jack took me out and showed me the elegant Victorian mansion, built by Calvin Holmes on the Knight's Valley ranch. It is now a California historical landmark.

Jack has since mailed me a paper showing the final dispensation of the ranch property: "Known locally as the Fountain Grove Ranch. They bought this ranch in 1853, $1.00 per acre for the flat land and .50 cents per acre for the hill land [just one Arkansas cow would have paid for 100 acres]. About 15 years ago Hewlitt-Packard purchased part of the ranch about 200 acres for about 3.25 million. About 10 years ago Sheriton hotels purchased about 500 acres for about 23 million. The flat[land] now would sell by the square foot." Truly cattle were worth more than the dust itself.

6

The Open Range Saga

THE OPEN RANGE CONCEPT

"The buzzards will soon show you where your cattle are—and if you don't git outta here the buzzards will be lookin' for your carcase too."

These words were spoken over the barrels of a shotgun to an Arkansas stockman who was looking for stray cattle. For over two hundred years Arkansas cattle have ranged out, run on open range, or free range, as many called it. Most of the old-time stockmen liked taking advantage of the open range. It produced beef at lower cost, and it was legal. "But we've got another law, the law of the shotgun," as one opponent of the open range told me.

After the earth was created, as Psalms 50:10 points out, "God owned the cattle on a thousand hills," and there were no stock laws. Anyone who wanted to farm or raise a garden simply fenced it in and the rest of the whole world was pasture land. Surprisingly, this view was the governing principle in many parts of Arkansas until a very few years ago. This was the original open range concept and differs from what is called open range in some western states today where large tracts of range land are leased and grazed by several ranchers. The open range of Arkansas was sometimes called "free range," and there were no restrictions until and unless a lot of farming, or urban development, or people from other areas moved into an open range area. There generally were few problems with the early open ranges. Farm and ranch people in Arkansas tended to get along.

Every question, every argument, has at least two sides. In this case, like a cube, the argument has at least six sides. So let's look at three main arguments against the open range—three views from down the shotgun barrel, so to speak—and then consider the three views of the open range stockmen.

The first objection to having the range open was that it was ecologically unsound and ravaged certain types of plant life. This would be a more intelligent objection if we would, or could, talk to some of the old-timers who lived in the areas where open range was practical and practiced. In the early times before the coming of the whites, buffalo ranged in large numbers all across Arkansas. Joutel, the chronicler for La Salle's last voyage, mentioned "most lovely plains" and large numbers of buffalo and antelope. Ecology is, in some respects, the study of the relations between different animals in an environment. The buffalo helped create a type of environment. They ate down and trampled the coarser vegetation, thereby helping to maintain those "most lovely plains" that were such fine pasturage for the antelope and other smaller grazing animals. They started a beneficial chain reaction.

After the demise of the buffalo, open range grazing by the French, Spanish, Cherokee, and later pioneers' cattle could and did help fill the ecological gap left by the buffalo. The transfer was gradual, and for a while range cattle grazed the same prairies with the buffalo. Where in eastern Arkansas Joutel had observed in 1687, ". . . the plains lying on one side of it, are stor'd with beeves (buffalo) wild goats, (antelope), deer, turkeys, bustards, swans, ducks, teal and other game," Thomas Nuttall recorded in 1819, "The cattle throughout this country are generally left to provide for themselves, and suffered to range at large." And later near the same area, "while passing through this prairie, I observed five deer feeding, . . . the bison (improperly called buffaloe) is also met with occasionally."

In his book *Sawmill*, Kenneth L. Smith comments on the early virgin forest of the Ouachitas, "Virgin shortleaf pines in the Ouachitas grew in an open forest of trees widely spaced with little undergrowth and a thick carpet of grass. A person could ride a horse, or drive a team and wagon, through these woods." I have heard old-timers say many times that there was hardly any brush when we had open range. And so, between the killing of the buffalo, the logging of the virgin forests, and restrictive stock laws, the environment has suffered.

Many hunting magazines have expressed opposition to cattle grazing in the National Forests. They say it is detrimental to the reproduction of their target animals. From the standpoint of my observations and research, this simply is not true. Down the creek a mile or so from where I sit writing this is a pasture where I used to fence in my cattle during hunting season. And it became quite overgrazed. However, I always saw more deer there than up in the areas that were seldom grazed. The overgrazed area had not been improved or fertilized. I believe the reason is that without man's domestic cattle the environment is incomplete. Many old-timers felt that it was more important to produce beef for the nation than to provide target animals for a few. But I believe that the truth of scientific research will show that open range grazing of cattle and hunting can coexist to the benefit of each other. Some of the restless anti-range groups say the cattlemen are out to "get rich quick." The "get rich quick" cattleman, as far as I can tell, is a non-existent species.

On my 1989 cross-country ride I spent a couple of days at the Brown's Park Wildlife Refuge in northwestern Colorado. In an interview with the ranger there I learned more about the harmony that can and should exist between domestic and wild animal life. Jerre Gamble told me, "I have four things at my disposal for reducing excessive plant overgrowth. I can use fire, chemicals, machine cutting, or allow cattle to graze. I prefer cattle grazing, because it is cost free, and also is a more efficient recycling of nutrients. Of course overgrazing cannot be allowed." Later, in Nevada, I was told that after cattle were removed from the Ruby Marshes, wildlife had diminished.

The second objection to the open range was that it was difficult to raise a garden or other crops where you have open range. The answer to this objection is simple: gardens and croplands can be fenced. Some cattlemen have offered to fence gardens for free to keep down trouble.

The third of these objections to open range was that cattle ranging out were a hazard to traffic on the highways. The answer: historically, good open range areas were not near high-speed highways. Millions of acres of free range were crossed only by county roads or slow mountain roads that were safer if an occasional cow slowed traffic down anyway. Cheap range has always been a necessity for beef-producing ranchers. The feed lot presents a different situation, where grain production is all important. But for the cow-calf operation that is the traditional ranch of the colorful West, cheap range land is a must. It is the cow-calf operator who must keep the price down so the feed lot operator can make a profit and produce beef that you and I can afford. The Ozark and Ouachita rangelands were primarily used by cow-calf ranchers.

Agitation built up and continued against the open range until many entered the argument who were new to the country and knew little of the country and nothing of the economic value of the range. Cattlemen had the same success resisting the road laws and range laws as the Indians had had resisting the wagon trains and railroads. Stock laws began to whittle away the open range, only certain parts of counties to begin with, until open range, even in the wilderness areas, is on the "extinct nostalgia" list.

But before the open or free range had been peopled to death and legislated away, Arkansas had contained millions of acres of valuable rangeland in the Ozarks and Ouachitas. From the 1750s when the French government gave any "worthy but poor" French girl, "one cow and calf . . . a gun and ammunition," along with other valuables to each soldier who would marry and settle down, Arkansas had been open range territory. These vast woodlands and meadows were laced with thousands of miles of natural water troughs, creeks, and rivers, flowing over natural limestone and sandstone filters. In *Folklore of Romantic Arkansas*, Fred W. Allsop says, ". . . in the '30's to '70's [1830–70], there were few wire fences, the grass was knee high, and long-horn cattle and razorback hogs were in the heyday of their glory. These were the days when at stated intervals 'round-ups' were held for the branding of stray cattle."

Early in Arkansas's history, the natural prairies had been relegated to farming, and so, for the most part, the rangeland consisted of woodlands with few meadows. The question that comes to the minds of most is how in the world could cattlemen have ever kept up with and rounded up cattle under those conditions? A friend of mine, who has since passed on, once told me that he and his family used to raise cattle in the White Rock Mountain area of Franklin County and ranged "as far as we could ride a horse in a day in every direction." I asked him how they ever rounded them up in that rough timbered country, and he answered, "on hard-tailed cowponies." Years ago I used to see very large old corrals in this area.

Some stockmen depended on the attraction of salt to help gather their cattle. They sometimes used "lick-logs" as gathering points for their cattle. An interesting and humorous story was recorded in *Folklore of Romantic Arkansas*:

> In early times the frontier people of Arkansas who owned cattle were accustomed to provide "lick-logs." For the benefit of those who do not know what lick-logs are, I will say that they were simply fallen trees with notches cut in them two or three feet apart and a few inches deep. In these primitive receptacles the salt would be placed for the cattle two or three times a week.
>
> The term "lick-log" was sometimes applied to preaching places also. Mr. Washburn and a Baptist preacher happened once to lodge together at a place where there were a number of Indians. The ministers were talking about the experiences of their respective labors. The Baptist brother remarked that at a *revival* he had converted and baptized a number of people, "And, by the way," said he, "they were nearly all Methodists formerly!" "Oh," replied Mr. Washburn, "then you and I attach a different meaning to the word 'revival.' I mean a change of the heart from sin to holiness."
>
> "Well, however that may be," said the Baptist, "they came to my 'lick-log' and I put my mark upon them."
>
> An indian present, who had been listening, exclaimed with the peculiar shrug and grunt of the aborigine:
>
> "If any man puts his mark upon my cattle when they go to his *lick-log*, I call him *cow-thief!*"

DIPPING VATS AND RANGE RIDERS

The spreading of external parasites, especially ticks, has been attributed to cattle drovers. In 1915 the state of Arkansas passed act No. 86 that required the dipping of cattle for the "eradication" of ticks. The method didn't work quite as well as anticipated, so in 1947 and 1951, the law was modified to require "dip[ping] cattle for the purpose of reducing ticks in the state of Arkansas." To make sure that this law was carried out as stated, stock range riders were hired, and by 1951 their salary was up to "$200 per month from May 1 to November 1, to be paid by the county." That was more money than most cowboys on big ranches were getting in those years. Naturally these range riders had a zeal to carry out their jobs.

The law stated: "dipping shall be carried out once each month between May 1 and November 1 of each year." The provision further stated: "where refused to dip cow as ordered officers could take cow, have her dipped, and then hold her until fees for dipping were paid." This law was contested in 1930 in *D. Humphrey V. Tinsley, 181 Ark. 71, 25 S.W. 2d (1930)* (decision under prior law) and the stock owner lost the case and his cow.

An attempt was made to round up and dip some of Arkansas's wild horses as late as 1931.

People living in the "natural state" naturally resented this law. Dr. John Ferguson of the Arkansas History Commission told me that the resentment reached the explosive point in Howard County where he grew up. He said sometimes late at night they would hear a loud boom and someone would say, "There goes another dipping vat." Dr. Ferguson also told me a presumably true story that presents the resistance of a seemingly "helpless little old lady" to this overbearing law.

This lady evidently was unable to do the dipping herself, so the range riders were doing the job for her, and she was expected to foot the bill. The little old lady stood meekly by, with one hand under her apron, while her cattle were being

133

dipped. Imagine the surprise of the range riders as she whipped out a pistol from under her apron and demanded that the riders dismount. She proceeded to run them through the evil-smelling dip solution!

In *The Voices of Moccasin Creek*, Tate Page accurately sums up the feelings of some of the rugged mountain men's feelings toward this law. These old-timers had relied on burning the woods to control both ticks and brush. But now they were confused. "They pointed out the fact that one group of government men were saying, 'Don't burn the woods.' Now others were saying, 'Get rid of ticks.'" They were told this was to control "tick fever." These old-timers had not even heard of "fever" ticks, but their reasoning was, "If'n they be fever ticks a-comin' an' they's dangerous, we better burn hell out o' them woods come spring."

Page has the last word on Arkansas's experience with the dipping vat law: "The irony of the dipping vat project forced upon these people is evident to anyone who knows the mountains. Cattle were tick-carriers, but they were of little significance when all the other tick-carrying wild animals were considered. Rabbits, wolves, and their cousins carried untold millions of ticks. The fever tick extermination was another government exercise in futility. There have never been simple answers to complex problems though simple men have persisted in trying to find them."

SIXTY THOUSAND OLD MARKS AND BRANDS

Where open range grazing of cattle is practiced, branding is necessary. Where rustling or stealing is a problem, it is especially advisable. It should come as no surprise that thousands upon thousands of marks and brands have been recorded in the state of Arkansas.

When I started research on this book I consulted a study on the subject that dealt with the whole nation's brand system. After showing the many brands that most western states had, it stated that Arkansas had 176 brands. It was not stated where this number came from, but when I counted the marks and brands recorded for Crawford County, where I live, the number was eleven hundred. Stone County records almost two thousand, and Arkansas County has over three thousand marks and brands.

Those old marks and brands books are beautiful. They are often bound in leather, sometimes tan split, sometimes beautiful red leather, and stamped in gold on the cover is "Marks and Brands." Even the handwriting of some of those county clerks from over a hundred years ago is more beautiful than much of what hangs in our art museums today.

Among the old French records of Arkansas Post, an entry dated February 2, 1778, shows the name Sami Rener and his mark, "S." Following his name appears Peter Presley, Senr., and his mark, "I" (either the letter "I" or number "1"). These are names on a petition. No mark is shown with the other names. These might very well be the oldest brands in the state.

Cattle would have been ranging there at that time and brands would have been necessary. The oldest recorded brands on livestock in the state were the horse brands of 1820. These were shown in old stray or "estray" books. These were record books kept by the county clerks to record stray animals taken up. The oldest stray books I have found were one in the courthouse circuit clerk's office at Dewitt in Arkansas County (see chapter 2) that dates from 1820 to 1844 and one at Walnut Ridge in Lawrence County that dates from 1822 to 1853. For the next century and more these old records of estrays tell their story all across the state. The oldest brand book I found in the state was at the Old Washington Historic State Park in Hempstead County. It dates from February 24, 1821, to the latest entry in 1830. This earliest dated entry is on the second page and is the letter "D" registered to Churchill Fulchear. The first entry on the first page is not dated and is for a man named Christopher Antony. He recorded a "C2" brand and his earmark, an underslope in each ear. It is a pity this entry was not dated as I was told that Mr. Antony came to that area in 1814.

At Walnut Ridge in Lawrence County, the office worker at the county clerk's desk said she didn't know where the old brand book was but that I was free to look around. On a top shelf to the left of the other marriage records, I found it. A well-preserved book measuring eight by twelve inches, bound in beautiful maroon leather and stamped in gold: "Marriage Record, 1821–1837, Marks and Brands Record, Jan, 1822–Nov, 1853, Execution Record, Jan, 1822–Aug, 1849, Stray Book April 1822–March 1853." I took this out to the office where several women were at their desks and said, "There *has* to be a point of humor here somewhere," pointing to the book. Then I got a laugh. This was, to my knowledge, the second oldest brand book and the second oldest stray book in Arkansas, but I'm quite sure it was the oldest in the entire West to combine marriage records, cattle records, and executions in a single volume.

EARMARKS

These are a few of the most common earmarks registered in Arkansas. Earmarks are read as the cow faces you.

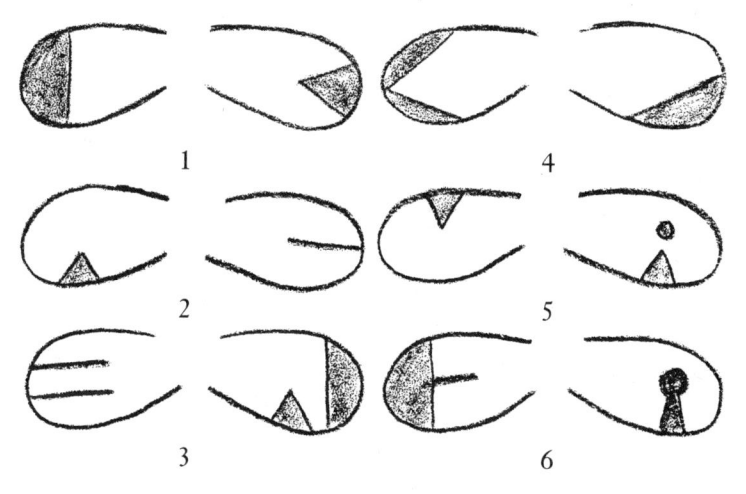

1. Crop off the right and swallow fork the left. 2. Underbit the right and slit the left. 3. Double slit the right and crop off and underbit the left. 4. Sharp ear the right and underslope the left. 5. Overbit the right and hole and underbit the left. 6. Crop and slit the right and keyhole the left. The earmark illustrated at the top of the page is from Stone County, Arkansas, and reads, "Crop off underbit and hole in each ear."

BRANDS

Many early brands were simple letters and numbers. Many of the letters were the stock owners' initials. Some more complicated brands were seen very early, but most of the intricate brands developed later. Brand examples shown had many duplications throughout the state before the state central system took over in 1959. Over sixty thousand marks and brands were registered in Arkansas from 1820 to 1959.

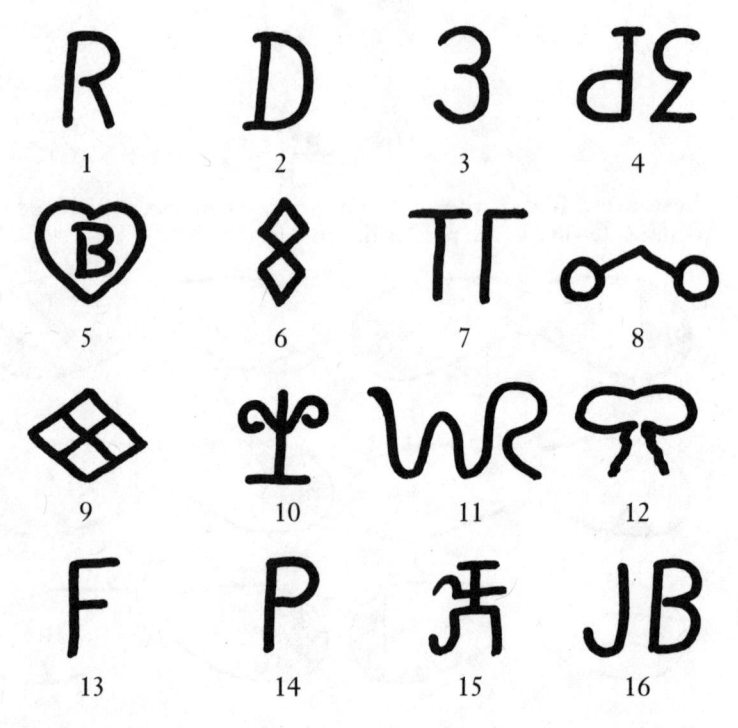

1. Horse brand from a stray book, Arkansas County, 1820. 2. Brand registered to Churchill Fulchear, 1821. This is the oldest dated brand. It is the second brand listed in the state's oldest brand book at Old Washington, Hempstead County. 3. Brand registered to J. Potts in Pope County, 1889. 4. "Inverted 3 P" brand from a stray book, Arkansas County, 1820. 5. "Heart B" brand registered to Edmon H. Brenham in Miller County, 1886. 6. "Double diamond" brand registered to Robert H. Crockett in Arkansas County, 1857.

138

7. "T inverted backwards L" brand registered to Thomas Linkhorn in Lawrence County, 1822. This is the oldest brand registered in Lawrence County, which has the second oldest brand book in the state. 8. "Bridle bit" brand registered to to G. W. Causey in Ashley County, 1886. 9. "5 diamonds" brand registered to J. L. Forline in Logan County, 1911. 10. "Old Mexican flower" brand registered to Wayman Harper in Montgomery County, 1938. 11. "Running WR" brand registered to Winthrop Rockefeller in Conway County, 1954. 12. "Bowtie" brand registered to Ben Chism in Johnson County, 1908. 13. This is thought to be the old Fancher road brand. 14. A Potts family branding iron found at Potts' Tavern. 15. A "Spanish brand" listed in a Hempstead County stray book, 1887. 16. An unknown iron found at the old ghost town of Schaberg in Crawford County by Janet Denton Cordell, the author's daughter.

As to the oldest earmark in the state, in describing the hardships and trials of the remnants of the De Soto expedition, Garcilaso de la Vega wrote: "They came upon a sow which had been lost on their trip out, and that this animal had dropped thirteen pigs, all of which were now large and marked on the ears, each with a different mark. It must have been that the natives had distributed these pigs among themselves and identified them with their own particular signs." Later Garcilaso continues: "To each of the friendly caciques, they presented two sows and one boar, thus making it possible for them to raise swine." According to the most recent De Soto studies they must have been somewhere in southern Arkansas. This was in 1542, and I believe would predate any earmark west of the Mississippi.

Early Arkansas law had required that "Every person in this state who has cattle, hogs, sheep, or goats shall have an earmark and brand." It was further stated: "It shall be the duty of the clerks of the county courts in each county to keep a well-bound book in which they shall record the marks and brands." When cattle changed hands the law stated: "A person purchasing or acquiring cattle or other stock, where he brands or marks them with his brand or mark after the acquisition of animals shall do it in the presence of one (1) or more of his neighbors." This was listed under rebranding or remarking, assuming the animal was already marked or branded.

In going through the old brand books several interesting points emerged. In the oldest of the records, earmarks were sometimes used without a brand. Old estray books sometimes showed cattle earmarked without a brand, but the horses were more often branded. The branded horses were usually small, from 10 to 14 1/2 hands high (measured at the withers). This suggests to me that the Spanish mustang types were the toughest range horses, and they were often turned out when not being used. The taller horses may have been of Thoroughbred stock more recently brought in and more valuable and so not ranged out. Sometimes, however, these tall horses were branded. Generally it seems the smaller horses were in the oldest listings (from 1820 to 1840 or so).

As time went on, most cattlemen registered an earmark and a brand, and the estray books reflected this. At first, in most brand books, simple letters were used. These were often the owners' initials. Later, diamonds, bars, slashes, circles, quarter circles, wings, rockers, drags, etc., were added to make the brands more decorative and harder to change. I found registered brands where the position stated was for the horn (of cattle) or the hoof (for horses). However, practically all were to be burned into the hide. (Left or right side, hip, shoulder etc.)

Quite often in the estray books, a "Spanish brand" will be mentioned. This was a complex brand used by the old Spanish, Mexican, and sometimes the old French cattlemen. An ordinary brand may be "read" or "called," such as the simple letter "R," a rocking "R," a bar "Y," etc. But some of the complex brands from Mexico would be called just

"Spanish brands." Many of these brands may have been from early Spanish settlers. These could have come from animals traded from the Comanche via Fort Smith, or some other border town. In any event, I have bumped into "Spanish brands" in old estray books all across the state.

In 1868 Arkansas passed a law requiring anyone driving stock through the state to have the brand registered. This was called the drovers' law and drovers were required to register that brand with the state before entering. This was about the time the big Texas herds were beginning to move north, some of which passed through Arkansas.

The key position that Arkansas held in the development of the West naturally caused me to expect to bump into some of these old drovers' brands. The herds passing through and from this state to California before the Civil War would have done so before this drovers' law. However, following the Civil War, an unknown number of Texas herds passed through Arkansas bound for the northern market. According to the law, their brands should be on record in Arkansas.

I had hoped to find some of these old brands at Fort Smith, an old frontier border town, but the old brand book for Sebastian County had been lost. One Texas herd passed through Pea Ridge, but the old Benton County brand book is also lost. So many valuable records were lost during the Civil War, and the carpetbaggers that took over following the war had little interest in preserving these records. But not all was lost.

THE PINE BLUFF STORY

What a surprise awaited me at Pine Bluff in Jefferson County. The county clerk was very helpful and dug the old brand book out of the courthouse basement. She said that Texas and Arkansas had had a good relationship during and following the Civil War and that prior to the siege of their courthouse by General Powell Clayton in 1863, all or most of their records had been moved by covered wagon all the way to Texas, and thereby preserved. Their brand records date back to September 1861.

In 1869, according to this old brand book, Texas brands began to appear. This would have been during the heyday of the Texas drover period. From August 4 to September 4, 1869, 148 Texas drovers' brands were registered. Over seventy Texas brands were registered on one day, September 4. Twenty-two were registered by H. B. Elliot of Bell County and fifty-five by E. M. Mahan of McClellan (possibly McLennan?). So many brands registered by one man would indicate that herds were made up of cattle from many different owners, a common practice in that day and time. A few Texas brands continued to be recorded into the 1870s.

Why were cattle driven from Texas to Pine Bluff in southeastern Arkansas? I asked the same question and no one seemed to have the answer. But the record of the brands and a story, possibly a lost chapter in the drama of the West, had been burned into the hides of untold numbers of Texas longhorn cattle. And those priceless records had joined others that had been shipped to Texas and back by covered wagon for safekeeping. Texans involved in the preservation of those Jefferson County records knew the route to Pine Bluff and knew that it was considerably shorter than the trail to the Kansas markets. They would have known also that Texas drovers had on occasion fared badly in Kansas and Missouri due to slow-dying bad feeling between the blue and the gray; some Texas drovers had even been tied to trees and beaten while their cattle were stolen. I began to suspect that Pine Bluff may have been a far more important shipping point for those northbound Texas longhorns than historians had realized.

The county clerk at Pine Bluff again was of help to me. I was given stacks of information, including back issues of the *Jefferson County Historical Quarterly*, and these facts emerged.

In the late 1800s and into the twentieth century, Jefferson County, along with other Arkansas counties, had been a source of abundant feed for livestock. Especially abundant in

Jefferson County were cottonseed meal and hulls. Several feeding yards had opened in Jefferson County to fatten cattle and hogs for market. Even before the advent of railroads, a line of river steamships had operated year-round between Pine Bluff and Memphis. Add to this fact that one of the thoroughfares in Pine Bluff that leads toward the river is named "Texas," and you have several pieces of a puzzle that, along with the old brands themselves, show the close connection between Pine Bluff and those Texas drovers.

BRANDS IN CONTEMPORARY ARKANSAS

In 1959 Arkansas passed Act 179 "to provide for the Central Registration of all livestock brands used in the state." This act is carried out by the Arkansas Livestock and Poultry Commission, Division of Brand Registry. Currently 1,126 brands are shown in the state registry. A new book is issued every five years.

Fifty-two out-of-state brands are shown in the current state registry. One is from Canada. The other states showing cattle brands registered in Arkansas are Arizona, California, Colorado, Florida, Kansas, Louisiana, Mississippi, Missouri, Montana, Nebraska, New Mexico, Oklahoma, Tennessee, Texas, Utah, and Wyoming. The District of Columbia has a brand registered as well. Texas shows the most brands registered here, with twelve shown. The District of Columbia brand is the "double moose antler," an old German horse brand, registered by the American Trakehener Association.

In 1988 I sent a questionnaire to the owners of all the current brands registered in Arkansas. The questions were on subjects from historic brands to current brands. One interesting historical fact I learned was that most of the current brands were designed by their present owners; however, quite a few were inherited and are very old. Not everyone answered, but I was helped tremendously. A great part of the information in this book was obtained from following leads given by respondents to this questionnaire. I am thankful for this help.

Sometimes I followed up on unanswered questionnaires. By looking through the brand registry, I discovered that until a very few years ago, Wells Fargo Leasing Corporation of San Francisco, California, had a brand registered in Arkansas. They did not answer my questionnaire, but after my cross-county horseback ride to California, a friend of mine, Sandy McAuliffe of Fullerton (a Los Angeles suburb), called the Wells Fargo Museum there. The curator said he knew nothing of any brand ever being registered in Arkansas. Sandy called Little Rock to double-check the Arkansas registry. They confirmed that Wells Fargo had been registered to do business in the state. There were records that indicated Wells Fargo used to haul fresh strawberries out of Arkansas. Sandy said, "Yes but you don't brand strawberries," so we kept on the trail. Before I left Los Angeles, the curator of the Wells Fargo Museum called and said, "Denton was right; we did have a brand registered in Arkansas, but I have absolutely no information on it."

The early state brand books showed their brand, and it is listed in the 1973 edition as a connected WFL, standing for Wells Fargo Leasing Corporation, San Francisco, California. Position, right hip of cattle. The brand was registered for Benton, Washington, Crawford, Franklin, Sebastian, and Logan counties.

One of the out-of-state brands was for Oppenheimer Industries, Inc., of Kansas City, Missouri. The older books listed over a hundred brands for this firm. Each of their brands is a "gunsight," a circle with a straight line through the lower part. Following this gunsight brand will be found one or more other letters or symbols. All these different symbols puzzled me at first until I learned that this outfit was an investment firm. The arrangement was that different farmers and ranchers grazed Oppenheimer stock for a share of the profits. The stock was owned by many different investors who might never see the cattle but would have a brand.

The effect of having many wealthy investors associated with one company, it was explained to me, was that money was taken from wealthy, urban areas and spread out to poor, rural areas in several different states. The final result would have been increased employment, sale of feed and horse and cattle equipment, and so on.

I talked to one of Oppenheimer Industries' former secretaries who told me, "I worked in the trenches, you might say. Receipts were sent to me from all over the nation, right from the corral chutes where the branding, earmarking, and vaccinations were being performed. These papers would sometimes show sweat and blood or other corral stains."

There are untold numbers of equally interesting stories behind the carefully kept records of over sixty thousand old marks and brands in Arkansas.

MEN AND WOMEN OF THE OPEN RANGE

Logan France

"Here comes Logan with the cattle," the little boy would yell, and his sister, Glaphyra, would rush to the front porch to watch. Her eyes would sparkle as Logan France, then about fourteen years old and his brother Charlie, about twelve, drove the small herd of cattle through the streets of north Fort Smith, Arkansas. They had "drove 'em down" from the mountains and were heading at day's end for the corrals by the slaughterhouse, a drive of slightly over thirty miles.

"My dad would run anywhere from one hundred to a hundred and fifty head of cattle on the open range, and ever so often the slaughterhouse would order about twenty-five or twenty-eight, hardly ever thirty head of good, fat cattle, and pay Charlie and me five dollars a piece to drive 'em down. We could get a room at the Ward Hotel with a double bed for fifty cents and that left us each four dollars and seventy-five cents profit for the drive. The next morning we'd eat our breakfast there in Fort Smith and be back to Mountainburg in the early afternoon. In them days there was little ol' stores all along and we could get a sack o' that ol' sugary candy and five or six apples for a nickel and we'd just ride along, on the way back home, eatin' apples and candy."

Logan was in his early- to mid-eighties when he told me this story, and his wife, Glaphyra, who was listening, added the part about Logan's being her childhood hero and her running to watch when someone yelled, "Here comes Logan and the cattle."

Roping, riding, and driving range cattle was a way of life that Logan France had grown up with. He told me of writing his first check to pay for cattle when he was a lad of fourteen. This was in the upper Clear Creek canyon, and he said he leaned against his horse and used the seat of his saddle as a desk and a stub of a pencil he carried in his pocket to scribble the man's name and the amount. The slaughterhouse at Fort Smith trusted him with pre-signed checks.

Logan France didn't have much of a formal education. His most important education, the one that counted, was in a classroom with no walls. "We had all kinds o' horses, some good 'uns and some bad. We usually had good saddles that you could tie anything to. We couldn't always afford cowboy boots for us kids, but we buckled on our spurs in the mornin' just as regular as we'd lace our shoes." I imagine the "school of hard knocks" had gouged Logan France more times and more severely than he had spurred the sides of the horses he rode.

He told me of roping a wild bull in the upper Clear Creek country. The bull was owned by Eddie Bellas and had gotten so wild that he'd attack anyone trying to catch him. He would even charge a man on a horse. Eddie had offered twenty-five dollars to anyone that would catch him. That seemed like a lot of money to Logan, so the first thing he did was make sure of the reward, and then he got on his "little sorrel, that was a real cowhorse."

As he approached the bull he stopped to tie his lariat hard and fast and checked to make sure the cinch was good and tight. Logan made his sprint for the bull and the first throw was good. The bull headed for Logan and his horse but Logan reined the little sorrel hard to the left with enough speed and power to throw the bull on his side. He said the bull weighed around 850 or 900 pounds, but, with the rope choking him and the pony holding it tight, Logan ran to the downed animal and, by holding one foreleg bent, held him down. Then he moved his horse for slack to make a loop around the bull's nose so he could be led without choking him.

When all was ready he carefully gauged the distance to his horse and ran for it. He said he was back in the saddle again just a second before the bull got to his feet and headed for him. "I had to throw him three or four more times to teach him to head yon way instead of towards me," was Logan's summary of the bull's education. He then led him to the nearest road where he could be loaded into a truck.

The most interesting story that I got from Logan was the one about roping an African lion. When I asked him about it, he said it was an "awful thing" that he'd done. "Why, that thing could o' killed me as fast as lightning."

He introduced the story by telling of how his dad would be gone for several days and nights at a time, buying cattle. He said people would sell mostly their outlaws, whether cattle, horses, or mules, and that after his dad had bought them, he would send Logan and Charlie, even when they were very young, to bring 'em in. Logan's territory seems to have been the Clear Creek canyons and valleys that stretch from the creek's head in southern Washington County to its confluence with the Arkansas River in Crawford County. Logan's cattle-catching experience was not limited to domesticated cattle. He had grown up catching and driving wild stock as well: he had caught wild cattle, horses, mules, and razorback hogs, until his reputation had spread and he was in demand to catch wild stock of all kinds.

His most exotic catch happened about three miles north of Mountainburg, where a woman named Ms. Hays used to own a roadside zoo. She had bought an African male lion and

147

chained it up. As the lion grew bigger and stronger it had broken the chain, and Ms. Hays sent for Logan France. She said she had a lion she wanted him to rope. This didn't accurately sink in to Logan's mind. "I never dreamed of nobody havin' nothin' like that. She said lion, but I just thought it was a big ol' Maltese cat o' some kind."

Charlie, Logan's brother, met up with Logan, and Logan told him about the cat. "I wanna use you." He told Charlie, "Ms. Hays wants me to rope a cat or sumptin' she's got loose up there." When they got to the zoo, Logan and Charlie each chose a lariat from the several that were always behind the seat of the pickup. "Let's go down here and see what it is," Logan said.

Ms. Hays met them and said, "It's right down there; it was eating a duck when I left." Logan continued, "Well an African lion, the color of 'em is just like the color of a dead oak leaf, you know. Well I had the coil in this hand and the loop hung over my shoulder. And I walked up, I'm tellin' you feller, as close as from me to that woman right yonder." He was pointing to his wife about ten or fifteen feet away. "It kinda turned it's head and snarled, . . .why them teeth looked as long as my fingers, feller." Logan's fingers are quite large. "I just eased my thumb under that loop and when that loop slid down, it jumped to its feet . . . and I [loosened] that rope as fast as I could but I had too big a loop and it jumped through it. Charlie run and got over the wire fence, and I said 'Chuck, walk up the fence, and let it come down the fence and I'll rope it.'"

When the lion came by, Logan was ready with a smaller loop, and when it "hit the end of that slack, I was braced and it was hard to hold. I drawed it up tight and threw it. I told 'im [Charlie] get your rope on right quick!" Charlie got his rope on but not tight enough or soon enough, and the lion "hooked a claw in his loop and throwed it off." At this point Logan had no way to keep the cat from getting on top of him. "I was holding tight," he said and "it's a raisin' cain . . . I said, 'Get a rope on 'em Charlie, a foot or anywhere, get a rope on that thing.' Heck! You know that thing could get you, just before you could say scat. He got a rope on its leg . . . and I told Ol' Slim Harrison that worked there to 'bring that wheel barrow down here.' We had about a hundred yards to take 'im to a buildin' made outta concrete blocks with a cement floor and a three-inch pipe right in the middle, and a cement top on it. There was a big ol' monkey in it, and I told Ms. Hays to git that monkey outta that cage. She said, 'I don't guess we can chain it up anymore,' and I said 'Chain it up your foot, woman! You don't chain up lions, you cage 'em.'" By holding the ropes low and tight from opposite directions, Logan and Charlie held the lion in the wheelbarrow, and Slim, by extending his long arms, was able to keep clear of the slashing claws. Slowly, they backed the lion up to the cage of concrete and iron bars.

After the job was done, a highway patrol car drove up. (I suppose the loose lion had been reported to them.) They looked at the lion and told Charlie, "We don't believe that anybody roped something like that and put it in there." Charlie yelled at Logan, "Hey wait a minute, they said they can't believe we roped that lion and put it in there." Logan said, "Come on, Charlie, if it has to be turned out and roped again they'll never believe it either."

Throughout his life Logan continued to upgrade his horses and cattle. When quarterhorses became popular he became a successful breeder. He had one good cutting horse that had won many contests. Logan said, "What I'm tryin' to tell ya', he could cut the baking powder out of a biscuit without breakin' the crust." He and his son also raised and trained good roping horses. One of them, he said, was in a competition as far away as Madison Square Garden. He is an outstanding example of the kind of person the open range produced.

The Fanchers

Not all the Fanchers were killed in the 1857 massacre in Utah. A son and a daughter of Alexander Fancher, the captain of the train, were returned to Arkansas. In addition to the survivors, there were other relatives in Arkansas that were not on the expedition. And of course there are many female Fancher relatives who don't carry the Fancher name. The current Arkansas brand book lists one brand under the Fancher name, a half circle "F."

Larry and Suellyn Fry acquainted me with the history of several of the Fanchers of northern Arkansas. Larry's mother was a Fancher.

Horses and cattle seem to have always been associated with Fanchers and they still are. Larry Fry and his father have a beautiful place and a fine-looking beef cattle herd on Osage Creek in Carroll County. Their saddle shed shows a large collection of bits, spurs, bridles and saddles, both antique and recent. This varied and interesting collection is a reflection of the stories Larry and his father tell.

James Polk Fancher and his sons Lee, Sam, Denton, Grover, and Henry, they told me, were involved in cattle buying, trading and driving from the late 1800s to the 1960s. These men regularly drove cattle from the rough country of Sweden Creek in Madison County to the Arkansas River and back again.

Lee Fancher, when only ten years old, was the outrider with a herd being driven from Arkansas through the Indian Territory. He was ranging a little too far out and was surrounded by Indians. James Polk Fancher rode out and confronted the braves and must have known of the fascination the Indians had for red hair. Lee's hair was said to be "very red," so Polk said, "Lee, take off your hat." Then, with that flaming bush on display, Polk proclaimed, "I'll kill any man that touches a hair on his head!" The bluff worked, and Lee was saved. Lee later ranged cattle in Arkansas and Missouri. It was said that he once rode a horse from Kingston, on the Kings River in Arkansas, to Kimberly, Missouri, and back on the same day. This was a distance of a hundred or more miles.

Denton Fancher was known as a prominent stockman in

northern Arkansas, often driving cattle and other livestock long distances to market. He was said to be always roping something, or playing tricks in typical cowboy fashion. He and his brothers were apparently excellent horsemen who rode the best of horses.

The women of this distinguished clan were not to be outdone by the men. Mary Fancher was said to be not only beautiful but, like the others, skilled with horses. The story is told that during the Civil War (or during the chaos that followed), she was being pursued by bushwhackers. They were gaining on her, and the outcome didn't look good. But she realized the advantage of a lighter load for her horse, so, as the Frys put it, "She shucked the saddle at full gallop." One can only imagine her glancing over her shoulder while releasing the cinch, and with a handful of mane and a skillful leap, continuing to "ride like an Indian" while the heavy saddle tumbled away into the brush. She outran the bushwhackers.

Female bronc riders, champion ropers, long-distance riders, and beauty queens have ridden across the pages of Arkansas's history. A part of the landscape of one of our great western states, Rock Mary, Oklahoma, was named in honor of an Arkansas horsewoman.

The Bassett women of Wyoming and Colorado filled a book—*The Bassett Women* by Grace McClure—with their exploits. Elizabeth Bassett, the matron of the Bassett women and said to be the head of the Bassett gang, was born and grew up in Arkansas on a horse ranch. She was reputed to have been as "good a cowhand as any man. Any of her cowboys would have died and gone to hell for her," and she "died a southern gentlewoman who bested many strong men in a rough competitive world." The story of Arkansas and the West abounds with strong women.

The Blond-Haired Gold Digger on a Splendid White Steed

This title has the sparkle of a typical fantasy, but throughout its fabric runs a golden thread that holds a promise of truth. It has been handed down to us from the Cossatot River country in Sevier County by a physician named Ferdinand Smith, who practiced medicine in that area in the mid-1800s.

It was said that Dr. Smith was also an amateur historian who listened to the stories told among the pioneer settlers while he was caring for their sick. Those old country doctors, as they rode on horseback, or by buggy or wagon, were often paid for their services with garden produce, chickens, eggs, or livestock. It is entirely possible that, at times, Dr. Smith's only pay was an interesting story. The time frame of this story was many years before the arrival of the Choctaw Indians.

The story centers around an old trading post near where Lockesburg, Arkansas, is today. In those days Arkansas bordered Mexico at the Red River. The trading post was typical of so many scattered throughout the wilderness frontier in those early times. Invoices of the time reveal that an outpost like this would have sold flour, salt, whiskey, coffee, tools, and a few other goods. Items shipped out, via small streams to the Red River, might have included deer, buffalo, and bear skins, and, in this case, gold.

The picturesque, idyllic setting of the little Indian trading post got a little more picturesque and idyllic about once a month, when, as the story goes, a blond-haired, fair-skinned woman rode in on a splendid white horse, with Indian footmen following. The Indians were said to respond to her every command without hesitation. The woman was described as wearing leather garments and being adorned with gold. Her purchases, besides food, included mining tools, and she paid in gold nuggets.

Both the blond-haired woman and the Indians were secretive and spoke very little, and when the lady spoke, it was in Spanish. Of course, she would not answer inquiries about where she got the gold.

Attempts to follow the blond gold digger finally caused her to quit the country, and she was never seen again. However, a mine shaft was found in the Cossatot bottoms years after her disappearance. Over the years many people dug into the shaft, but the digging was interrupted regularly by the flooding of the Cossatot River. At different times mining tools were found, some identified as having been made in Seville, Spain. The last diggings were made in 1927. That year was marked by floods from the Carolinas to Arkansas, and the Cossatot River, taking sides with the mysterious blond miner, laid the secret to rest.

The story indeed sounds like a fantasy, but certainly a beautifully gilded one. I will add this final nugget. While I was researching the history of Sevier County, I found this item, with a 1913 date: "The Mexico Mining and Development Company said they owned a map showing where Spaniards mined over a hundred years ago in the vicinity of De Queen." De Queen is just fourteen miles from Lockesburg, the site of the old trading post.

Mary Conway: A Raven-Haired Girl on a Black Thoroughbred

On April 11, 1849, seventy-five covered wagons, over a thousand head of livestock, including teams, and four hundred seventy-nine men, women, and children rolled west out of Fort Smith. When the wagon train rolled out of Fort Smith, it rolled out of the United States. Fort Smith sat on the extreme western border in those years.

This was the Fort Smith Company, composed of travelers from many different places, commanded by Captain Dillard. They were traveling near the Clarksville Company, and Mary Conway, a black-haired young woman of seventeen, was along, riding a black horse. She was the daughter of Dr. John Conway, a surveyor. She was the oldest of four daughters and had six brothers. Her father had provided her with the horse to ride on the trip. She apparently rode on horseback all the way, a seven-and-a-half-month trip.

Mary had seven Conway uncles. One was Arkansas's first governor, James Sevier Conway. Another was Arkansas's fifth governor, Elias Nelson Conway. One of her Conway uncles was a congressional delegate, and one was a state supreme court justice. She was said to be quite popular with both the military escort and the emigrants in the wagon train. She seems to have won the respect as well as the admiration of the company.

An observer with the wagon train described in colorful terms the ending of a typical day on the Plains:

> Now comes the busy scene of pitching tents, collecting wood, preparing food, etc. The sound of the axe, the metallic ring of the blacksmith's hammer, the merry voice of the children, the lowing of cattle, the braying of mules is heard. Some children are playing near the water . . . and under a large, shady cottonwood tree on the bank of the stream I see a young lady, who has just alighted from her black palfrey, enjoying the luxury of a camp seat, after a fatiguing day's ride. Habited in her riding dress and with bonnet on, a veil thrown carelessly aside, she is twirling listlessly a switch, and giving heed to the conversation of a young emigrant who is sitting contentedly at her feet.

As the train progressed west and passed a peculiar rock formation, one of the army officers, Lieutenant Simpson, climbed to the top. Captain Marcy called to him to unfurl a flag, which he did, and then Simpson records: "A person present suggesting that it be named after an Arkansas young lady (as much esteemed by the emigrants with whom she was in company, as she is by the officers), I immediately fell in with the suggestion, and thereupon with waving flag, proclaimed it to all concerned, that thenceforth, in honor of the said lady, the rock should be known as Rock Mary. Rock Mary, then, is the name of this fantastic formation." This rock is found in western Oklahoma.

A romance developed between Miss Conway and Lieutenant Montgomery Pike Harrison. In honorable fashion Lieutenant Harrison talked to Dr. Conway and Mrs. Conway about marrying Mary. They did not object but stipulated that the marriage be after the Conways got to California.

The mining companies had expected that, as Mary Conway

wrote, "[T]he government would furnish an escort from Santa Fe to San Francisco; but to our great disappointment, we will have no such protection." This meant that she and Lieutenant Harrison would part in Santa Fe, as Marcy and the troops had been ordered to return to Fort Smith. It was said that everyone in the company loved both of the sweethearts and were sad at the parting. One of the party wrote, "I noticed Miss Mary as we were breaking camp this morning and her eyes were red from weeping. I hope that they will meet again."

Doubts had been voiced that Mary Conway could endure the trip, due to her tender years. However, she did endure the trip, even though as she later wrote, "[W]e have been traveling in a dangerous part of the country, where the Indians have been committing depredations on the whites, and they actually murdered two men within three miles of us."

Farther west, in the Arizona desert, an army officer who had been hearing reports of Miss Conway said he had saved for her arrival there "a bottle of Molasses and a lump of sugar since three weeks. I found more than I had anticipated." He described her as "an angel in such wilds!"

Meanwhile, Lieutenant Harrison had not fared so well. He had often expressed a trust in the Indians. He had stated that he would, if approached by Indians while alone, face them in a friendly and calm way. On October 7, 1849, after camp was set up, Lieutenant Harrison went for a lonely ride and never returned. Captain Marcy's report to the war department, aided by his Indian guide's reading of the signs to reconstruct the details, describes what happened.

> The murder was committed by two men. They had two mules and one horse with them. They came down upon their victim at full gallop, but finding that he was not disposed to fly, but on the contrary walked his horse towards them, they also pulled up to a walk. The parties met and rode a short distance together, then dismounted, and seating themselves on the grass, smoked together. Here they got possession of his rifle, on pretense as supposed, of examining it. As this

was the only weapon he had with him, they then overpowered, tied him, and placing him upon his horse, led the horse between them into some timber, skirting a ravine, where one falling behind, shot him in the back of his head, the ball found in the brain, indicating that the deed was committed with his own rifle. Hastily stripping him, they scalped him, threw his body into a ravine, and taking everything but one boot and his saddle, made their escape. Some miles farther they halted, and lighting a fire, had prepared some meat for cooking, as the raw meat was found spitted and the fire smouldering. They left here very hastily, as a pair of moccasins, a lariat, and some other articles were dropped in their hurry, occasioned doubtless by hearing the report of the howitzer which was fired from camp at sundown as a guide to the missing officer.

Montgomery Pike Harrison was born in Indiana and graduated from West Point on July 1, 1847. He had served at Fort Smith from 1848 to 1849. His grandfather was President William Henry Harrison. His younger brother, Benjamin, was later a president of the United States.

And what became of Mary? According to Grant Foreman in *Marcy and the Gold Seekers,* one of her nieces wrote, "Aunt Mary . . . married a sea Captain," and "had four sons and two beautiful daughters; she retained her charm and sweetness all through life."

WOMEN IN THE RODEO AND ON THE RANCH

At least since the close of the nineteenth century, and into the twentieth, Arkansas women have continued to ride and rope alongside men. In 1896, a woman for the first time in the United States officially entered a rodeo and rode a bucking bronc. She was Annie Shaffer of Fort Smith, and the rodeo was at Fort Smith. Several years earlier, that little frontier town had witnessed another illustrious horsewoman, Belle Starr, put on a show. At the Sebastian County fair, two legends took part in a fake robbery as the "Bandit Queen" forced the "Hanging Judge" Isaac Parker, at gunpoint, to step from the stagecoach and hand over his money. Belle Starr had often ridden those streets on a long-legged horse carrying a long-barreled pistol when it was not a staged event. Her old sidesaddle is in a Fort Smith museum.

While interviewing the granddaughter-in-law of James Moose at Morrilton, I noticed pictures on the wall of her daughter and granddaughter. I was told that they were Kathy and Tracy Kordsmeier. They both rode in rodeos and have won a fair share of saddles and ribbons. Here we see the pioneer tradition, the strength and the adventuresome spirit that have been handed down. In looking over my old copies of the *Western Horseman*, I noticed a report on the National High School Rodeo Association finals for that year in the November 1987 issue. The event was held at Pueblo, Colorado, and the article said there were "more than 1,200 high school students, bringing with them years of hard practice, honed skill, intense desire, youthful enthusiasm, and, above all, the spirit of the West." I also read, "In the breakaway roping . . . Tracy Kordsmeier, of Morrilton Ark., finished third." When Tracy charged out of the chute that day at Pueblo, Colorado, she was practically right on the trail her great-great-grandfather, James Miles Moose, had ridden with a herd in 1852. Tracy Kordsmeier had certainly helped bring "the spirit of the West" to Pueblo that day.

There seems to be no end to these romantic and adventurous stories, and Arkansas's frontier past features brave women just as much as it features brave men.

OLD TIME BRONC BUSTERS AND HORSE TRAINERS

Students of the historical movements of cattle herds must not overlook the importance of horses or the importance of the men who trained them. Before the advent of large stock trucks, horses were the only good way to move large herds.

Horses are beautifully coordinated, athletic creatures, but as far as a rider is concerned, they are born without steering wheels, brakes, or safety belts. This meant that horse breakers or trainers were important, and, considering the thousands of horses that were used, they did not have the time for the job that modern trainers have.

To the better trainers, "breaking horses" didn't mean breaking horses' spirits. It referred only to breaking their bad habits and training in some useful ones.

Arkansas has a long history of colorful, expert horse trainers. Denton Offut, for instance, was a horse trainer, or "horse tamer" as he was called, in 1849 in the Fort Smith area. The *Fort Smith Elevator* of September 12, 1902, described a street scene in that town in the early spring of 1849.

> His skill as a horse tamer was remarkable. Passing through the crowded streets you would hear a drum and see him tapping it, and an unbridled horse that he had broken, tamely following him as he lectured to the crowd. He was known in Kentucky as the 'Whisperer,' from his methods. He would get a vicious horse in a stall and avoiding the bites would cautiously stroke the nose and whisper in the ear. The subdued horse would finally suffer handling and bridling. The whisper was a fake to deceive the crowd. The secret was a strong perfume on his hand that has a singular influence on the animal. . . .

The writer's mention of "a strong perfume" may have been just an opinion. It reminds me of a similar opinion mentioned about my friend Otis Parker, the next trainer we will consider.

Otis Parker: "Rolling with the flow"

When I first met Otis Parker he was already an old man. He was a tall, long-legged, and slim black man, and I liked him from the start, especially after seeing how beautifully he dealt with horses. He stood by a horse he had been training and told me, "I can roll on, and I can roll off." Then he demonstrated his technique. He laid a leg over the horse's back and almost effortlessly rolled on. He said, "If they start to get excited, I just roll off," and he did.

Several years ago Otis rode over the greatest divide, and the world lost a good man. He had ridden with trail herds in Arkansas and had trained five-gaited horses for many years for horse breeders in the Fayetteville, Arkansas, area. He trained "Old Glory," a Tennessee Walker from Fayetteville that won a blue ribbon at Madison Square Garden, and he was often called on to catch semi-wild cattle that had either ranged out or had escaped from ranches in several counties of Arkansas.

Otis and I discussed horse training several times. He said, "When I was young, I thought it was a horse's nature to buck, but I found out that that isn't so." He told me a story of a Fayetteville horsemen who had brought a "bunch of half-wild range horses" from Oklahoma. Otis said the horses were giving the horse breakers a hard time, and they called on Otis to help them out. Otis said, "They led the horses up to me one at a time, and I would get on one, ride 'im down the road and back, then get off and they would have another horse ready, and I would ride him the same way. They asked to see my hands; they thought I had some kind of a drug that I was using, but I didn't." It was then that Otis demonstrated to me his roll on, roll off system.

Otis Parker lived in the southeastern part of Fayetteville when I met him. The town had grown up around him, but he still had his horse stable and corral. He said that sometimes when a horse was brought to him for training, he would unload it by the side of the street and ride it into the corral, even though it had never been ridden. Otis Parker never retired from horse training. At the age of eighty-six, he was still breaking horses when he died of complications from a stockyard injury.

Not long ago I talked to his daughter Bernice. I asked her if Otis used sophisticated bits and rigging in his training as many modern trainers do. A beautiful smile spread over her face as she answered, "No . . . he just used a soft braided rope on their neck to teach them to give to a pull, then he'd get on." Otis could soothe a horse with his hands to a remarkable degree.

As a black man, Otis Parker had battled some things besides broncs, and I think he had ridden the buck out of all of them. But the big surprise for me was when Bernice told me that she was a Duke University graduate, and that Otis had put his other children through universities as well.

Otis was a horse trainer who put his children through college and a horse through Madison Square Garden that earned a blue ribbon. Certainly Otis Parker had earned his mark of distinction.

Aaron Davis: Spoiling Broncs for a Living

The same day I talked to Otis Parker's daughter, Bernice, I visited my friend Aaron Davis in Farmington, Arkansas. Over a cup of coffee we discussed Otis and his training, and Aaron told me of working with him in some horse-breaking adventures.

He said he had gone with Otis to haul two unbroken fillies in the Fayetteville area. These were two-year-olds that had not even been trained to lead. The roads were bad and they had parked their truck about half a mile from the horses. Aaron said they had taken a half hour or so to teach the young horses to lead and were heading towards the truck, when he noticed that Otis had rolled on one of them and was riding her. Aaron then did the same, and they rode on down to the truck where they loaded the "unbroken" fillies to take them in for training.

Aaron Davis is a horse trainer, saddle maker, and an old-time cowboy. He grew up in Oklahoma. When he was about eleven years old he started helping his dad train bucking horses for Buetler brothers (a rodeo stock contracting company). His job then was to ride for eight or ten seconds. If he hadn't already been bucked off, he would have to fall off or jump. They had to spoil the broncs to buck. I don't know if

Dr. Spock has heard of, or would approve of, this child psychology for raising broncs. Or was it a bronc psychology for raising children?

Sam Allen: An Old-Time Bronc Buster

I have known Sam Allen for many years. He has many friends in Arkansas, and he has broken and trained scores of horses and has ranged cattle in the state. He also cowboyed in Texas in the old days. He told me the story of how some of the old big ranches would try out a cowboy in those days. He said they would assign you a horse and when you went to saddle up on that first day, "The boys would all gather 'round the corral to watch, and then you knew you'd been given a real dandy." One can easily imagine some of those rides.

I learned a new horse-breaking expression from Sam. When horses would buck and fight real hard, he said, "They throwed a ring-tailed hissy." Sam broke a lot of horses that were good at throwing "ring-tailed hissies," and when he finished, even inexperienced riders could handle them. Sam showed me how to use the "running W," a rope arrangement that aided him in training stubborn horses. The running W is designed to pull both front feet out from under a bucking horse, leaving it on its knees and chin. By the second time this happens, most horses decide, as Sam put it, that "buckin' ain't really what they wanted to do."

Sam also had broad experience working with stock animals. Once I bought a half-brahman cow from the stockyard at Rogers, Arkansas. Sam ran the stockyard there in those years, and he said it would make me a good range cow. I asked him if I could brand her there in his loading chute before I loaded her, and he agreed. However, while my iron was getting hot (I had built a fire near the chute), she jumped so many fences back and forth that I decided that she was out of my class, and I traded her to him for another one.

Sam always had horses around, and once he shared with me his feelings for a good horse. "These modern kids talk about their fine cars, you just give me a good horse with a good saddle, and a pair of old worn soft chaps; there's no Cadillac in the world that can give me a better feel." He once sold a quarterhorse stallion for me, but mostly we traded stories and I learned a lot from him. I will always remember him as a good man of the old school, a cowboy, a friend, and a wild horse breaker.

George Ogle: Think Like a Horse

George Ogle, another horse trainer in the Fayetteville, Arkansas, area, gained quite a reputation around Fayetteville for handling bad horses and taming some of the mean ones. He also shod horses, and I have an old pritchel (a horseshoe punch) that he made for my brother-in-law years ago. George had quite a background of cowboy credentials, including, I believe, riding on the buffalo roundups in the Wichita wildlife refuge in Oklahoma.

A common problem in horse breaking (especially for less-experienced horse handlers) is the tendency of horses to rear up. It is usually caused by a harsh bit or harsh hands, and it is a dangerous habit if not broken. George told me of one horse he had to cure that would rear up, fall over backwards, then lie there and refuse to get up. Now George's technique for reversing a bad habit was to convince the horse that he liked to play the horse's game better than the horse did, but George would play it in such a way that the horse got tired of it before he did. His rearing cure worked like this: George got on the horse and teased him into rearing up, but before he could go over backwards, George stepped off, about at the straight up point, and held onto the reins and *pulled* him over backwards. About this time the horse thinks, "Hey! That was my game, you spoiled my act!" Before the horse could decide not to get up, George—a large man—sat down on the horse's neck and wouldn't let him get up. Then he called to his helper for his whip and convinced the horse that lying there wasn't much fun after all. This may seem like harsh treatment, but that kind of bucking habit could easily kill someone, and Ogle said it worked. I can see the logic. The horse decides, "This guy enjoys this act more than I do; I'd better give it up."

For years I had heard that George Ogle was rough, but I enjoyed his company as I visited with him on his front porch one summer day, and I learned some horse psychology from him. Horse training and bad habit breaking is a skill and an art, and the old-timers sometimes developed their own methods. Even though some of these old-time training techniques may seem a little rough, it is really a rough, tough game, and you also have to love horses to get involved and make the game work.

The horse trainers I have discussed here all seemed to love horses and had well-disciplined horses to their credit.

RODEO: THE SHOWCASE OF OUR WESTERN HERITAGE

Nobody knows how old American rodeo is. Several western towns claim to have staged the first formal rodeo, but rodeo, of all sports, bucked out of the chutes of our covered-wagon past, kicking over all traces of formality. The rootstock is probably deeper and has more forks than any of us realize.

The word "rodeo" is Spanish and comes from the verb *rodear*, meaning to surround. Back in the old days cattle ran back in the hills and canyons and sometimes got a little wild, so when you tried to "bring 'em in" for branding or shipping, you may have found yourself staging a "rodeo" without intending to. When the area that is now Arkansas was under Spanish control, it is altogether possible that the word "rodeo" was applied to rounding up a few head of cattle from time to time. Herds of cattle ran on open range near what was then Fort Carlos.

Roping or lassoing animals goes far back in history. It was not an unknown art on the western frontier in the 1850s drover period. Captain Randolph Marcy, who escorted the first wagon train west from Fort Smith in 1849, advises westward travelers on how to make a rawhide lariat "upon long journeys" when the ones they had "wear out or are lost." He says the ones braided by the Indians are "better for lassoing animals, but they are not as suitable for picketing as those made of other materials, because the wolves will eat them, and thus set free the animals to which they are attached."

Pope County, Arkansas, saw several roundups of cattle herds that were driven to California in the 1850s, and one of its old-time residents tells of some of the early day junior mini-rodeos. As Tate Page relates in *The Voices of Moccasin Creek*, "When the cattle buyers came, and most of the cattle were driven in out of the woods, the numbers were astounding. When the cattle were lotted [or corralled] at night, the younger men would slip out and ride them, or more often be bucked off. Grandpa didn't like for the cattle to be bothered, but he overlooked the actions of the boys."

Many rodeo champions got their start at a young age. Denny Flynn of Charleston, Arkansas, the world-famous rodeo star, told me that he started when very young, helping calf ropers. After he untied the calves, he would jump on them and ride to the other end of the arena. I tried that in my uncle's pasture when I was a kid. I tried to get on a small but rank bull by grabbing his tail. The faster he ran, the longer steps I took. In the end I had a severe fall without even having a ride. I came to enjoy roping more than bull riding.

We are told that the only difference between men and boys is that men play with bigger and more expensive toys. With this in mind we can easily imagine these ranch boys growing up looking for bigger and meaner bulls to ride. And those who enjoyed roping would get together weekends to show off their skills. By the time they started betting on who was best, rodeo was born.

From this viewpoint of rodeo's origins it is easy to see why the spirit of the Old West is so often seen among rodeo contestants. Our pioneer forefathers were strong and not afraid to face danger, and they had to share and cooperate just to survive. We see this among rodeo people today. Looking into the steady gaze of our young rodeo cowboys we see calmness and serenity, balanced by a love of excitement. A bull or bronc rider will possess the courage to risk life and limb to win a contest and yet be willing to share his knowledge, and his last buck, to help a cowboy competing against him. I have heard many rodeo cowboys say that it is the kind of people that make up rodeo that keeps them at it.

At the Steer Palace, a rodeo and roping arena near Alma, Arkansas, I met Andy Jackson. Andy competed in high school rodeo and was the state champion steer wrestler one year and had scored high nationally. At one contest, I was waiting to watch his turn when a contestant before him put his steer down in 3.8 seconds. It was to be some time before Andy's turn came up, so I went over to meet the guy with the 3.8 second score. He was a professional from Oklahoma, and we talked awhile. He said he had been a professional football player and had made the switch to rodeo because of the people. "There's no comparison," he said, "in pro football the competition is felt differently. It's like they want to hurt you. In rodeo you get the feeling of family, like caring for one another." As we talked I was watching Andy, sitting on a well-muscled buckskin quarter horse, relaxed and looking solid. Only one contestant before him. I felt a moment's pride, almost as if he were my own son. Could he make a run at a 3.8-second score?

The cowboy before Andy made a good run and a fair score. Andy rode into the box; the buckskin seem a little "strung up." He walked him out and re-entered. For just a second, horse and rider stood like a statue, every nerve and muscle tensed like a panther ready to pounce on a deer. A slight nod of Andy's hat brim, the clang of the gate, and the stopwatch is ticking. A blur of action, the steer sprints away; in two seconds the buckskin has overtaken him. Andy leans far out, right hand over the steer's neck, kicks loose from the saddle with both hands on the steer's horns now; with a twist of powerful shoulders coordinated with the thrust of his weight and the steer is down and the stopwatch stops. The score: 4.8 seconds, just a second behind the pro.

I turned and said, "You can't let any grass grow under your feet with competition like that on your heels." The pro answered, "The kids in this area make pretty good rodeo cowboys. Most of 'em grew up on farms and ranches and have been around livestock all their lives."

Team roping is an event that seems to resemble useful range skills to a great extent. It has became popular all over the nation. In 1987 Arkansans Shawn Harris of Vilonia, Arkansas, and Mark Lee of Greenbrier, Arkansas, had the best score at the National High School Rodeo Association finals at Pueblo, Colorado.

Bobby Hurley of Clarksville, Arkansas, and Dennis Gatz of Ceres, California, ranked third for 1989 in the PRCA world standings in team roping. Hurley's father brands a "BH" and raises Longhorn cattle. Bobby and Dennis have qualified for the National finals Rodeo three times, and won in 1988.

Denny Flynn went on to rodeo in several events. He was state champion in bareback bronc riding and placed in bulldogging. After his early success Denny went on the professional rodeo circuit for twelve years, specializing in bull riding, and in that event he smashed records on national and international levels.

In those twelve years Denny Flynn won the National Finals bull-riding event three times, thus setting a record, and was runner-up world champion three times. I met a young cowboy-saddle maker in Wyoming on my cross-country ride who said he considered Denny Flynn the greatest bull rider of all time.

On July 23, 1975, at a Salt Lake City rodeo, Denny was gored by a bull that he thought had killed him. The horn had penetrated to within a few inches of his heart, but he was back on the bulls at Madison Square Garden by October, and four months after the injury, he won the 1975 National Finals bull-riding championship.

On Labor Day, 1979, thousands of Denny's fans witnessed a ride they will never forget. This was on the 1978 Bull of the

Year, Red Lightning. In 1979 Red had bucked out of the chutes forty-nine times and had been ridden the full eight seconds only six times. Denny had been on Red six times. He was bucked off the first time, but he had scored the full eight seconds every time after that. He claimed he had won $21,000 on that one bull. However, Denny mentioned that Red Lightning had started spinning to the right, and he didn't know if anyone had ridden him since. "He bucks harder to the right," Denny said.

That record-making ride was put on at Palestine, Illinois. *Western Horseman* magazine described the first few jumps of the 1,600-pound bull, "Red Lightning cleared the chute gate like a four wheeled nuclear bomb. His front feet were three feet off the ground and his back hoofs higher than the chute itself."

Denny was expecting the sudden switch to the right and later remarked, "Then, when he blowed up and turned back to the right, well, he just kicked right over his head. It seemed like his front end just dropped out from under him." *Western Horseman* described it as a "360 degree mid air spin."

The announcer, John Hutson, says of the ride: "The bull did everything right. He had the drive, the power. The way he left the chute, and the speed he picked up as he went, was phenomenal.

"Denny became a part of the bull. I've never seen a man so much a part of an animal. It was like he was glued . . . you have to know Denny Flynn as a human being to really appreciate what happened that night . . . you see something like that . . . you won't forget it in your entire life."

Denny rode until the buzzer sounded and jumped off. He said it seemed as if it was fifty feet to the ground, and when the score flashed up on the board it read "98." The highest score ever made on a bucking bull; it's in the *Guinness Book of World Records*.

When I met Denny I could understand why John Hutson said you would have to know him to appreciate his riding. I helped him design a couple of brands. One was a "bucking 98" and the other a "flying double F." He wanted the two "F's" to look like a horned bull's head.

I didn't notice him with the typical "bull riders' lump" in his jaw, nor see him light up a cigarette, so I asked, "You don't use tobacco do you?" Through a youthful grin, he answered, "No, I don't chew or smoke or drink. I cuss a little; I shouldn't, but I do."

The rodeo riders we see today are showy. They may not be real range riders, but they are for real. You might compare them to flowers growing on the tips of branches. These branches are growing from sturdy trunks, our pioneer forefathers, that put down their roots a long time ago.

The story of Arkansas's adventurous past has been only partially told and practically forgotten. A long time ago, the Quapaw canoes glided downstream to the mouth of the Arkansas River, and gave the land its name. The conquistadores marched over us with over a hundred horses and left. Over a hundred years later La Salle called our country "the finest in the world." Old invoices echo the past: a thousand bear skins and a thousand pounds of gunpowder. An old estate listing ten thousand pounds of tallow. A rusty branding iron wired to a century-old wagon wheel as a memento of a heritage.

Rutted wagon trails in Wyoming that led from Arkansas to California, blazed by the Cherokee, the Scotch, and many others so mixed up that nobody knows their lineage. Tens of thousands of cattle were driven over those old trails, so unpretentiously that history took little note.

But the adventure was there. The stampedes, the Indian confrontations, the desert stretches without water, and the celebrations at trail's end.

Arkansas's key part in the development and taming of the Old West has been ignored for far too long. It is a sad irony that the trails blazed by our ancestors have been so lost to the trail dust of time.

II

The Long Ride

7

Some of My Story

The Rocking Lazy "D"

White smoke rolled off the fire as more dry oak wood was piled on. The smoke diminished as the intensity of the heat increased, and red tongues of fire licked at the face of the branding iron until it, too, was red hot. At the other end of the corral a white-faced cow had been roped by the head and heels and laid on her side. The hot iron was pressed firmly to her right hip for a second or two and lifted to reveal a rocking lazy "D" brand, in which the color of new saddle leather was clearly visible. An underbit was cut in her left ear and vaccination shots were given, the entire operation taking less than one minute. As my next cow was roped, the first one showed little sign of pain or concern, nibbling grass at the corral's edge, now relatively protected from both theft and disease.

I had it better than most people running cattle because I made my living mostly as a woodcarver. I ran a few head of range cattle and horses and broke a few horses from time to time for others, but mostly I was a cowboy whittler. I could ride a horse I was breaking, look after my cow herd, and carry my carvings and tools in my saddlebags. I had laced a special leather pocket on my chaps to carry my carving knife. I was near my favorite things most all the time. I was in love with the life I lived in the free range territory in northern Crawford County, Arkansas. I knew that someday this way of life would end, by legislation or land speculation or misunderstanding or all three, but each day that it lasted I felt I was cheating on the rest of mankind.

In the mid-1960s I had registered the rocking lazy "D" brand. A letter on its side is a lazy letter, and a rocker underneath the lazy D makes it look like a cowboy hat, and that suits me fine. It sure made me feel good to see my little herd wearing that brand. I composed a song about it in those days that went like this:

> When th' sun peeks over th' mountain
> and kisses th' valley below
> then I catch my pal in th' ol' corral
> and away for th' day we will go
> a coffee pot I have not but a tin can
> in my rifle boot I've got a fishin' pole
> But I wouldn't trade th' days that I spend in this way
> for a ten gallon hat full o' gold
> If I don't find a half a dozen of cattle
> with th' brand of my rockin' lazy "D"
> Then I'll find me a spot, and likely as not
> I'll catch me a fish or two or three.

In the late sixties an outsider did haul cows into my area and turned them out. I didn't like it, but my bull thought it was fine and appropriated them into his bunch. That was in the spring. I decided that I knew how to handle the situation, but first I had to separate out the new cows. They were part Angus and some mixed colors. This was done at the old ghost town of Schaberg, where the railroad fence made a handy divider. An old, stubborn black cow was the lead animal of that bunch, and she clearly thought my cow pony and I couldn't drive her anywhere. I needed to move them to a corner of an old fence by the railroad crossing gate, where the separating would be fairly easy. Every time I would head them into an open field toward the railroad gate that old cow would cut back full speed into the timber. My good cow pony, Mirwan, would head her, with his ears laid back and teeth showing, in less than fifty yards, but she learned slowly and would try it again. Mirwan was warming up to the game and liking it better all the time, and since a horse has more endurance than a cow I soon had them herd-broken and relaxed. I put my herd on one side of the railroad fence and the other cows on the other. Then I drove my herd, with my bull, a mile or two up the creek to a place near what I called the Paradise Pool, not far from the King's Throne, one of my favorite hideouts. I drove the outsider's herd down the creek a considerable distance, far enough not to see them anymore all that summer. Late in the fall their owner trailered a horse down and rode by looking for them. I told him that I'd last seen them heading south.

I have always loved things relating to western Americana. One of my oldest recollections is of standing in an old wagon road in North Carolina where I was born, trying to rope a fence post. In 1945 I ran away from home and worked a branding season in Texas and New Mexico. In New Mexico we worked several ranches and branded a thousand or more Longhorn-Hereford cross cattle. I learned a lot in several different western states, but I have learned the most in Arkansas. At the Steer Palace, between Alma and Van Buren, I watched a professional steer wrestler put down his steer in 3.8 seconds. He was followed closely by an Arkansas teenager who put his steer down in 4.8 seconds. Later the pro told me, "This part of Arkansas has always produced some good cowboys. There are good ranches here and you grow up knowing horses and cattle."

That observation is generally true, but today many ranchers all over the West are losing their appreciation for the value of the horse for handling cattle. A horse can outthink and outrun a cow; if he can't, he isn't a cow pony. It's sad to me that we are forgetting how to use him.

I rode with my cattle a lot. They knew me. They knew my horse. When I rode up on the cattle in the woods or some creek valley they would just stand there chewing their cuds, and I could quietly drift them up or down the creek, wherever I wanted them to go. If they tried to cut back, I would swing wide and head them before a race could start. I didn't have to excite them. Horses are more practical, faster, and less likely to excite on any terrain—flat, hilly, wooded, brushy, or whatever—than trucks or four-wheelers if the cowboy knows his business.

One spring, when I drove my herd up the creek along with their freshly branded calves, a strange Hereford bull ambled down the mountain from the west. As I turned in the saddle at his approach I noticed that he was a little lean and guessed that he had wintered in the mountains alone. I let him drift in with my bunch because he seemed a little wild. I thought he'd soon settle down, and he did. By midsummer he was well herd-broken and was running with my bunch with no trouble at all.

He was unbranded, but I asked around and found that he belonged to a neighbor several miles to the north. He told me that the bull had gone completely wild and couldn't be caught. He had offered to give half of him to anyone who would butcher him in the wild with a hunting rifle. My young cowboy's ego led me to say, "I'll load him in my trailer and bring him to you." So we made a deal, and I brought the bull. "How much do I owe you?" he asked, and my young cowboy's ego said, "Oh, just buy me a tank of gas." So he did. In those days a tank of gas came to five dollars.

I've always regretted that I told him I had gentled the bull. I should have asked, "What will you take for him, just as he is, out there in the hills?"

During my years of ranging out I used several different horses. I had learned as a teenager in New Mexico to change horses often so as always to ride a fresh mount. There is a tendency, as the saying goes, to ride a good horse to death, but I always tried to ride the horse the most that needed training the most.

A special, good horse will always be needed at special times, but I would ride any horse I was breaking if there wasn't much to do but check on things in general. On one such occasion, I was riding a bronc with a strong tendency to buck. Most horses I broke didn't buck, because I used the best gentling methods I knew to produce horses without mean tendencies. But this one belonged to someone else, and it had more buck than brains. As soon as I led him through my gate, I got on him, and he started bucking high, in a small circle. I stayed with him and got him stopped as soon as I could and then headed him up the hill out of Schaberg. By then he was too tired to buck, but a car coming down the hill (a rare event in that place and time) stopped; the driver was a long-winded friend. I stepped lightly off, knowing that if I tried to make the horse stand he'd buck again. The man talked until my bronc was completely rested. As soon as he left I stepped back on the bronc and turned him up that steep hill again, urging him into a fast trot before he could remember to buck.

My horses were good. Star, a stout-built, half-Arabian mare, was the best trail horse I have ever ridden. She had a strong instinct for picking good trails over rough terrain, and she communicated her choices to me, but never argued if I overrode her choice. Usually at night I would be forced to give her her head in these matters. My only option then was to grumble a little when I thought she was going wrong and when she came out at the right place, which she always did, to stroke her affectionately on the neck just forward of the saddle.

Mirwan, a purebred Arabian stallion, was one of the two best cow horses I have ever ridden. The other was a buckskin quarterhorse in west Texas when I was a teenager. Mirwan is an Arabian word meaning "strong." He was a dark mahogany bay that I had raised. He was tough and fast and made it a matter of pride never to let a cow beat him. Some of my friends called him "the Bulldozer." He could smell the cattle, so that when the brush was too thick for me to see them, he would still make the right turns either to head them or to keep them moving straight, whichever we were doing. Another good horse was Misty (for Ozark Mist) one of my best-ever horses for riding cross-country looking for strays. She excelled at endurance. I have had many other horses of all kinds, but these have been my best cow horses.

The old ghost town of Schaberg was in the middle of the range area I used, with about three old houses left that were good enough to live in. I ranged my small bunch from a few miles north to a few miles south of Schaberg. There were several other brands ranging in the general area but it wasn't crowded. Mr. Taylor, a neighbor who branded the upside down "T," owned some cattle that were shot with a shotgun to drive them out of a garden. The owners of the garden knew they were in an open-range area, and their garden was not fenced. Mr. Taylor offered to fence the garden, but they had refused, so he moved his cattle. I had one cow shot, but she recovered.

The open range was good to me. Sometimes it was exciting and sometimes a little scary.

Like the mix-up when my neighbor and I and a few others had rounded up a hundred or more cows and calves at Armada, a place that is now just a name about a mile south of where I lived at the time. We were roping calves to be vaccinated, and I branded the few head I had there. Another cowboy and I each roped a separate calf at the same time. His was thrown to be vaccinated just as my calf bucked into his rope and got tangled. The other calf jumped up and began bawling and bucking, the way mine was doing. The other roper's horse, a young Thoroughbred mare, got excited and started bucking, too. Since both ropes were tied hard and fast to the saddle horns, the mare was forced to buck in a circle around me and my horse, Star. Star remained calm and kept turning with the action, but we were being wound up and tied like a package. Each revolution brought the bucking and kicking closer. I heard someone yelling, "Jump Ivan! Jump!" but I didn't want to jump down into that kind of a mess, so I stayed on Star. I always feel safer on a horse. Finally the roper managed to release his rope or cut it, the action stopped, and no one was hurt.

Range cattle develop behavior patterns like wild animals, and understanding those behavior patterns makes it easier to keep track of a herd. Over the years I got to know cow politics pretty well, so I could tell about what they were going to do at any given time. When my cattle were getting ready to move to a new area, they would start to campaign for it. It sounded something like a Democratic or Republican caucus, with all that bawling and carrying on. When I heard that noise I knew they were getting ready to drift, so I'd get behind them and make them go where there was more grass and then they would usually settle down for a week or so.

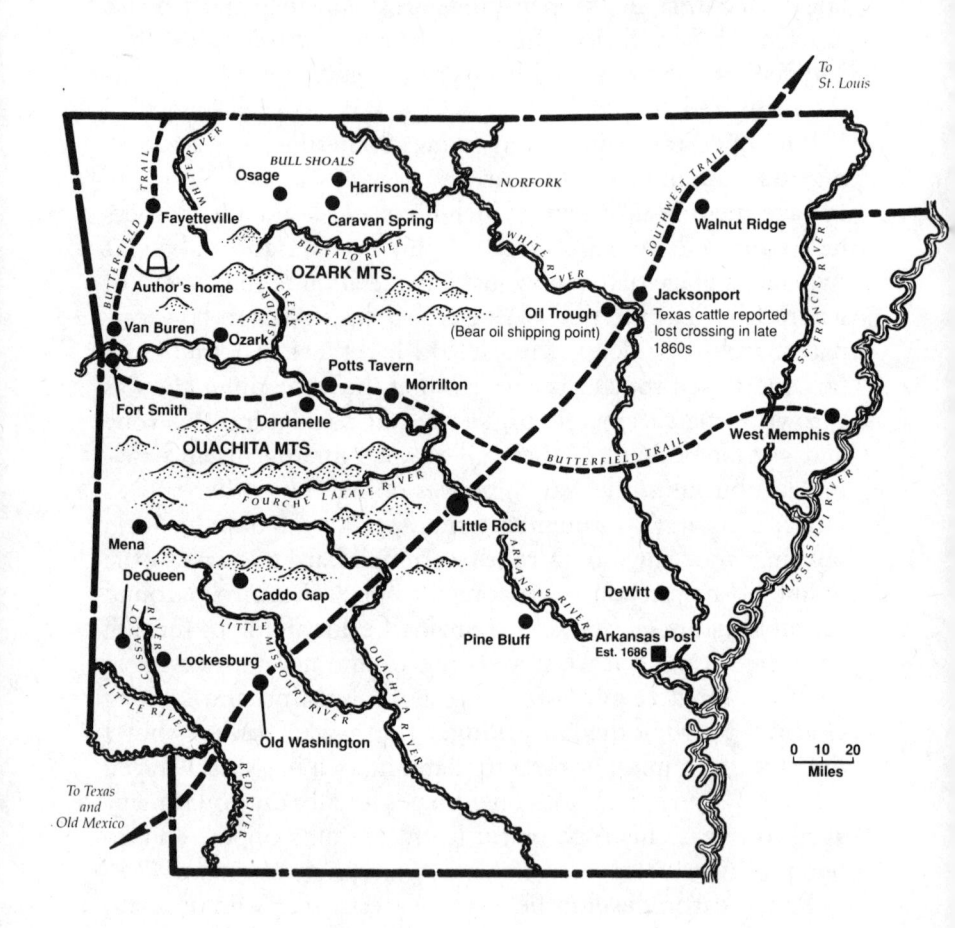

Before I learned to listen, my cows would sometimes drift seven miles down the creek to a little village called Chester where having cows in the streets was not uncommon in those days. When this would happen I would ride down, usually with one or two of my daughters, all of whom were pretty good cowgirls, and we'd tie our horses in front of one or the other of the two old wooden grocery stores there and have a bottle of pop before starting the seven-mile drive back up the creek.

On one such trip my bull got a little stubborn and I didn't have any cowgirls with me. He headed up a street that led up the mountain, running straight toward a large man who was bent over under the upraised hood of his car. The bull didn't turn until he was about ten feet or so from the car. I reined Star up just as the man raised his head, and I asked him if there was a fence up there, motioning toward the brushy hillside, that would block the bull. He said, "What bull?" I didn't say any more, but headed Star up the hill. When I looked down into Chester I saw my enormous bull amble into someone's garage. As I started down he came out and went into a garden near the garage. We played that game until he gave up. Then we went on back downtown to pick up the cows and start the seven-mile drive back home. There I changed horses and drove them all the way up beyond the King's Throne to some old fields they knew pretty well. They settled down there for a week or so while I studied cow politics. I don't think my cows ever went back to Chester.

I had many secret places like the King's Throne, Paradise Pool, and the old hollow tree at Armada where I kept a few supplies. The King's Throne was at a narrow place in the canyon where a rill entered the main creek. I could spend the day there carving, and if the cows came by heading for Chester I would know it. There was an overhanging rock ledge making a small cave where I could keep dry wood, coffee, sugar, and cooking fat, and there was a good hole where I could swim and catch fish to fry. Sometimes I would spread my chaps on the large flat rock I called the throne and take a nap. The close smell of chap leather and of my horse tied nearby blended with the music of the creek to bring me as close to paradise as I have ever been.

On the other side of the creek runs an old stagecoach road. Legend tells of a robbery near the King's Throne in the late 1800s. I was told by an old-timer that when the stagecoach got to Winslow at the north end of the Canyon, a posse ran down and killed all of the robber gang, but the money was never found. I don't know how old the road is, but it's deep rutted, and oak trees have grown up in it that are wider than I am. I think it was a spur of the Butterfield Route. Riding along it causes the mind to drift far back in time. The first branded cattle ranged here, and all across the hills and valleys of Arkansas, before our grandparents and their grandparents were here.

8

The Quest

> *Life begins as a quest of the child*
> *for the man*
>
> *And ends as a journey by the man*
> *to rediscover the child.*
>
> —*Laurens van der Post*
> *"The Lost World of the Kalahari"*

April 19, 1989. The night was cold, but I was sleeping so soundly that when I woke up around midnight, I was disoriented and for a while I couldn't figure out where I was or what I was doing there. I instinctively found my flashlight, and after shining it around my bed, I realized that I was in my tiny tent with only a saddle blanket under me for a mattress. I opened the flap and by the flashlight's beam spotted my horse, Lad, dozing peacefully on his stake rope a few feet away. He seemed oblivious to the chilly moonlit night. Frost was forming.

At that instant the reality of where I was hit me. I was camped in a small, piney field near Proctor, Oklahoma. I shined the light back inside my tent, and my mind tried to mumble, "It's O.K., it's only a practice run," but by then I was fully awake and reality was upon me, and I thought, "Oh, no, this is for real, I'm on my way to California on that little horse, and this little tent is to be my home for over two thousand more miles." I lay back down and sank to a new low. I pulled my only army blanket and my saddle blanket up. I bunched up like a squirrel in a hollow tree and was warm enough to sleep until the first light of dawn awoke me.

I had hit a new low. Although for the remainder of the 2,500-mile ride I had more lows, they were not despairing lows. I never regretted the ride I had undertaken, never once considered giving up my quest. As a child, back in North Carolina, one of the first teachings of my mother that still sticks in my mind was the old adage, "Once a task is begun, do not leave it 'til it's done, be it large or be it small, do it well or not at all." This time I had taken on a large task, and I intended to do it well.

I had been making preparations for this ride for over a year, but my daughters said I had talked about it for as long as they could remember. I don't know how long I had carried the dream, but I remember that when I was a teenager in my native North Carolina I had had an overpowering urge to ramble west, to sleep on the ground in a different place every night—by the road, under bridges, or wherever I could find a good place. I guess I wanted to find the man inside me, so I ran away from home when I was seventeen and didn't write a letter with a return address until I was over a thousand miles away. Now, I suppose at sixty-one I was beginning a journey to rediscover the child inside me. In any case, my Arkansas to California horseback ride helped me to understand and trust myself more completely. None of my youthful ramblings were nearly as fulfilling, nor taught me as much about myself.

For years I have had a recurring dream. I am walking all over the United States. The country is a huge map. Sometimes the nation is no bigger than several city blocks, and I make tours all over it, exploring and searching, looking for something I don't understand, but mostly fulfilling the urge to ramble.

Many times on my cross-country ride I would dismount and walk to get the kinks out, and I would fantasize that the whole nation was really only a large map, and all I had to do was stroll across it. I must have walked a hundred or more of the 2,500 miles. The fantasy occurred only when I was walking.

The quotation at the head of this chapter was sent to me by Jose Lopez, whose friendship I made in Rocky Ford, Colorado. Perhaps the rediscovery of one's youth is the real "fountain of youth" that Ponce de Leon searched for. It is within us, and we can drink from it whenever we please.

The original reason for the ride, the conscious one, the one that sparked the flame, was adventure. I wanted to find out if western hospitality was still alive, how difficult it would be to find feed and water for my horse, what value the time to meditate would have for me, how it would affect my writing, how it would affect me as an artist. I wanted to set the West, past and present, the old and the new, side by side, through research and experience, and see how they compared.

A surprise for me, and one of the greatest benefits from the ride, was its research value. The trails I followed were lost trails, trails long plowed under. Many trails, like the Chisholm and the Santa Fe, have been ridden for over a hundred years, and written about in over a hundred books, so that the wagon ruts in literature are deeper than those in the ground. But here on the face of the earth and in the minds of a few old Westerners were still secrets waiting for me to discover. I could not have learned most of what I came to know even if someone had given me the keys to all the institutes of higher learning.

The year before the ride was spent completing the manuscript for the first section of this book and ended in choosing a horse, deciding on absolute essentials to carry with me, and studying the route beforehand. I would be following, as closely as practical, the old Cherokee Trail, a route used by the Cherokee Indians and their white friends in their 1849 journey to the California gold fields, and discussed in the previous chapters as a cattle drovers' route in the 1850s.

I made a special saddle for the ride, with a wooden tree. I used catalpa for the tree, because it's light, and with its extremely low shrinkage rate, it wouldn't be likely to warp out of shape. The total weight of the saddle was kept down to twelve pounds and eight ounces. The fork was the natural fork of the tree, as were many of the old-time saddles. I shaped the bars to fit Lad, the horse I had chosen. I rode him around some with just the tree, apart from the leather, to make sure there were no points that would gouge him and make saddle sores.

Many of my friends thought I should take along a packhorse, but I didn't because for the most part I would have to ride road shoulders, and in some places the traffic would be heavy. I would be freer with one horse, and it would take less time to set up camp and to break camp and to be on the go at the beginning of each day.

The problem was to keep the weight down. I could carry only what was absolutely necessary. This included feed for Lad. I took along a canvas nose bag, and to carry his grain I had a pair of pant legs cut from an old pair of denim jeans that I sewed shut with leather thongs and looped over the saddle horn.

This was the rest of my pack:

For Lad: A folding plastic water pail, a grooming brush, and a grooming cloth. These were kept rolled up in his nose bag. I also carried a laundry marking pen and wrote on the nosebag the names of towns and outstanding places we visited.

Food for myself: Beef jerky (with more to be mailed to me from time to time), dried fruit, parched corn, and a two-quart water canteen hung around the saddle horn.

Clothing besides what I was wearing: One pair of blue jeans, one shirt, one tee-shirt, one pair of shorts, two pairs of socks, two bandanas, one wool shirt for a jacket, one suit of cotton long-handled underwear, and a pommel rain slicker.

Bedding: One army wool blanket, to be carried rolled up in an eight-by-ten tarp tied behind the saddle. The long-handled underwear and the wool shirt were rolled inside the blanket. Lad's two saddle blankets constituted the balance of my bedding. The saddle blankets were the Mexican, all wool, woven type.

Miscellaneous: Two carving knives, four chisels, and an Arkansas novaculite sharpening stone, rolled up in a towel, several woodcarving blanks, a notebook and pen, press releases from the University of Arkansas Press, photocopies of newspaper stories with my picture for identification, a small tape recorder, matches, a mini-flashlight, a two-ounce, handmade aluminum digging tool to bury my trash, salt, a mini-camera, and film.

Lad is an Arabian gelding. I chose him for the ride because of the endurance and toughness characteristic of the breed. I also like a horse with spirit and style. The old-time Spanish mustangs were part Arabian, and many horsemen feel this accounts for their toughness and ability to survive under adverse circumstances. Lad possesses all these qualities: sometimes he survived on desert grasses only and had actually gained weight by the end of the ride.

The reality of the trip hit me pretty directly when I got the health certificate on Lad. It read: Origin, Mountainburg, Arkansas—Destination, Woodfords Station, California— Moved by Air__, Rail__, Truck__, Trailer__. These options were all marked through and "horseback" written in. The veterinary service was performed free, as a contribution to my ride, by the Broadfoot Clinic at Alma, Arkansas.

These words seemed to me like a passport to some distant country, and they made me feel like I was really nearing departure time. I went to sea for a year once, and it always thrilled me when the control station called us for our "Easy Tare Dog" (military lingo for, E.T.D.—estimated time of departure). It meant we would soon be casting off our mooring lines and starting the big engines.

I had set as my departure date somewhere from the first to the middle of April. This was the custom of the old-time cattle drovers and emigrants because they had to conform to the seasons. Any sooner and the grass would not be out enough for horses and cattle to live off the land; any later and the severe weather of the high altitudes farther west would take a heavy toll. The point at which I would cross the Continental Divide was left undetermined, because I would, in addition to having to follow nature's curves, have to conform to modern laws and ranchers' fences that forbid horses in certain areas. Nevertheless, I planned to stay as close to the Arkansas drovers' trails as my knowledge and other circumstances would allow. To step from the dust of documents to the dust of trails, I would have to talk and listen; and since God gave me two ears and one tongue, I figured I should listen twice as much as I talked.

My schedule did not allow time to take Lad on long rides to toughen him up, so I planned to do that as I went along. I finally settled on April 14 as the date for departure. The newspeople wanted to know ahead of time, so I gave them that date and held to it. As I rode Lad up to Artist Point for the kickoff ceremony, it started to rain. I was glad I had tested him with a full pack.

＃ 9

From Artist Point to the Oklahoma Border

The First Small Steps Were Big Ones

Artist Point is a gift shop on Highway 71, about seven miles north of Mountainburg, Arkansas. It's about a mile and a half from my place and around four hundred feet higher in elevation. From that vantage point one can view fifty thousand or more acres of Ozark highlands, hills, and valleys that had been a valuable part of Arkansas's open range for well over a hundred years. Standing there can inspire an artist and lift any spirit. Lad's spirits were lifted until he was downright snorty.

We were greeted by cheers as we approached. From the crowd gathered to see us off, and from the many kind words and blessings I had a feeling that the whole state was behind us.

Someone gave me a sprig of fresh apple blossoms (Arkansas's state flower) to remind me of the pleasant expanses back home when I was crossing the dry deserts over a thousand miles to the west. I was frankly and deeply moved.

It was beginning to rain as I rode up. The rain continued all through the event, and I hadn't been able to find a waterproof covering for my hat. Robin Kuykendall, of the Arkansas State Police, noticed this and gave me his. I used it, whenever it rained, all the way to California.

After the ceremonies, I rode back down to my place, which was on my route, and unsaddled. Though it was still raining, the reporters wanted more pictures and interviews, so I decided to make the next day my first full day. Some of the old-time drovers used the first day as a "test day," when they would travel only a few miles and set up camp to test the equipment. In one instance a drive covered only one hundred and fifty yards on the first day.

I used the remainder of this day to saw out some carving blocks to take along, as some of my collectors had already ordered hand-carved models of Lad. These would be carved along the way as commemoratives of the ride. This was to provide my main financial support for the five-and-one-half month journey.

The next day, April 15, I rode about sixteen miles and camped at an abandoned homestead just east of Devil's Den State Park. I planned on short, easy days to begin with to allow Lad to toughen and leg up, as the old horsemen would say. He seemed to be full of fire and had to be held in check most of the day.

During the first few miles I rode through an area where I used to range a few head of cattle wearing my rocking lazy "D" brand. This is the canyon between Winslow and the ghost town of Schaberg, a range long held as "common pasture" by stockmen south of Winslow. Logan France, the old lion roper who lives just south of Mountainburg, told me that he wrote his first check near here around 1909, when he was about fourteen. He had leaned against his horse and used his saddle for a desk. He was buying cattle for Fort Smith cattle buyers and driving them to their stockyards. He remembers being proud that at his age they trusted him with pre-signed checks.

This first day I also passed the place where, according to word-of-mouth stories, a stagecoach robbery had occurred back in the mid-1800s, before the railroad.

I ate a lunch of jerky and dried fruit while I was still deep in the timbered canyon. I came out on the Devil's Den road just west of Winslow. All along the way people greeted me and wished me well.

On the sixteenth I rode on through Devil's Den and over the hills to Cove Creek, a beautifully situated place with tall limestone bluffs on one side and sweeping meadows on the other. I took a bath in the clean water. I made camp near the road. Some of the people who drove by and saw my horse staked there stopped to talk awhile. Rose, my wife, had driven down and brought along my guitar, so after supper I played a few tunes.

After dark, as we were sitting around the campfire, some locals stopped by to visit and told us that we were camped at the mouth of "Lick Holler," so named because it was used as a natural salt lick back in the open-range days. The old-timer of the group noticed my guitar and said, "If you can play and sing some of them real old songs, I'd like to hear some." So I played and sang some.

On April 17 I rode by two little villages of considerable interest to anyone interested in western Americana. First was Evansville, the home in 1849 of Lewis Evans, captain of the Cherokee Mining Company, from which the Cherokee Trail took it's name. Then I rode by Cane Hill, birthplace of the famous pioneer quarterhorse breeder Coke Blake.

All through Arkansas and Oklahoma, the livestock showed a lot of interest in Lad and me. Whole herds of cattle would come as near as their fence would allow and trot along with us as far as they could. Near Cane Hill, a flock of goats ran toward us with enthusiastic bleats as though they meant to go with us. A huge tom turkey was following behind them gobbling at us, "Gobble, gobble!" with his tail flared out.

That night I camped at Lincoln, Arkansas, near the "Lindsey Prairie," where the Carter-Shores cattle drive of 1853 began.

Leaving Lincoln on the eighteenth, I stopped at Summers on the Arkansas-Oklahoma border to have new shoes put on Lad. Andy Anderson had been recommended to me as a good farrier; I would say he's the best. People noticed that Lad and I both had gray hair and asked our ages. "He's six," I said, "and I'm sixty-one." Oklahoma is known for its tornados, and as I rode across the border storm clouds with lightning were gathering in the southwest.

10

Through the Indian Territory

Oklahoma is OK!

"Back in the saddle again" is mostly a good place to be, but not during a severe thunderstorm, and that's where I found myself as I rode across the Oklahoma state line. The clouds were beginning to roll in as I stopped at the "Welcome to Oklahoma" sign to take Lad's picture, and I hadn't ridden a mile beyond it before I was back in my slicker. A slicker is way ahead of any modern rain gear. Mine is of the old design that protects me and my saddle all the way down to my boots and is fairly lightweight. With my slicker and wide-brimmed hat to keep the water from running down my neck, I enjoy riding in the rain. That is unless there is an electrical storm with it.

As the sky became darker, as thunder began to rumble and lightning played across the face of the clouds, I started looking for shelter. I could have put up the little tent carried in a three-pound roll in my right saddlebag, but I wanted to save that until nothing else was available.

About that time I noticed a farmer heading for his barn with a beautiful team of Belgium draft horses. I reined Lad off the road and headed for the barn, too. Each of the man's horses was almost three times as big as Lad, so Lad decided to show off his Arabian spirit. I asked the farmer, "What's the chance of getting in your barn out of the storm?" "Pretty good," he replied, "and I'll put you up for the night if you want to stay."

Doyle Murray's kindness was my first taste of Oklahoma hospitality; it set the tone not only for Oklahoma, but for the rest of the ride all the way to and including California. Many people along the way greeted me openly and told me, as Murray had, that they trusted a man more if he was riding a horse. Lad was to open doors for me that I could not have opened by myself.

The next morning Mrs. Murray fixed a fine breakfast, and Doyle insisted I take along a generous supply of feed for Lad. He seemed amused at my plans to make such a long ride on such a small horse.

Riding along the old drover trails, I should have been prepared to encounter living proof of the stories and characters I was writing about, but I was not prepared for the next person I met. Not ten miles into Oklahoma a man walked out into the road near Westville and stopped me. He had heard of the ride and told me that he was a great-grandson of one of the Arkansas drovers. He held a family history magazine in his hand and showed me a copy of the C. C. Seay letter, the story of an 1853 cattle drive. I said, "I'm featuring in my book that letter you're holding. I plan to use it just as it is."

He said, "Well, I just wanted to tell you that he was my great-grandfather, and I have the original letter in my bank box." And so I got to meet Mr. Billy Jack Smith. We visited awhile, and I rode on.

Just east of Tahlequah I had my first restaurant meal. I was beginning to learn just how good food can taste when you ride all day and only carry jerky and dried fruit in your saddlebags. I carried coffee and a coffee can to use for a pot, but in most cases the prairies are not safe places for a campfire. A waitress at the restaurant offered to water Lad while I ate, and she also gave him an apple, his favorite treat.

A little north of Tahlequah I tried to buy a full supply of feed for Lad. The lady at the feed store gave me a couple of gallons, which was all I could carry, but she wouldn't take any pay. Riding through Arkansas, Oklahoma, and Kansas often reminded me that we were in what is sometimes called the Bible Belt. Often when we were offered hospitality, I would notice the Bible open on the table. To offer refreshments was a part of the traditional customs.

By now Lad and I were starting to read each other's minds. Somewhere after the first thousand miles we became like a pair of drifters or hobos of the Depression days of the thirties.

Toward the end of the day of April 20, Lad was getting a little leg weary and kept wanting me to stop at every gate and ask permission to spend the night. He seemed to think that everyone would be as nice as the Murrays had been. I was starting to speak to him as if he were human (I've always done that with horses, to some extent). When I would notice that he wanted me to stop and ask, I would say something like, "Lad, they don't even have any horses here, there's no corral or any place for you to stay."

Late in the day he brought it up as we approached a sheep ranch, and I decided to stop and see. I reined him up in front of the gate and he stopped before I said, "Whoa!" After introducing myself, I said, "I'm riding this horse from Arkansas to California, and I need a place to stay for the night. If you have a place for my horse, I can sleep in the barn or anywhere, or if you have somewhere, I can put up my tent."

This was the home of Mr. Noble Ward, who accepted us without hesitation. He said I could turn Lad loose in the big corral, which hadn't been grazed for some time. This I did, and while I was going back and forth with my gear and fixing myself a bed in the hay, Lad stood square in front of me, looking me in the eye. I could see it written all over his face: "You see, I was right. These people are really all very nice to us, so why are you so bashful about asking?" I pushed him aside. It was pitiful, on the other hand, to see his face when we were refused.

After I got acquainted with Mr. Ward he said I could sleep in his attic, but I said that I would rather be near my horse. He invited me to watch the evening news on his TV, and during the conversation he remarked that there were not many rattlesnakes in the area, but there were quite a few copperheads. When I headed for the barn at bedtime, his dog, a big, black part pit bull, trotted along with me.

While I was arranging my bedding he kept sniffing at something on the barn floor, under the hay manger. Thinking it might be a snake, I got a shovel and my flashlight and tried to help him find it. When we couldn't, I decided not to let it spoil my sleep and went to bed, literally "hitting the hay." Then the dog came over and inspected the area all around my bed. At first the wet nose touching my neck was irritating, but finally I thought, "Maybe it is a copperhead he smelled, and he's looking out for his master's guest."

At last he curled up at my feet and spent the night there, except that two or three times an hour he would get up and circle my bed and then lie back down at my feet. I felt cared for and protected.

The next morning I found out that his name was Rambo. Good men like Noble Ward have good dogs like Rambo.

After we were on our way again, Lad developed what seemed like a severe case of impaction colic. He had been fed hay and grain all winter, and the change to green feed had been too sudden. I had grazed him some before we left, but the grass by the roadside was unusually rank, and he had pigged out. I guess the trek had given him an appetite bigger than his stomach. I knew the feeling. From Tahlequah on, whenever I left a restaurant my stomach would hurt.

Later in the day a kind lady phoned Dr. Mark Roberson, a veterinarian from Salina. He diagnosed the problem, treated Lad, hung around for about an hour to check on him, and gave me some medicine to carry along in case the problem occurred again, possibly in a remote area where I couldn't get help. When I asked for the bill he said there was no charge and looked thoughtfully at Lad. "I hope you make it, and I hope the little horse makes it." He also said that Lad was now able to be ridden, so I set off in the dark to find a campsite.

At a convenience store near the edge of the woods close to Spring Creek I asked and received permission to make camp. It was very dark by then, and I set up my tent by feel. The next morning Mark showed up at the camp to check up on Lad and left me with a sizable cash contribution for the ride. At this point I had more money than I had when I left Arkansas. Before I rode on, I stopped at the convenience store for a cup of coffee. The lady there told me that she had been instructed by the owner to give me whatever I wanted for breakfast at no charge. During the day it turned hot, but a brisk, cooling wind came up. I was determined to compose a song about each state as I rode through. Here is Oklahoma's.

> The wind of Oklahoma whips my pony's mane and tail and cools the sweat on my body, on the old Cherokee Trail,
> and the people in the country have that old-fashioned way.
> They cared for me and my pony. Oklahoma is OK.

Each song a state gave me I would sing several times a day until I had crossed that state, and I added verses to each song as I rode along. Lad was my drummer, his hoofbeats setting the four beats to a measure. To keep proper time I would always let his left front hoof strike the first beat of the four. Later that week I composed another song, one that I sang every day all the way to California, called "On Down the Road."

> On down the road, my pony prances.
> We've gotta get, on down the road.
> On down the road, we take our chances.
> We never know, what waits for us,
> On down the road.

Through the entire journey there was good and bad, but the good was most outstanding and the bad for the most part was humorous. On April 22, I stopped at a farmhouse to ask if I could use the phone. I had called the University of Arkansas Press the day before, when Lad was sick, and I needed to call again to report that he was OK and we were traveling again. I was met at the door by an old man who looked like he had survived from the days when Oklahoma was primarily outlaw country. He ignored my question about using the phone and, squinting intently at Lad tied to his gate post and obviously outfitted for the long trail, mumbled, "He looks like he fits the description of a horse stolen a few days ago in these parts." In spite of my insistence that I had the bill of sale in my saddlebags, I didn't get invited in to use the phone.

But I remember well the fine people like Fred Garcia who, when I stopped to water Lad, gave me a cup of coffee and later caught up with me in his auto to give me money for my lunch. On the night of April 23, I stayed with Mr. Forrest Qualls and his wife, Jeanette. Forrest had once been a neighbor of the quarterhorse breeder Coke Blake, mentioned earlier, back at Cane Hill. We discussed some of Blake's almost legendary ideas on breeding and training the quarterhorse. Forrest is a part of a dying breed, the old-time bronc rider, trainer, and horse trader. He told me of a horse he trained that "got to likin' to buck," and it seems that Forrest "got to likin' it, too." He said he would save "that ol' bronc" for Sundays. After mounting in the corral, he would have his wife throw open the gate with the "horse buckin' right through it." Forrest, astraddle the bronc, would be "hootin' and yellin'" for pure joy and exhilaration.

When I rode into Claremore we had been on the road ten days without a day's rest for Lad. Just west of town, Mr. Cliff Delay did me the kind service of keeping Lad on good pasture for a couple of days. My wife drove over from Arkansas to look me up, and in answer to her questions of my whereabouts a lady asked her, "Oh, you mean the old man from out of the past?" and so Rose was directed to me. We spent a couple of days seeing Will Rogers' old hometown of Claremore.

Riding west out of Claremore I soon entered Osage County, an area noted for its fine bluestem grass. I have heard old Arkansas cattlemen speak of driving herds of cattle to that country to graze the good bluestem for the summer. One night I stayed with Bill Whitlatch, part Osage Indian and cowboy who works the old way with horses. I had been on the trail for two weeks. Since I had made thirty miles the day before and this was Sunday, I enjoyed a good visit as Bill and I lingered over a fine, big breakfast his wife, Marilyn, had cooked. Lad had been turned out for the night in a large pasture, but when I whistled he came and we continued our westward trek.

In Ponca City, the Brace Book Store held an autograph party for my first book, *The Art of I. Denton*, and the good folks there all but gave me the key to the city. West of Ponca City the Kahles and Claybakers opened their homes to me. On May 6, Max Claybaker, who uses heavy-duty scales on his farm, weighed Lad. He weighed just 760 pounds. I weighed in at 160 pounds, and my entire pack and saddle weighed in at 60 pounds. This meant that Lad's total load came to 220 pounds. Other people helped add flavor to my research. Melvin Kahle, for instance, pointed out for me depressions in the prairie that are said to have been caused by the tens of thousands of Texas longhorn cattle on their way north over the old Chisholm Trail.

Although I had lived along the Arkansas-Oklahoma border for around thirty-seven years, I felt now that I was getting to know Oklahoma for the first time. When you travel this way, cross-country on horseback, making only twenty or thirty miles a day, you have time to speak greetings as you ride by, even if you don't stop. But occasionally someone would invite me to tie my horse and come in for refreshments, or if I stopped at noon to water Lad I would sometimes get invited for lunch. This happened at Walter Colby's, just east of Ponca City. Mr. Colby is an Osage Indian, and he told me that Colby, Kansas, was named after his grandfather. Another day as I was resting by the road, a Baptist preacher stopped to chat and offered a prayer "to assure the success of the ride." Then he gave me a twenty-dollar bill. You can't beat that—a prayer and twenty bucks at the same time!

Just before I left Oklahoma, I stopped at the little town of Manchester, just south of the Kansas line. Clouds were building in the southwest, it was hot, and tornado warnings were out. I ate lunch at a small restaurant, and then I took Lad's picture as he stood tied beside a sign that said, "Welcome to Kansas."

11

Kansas

A Land of Many Trails

The day I rode across the state line into Kansas I logged thirty miles. Severe storm warnings were out; it didn't look too bad, but at the end of the day I requested and was granted permission to sleep in a barn that belonged to Dick Moore. No storm came up that night, and the next morning as I was saddling Lad, Dick and his wife, Dixie, came out and invited me in for breakfast. After a good visit I headed north toward Harper, where I planned to drop in on Russell Smoker, a good friend who was a wheat farmer.

Many of the old drovers followed the Arkansas River around its great bend to the north, but I decided to cut across, not only to shorten the distance but to miss the busier sections. It's likely that some of the west-bound travelers must have followed Medicine Lodge Creek, as I intended to do.

On the way into Harper I rode by Chaparral High School, where several students and photographers from the journalism class came out for an interview. During the several days I spent with Russell I spoke to several of the classes.

Russell Smoker is also a woodcarver, so while Lad and I rested, Russell and I did some whittling. We each carved a horse. I gave him mine, because he was one of my backers for the ride.

On May 13, I left Smoker's and headed west on some good, sandy dirt roads he had shown me as a better route to Medicine Lodge. A cold north wind that had made progress toward Harper difficult had switched around and still blew against us until early in the morning, when it died down and a slow rain had started. Since there was no thunder or lightning I enjoyed the cool ride.

Leaving Medicine Lodge, I followed a road that led up Medicine Lodge Creek. Since traffic wasn't heavy, I set up camp on a grass strip only about fifty feet wide, between the road and the railroad. Lad was getting accustomed to most sights and sounds by now so I didn't think a train would bother him. I named it the "I be damn" camp.

Sometime before midnight, after I had fallen asleep, a pickup truck slowed down and stopped near my tent. A man got out and walked over to the front of my tiny home. I unzipped the flap to look out at a pair of cowboy boots and up into the darkened form of a tall man who said, "What's goin' on here?"

"I'm riding my horse from Arkansas to California," I answered, "and I just stopped here for the night." I smelled beer on his breath as he hesitated a second or two and said, "Well, I be damn! Well, I was on my way back from a ropin' at Sun City and I saw your horse and thought the horse might be loose."

"Did you win anything at the ropin'?" I asked him.

"I sure did!" he answered, "I won the jackpot. Made me some bucks! Well, I've got to be going, just thought I'd check on the horse." His buddy, back in the pickup, must have asked what was going on, because I heard another voice exclaim, "Well, I be damn!"

Many times people noticing that my horse and I were obviously rigged out for a long trip would stop their autos and ask, "Where you going?" As I answered, "California," I would look directly into their faces because I liked to see their eyes widen and their jaws drop. This got to be one of my favorite sources of amusement along the way.

Once while I was stopped by the roadside in Kansas to graze Lad, a rancher mistook me for a drifting horse trainer and stopped to offer me a job breaking horses. Anyone who kept horses would usually give me grain for Lad free of charge.

At Sun City the country roads were a little confusing, so I asked directions from some boys riding push scooters. One of them said, "Just follow us!" As we all headed downhill toward a bridge, with the guys coasting and Lad trotting, they asked me questions about my ride. Their jaws didn't drop when I said I was going to California on my little Arabian horse. They acted as if it were natural to ride your horse to California whenever you wanted to. At the bottom of the hill they turned off, they all waved, and one said, "This is as far as we're going, see you later."

South of Greensburg, in some of the most beautiful cow country I have ever seen, I washed a couple of pairs of socks in a creek and pinned them to my pack. They soon blew dry in the prairie wind.

I stopped at the home of Robin and Cindy Powell and their five children to ask about camping at an abandoned farmstead nearby, but they insisted that I stay at their place. They had an old school bus I could sleep in and lots of good grass to stake Lad on.

Robin had two good guitars, and we stayed up late pickin' and singin'. They gave me a children's book about a cattle drive from Florida, and all but the two youngest autographed it for me. Alisha wrote, "I liked the songs you sang." Josiah wrote, "I liked the picture of the carving you showed us. Thank you for showing us your horse." Caleb wrote, "I liked the saddle you made. Your horse was neat, too." On another page, in a mature hand, was written, "Ivan. We're glad you stopped at our home. Thank you for sharing with us. The Powells, Robin, Cindy, Alisha, Caleb, Josiah, Luke, Maggie." This book is one of my most treasured possessions.

Back on the busier highways, I became aware again of an annoyance and a danger that had been with me since eastern Oklahoma and would stay with me through Kansas and Colorado. This was the deer-warning whistle attached to many cars and trucks. It makes a high-pitched sound that people can't hear, but when you're sitting on a spirited horse and one of those whistles goes off, nobody has to tell you.

It was terribly frightening when I first experienced this horseman's horror. Lad had become used to traffic, and I thought we were doing fine when, at the approach of a truck, I felt him stiffen up and jump violently to one side. This happened off and on for several days, and I thought Lad was losing his horse sense until a truck driver told me about the whistle. Lad finally got accustomed to the thing, and if I stroked his neck as vehicles passed he would be fairly calm. But he would always stiffen up and stare at the source of the whistle. I suspect that the deer, too, will become accustomed to the sound and not respond, but the danger will persist for horsemen—especially children riding highway shoulders—who face them for the first time, so the benefit will be lost but the danger will remain.

At Mullinville I took refuge from an approaching storm on the porch of an abandoned homestead west of town. I put

Lad in the old corral and was going to sleep when Arthur Moyer found me there and invited me into town to stay with him until the storm front passed. I spent two days with his family and got to attend the graduation of the eighth grade at the Mullinville school. Arthur's grandson was one of the six students in the class.

While I was in Mullinville Lad escaped from the corral. I found him on the east side of town, at the home of Vivian Sloan, who had pastured him with her horses when he stopped there. When she found out who I was, she showed me a letter that I had written her in 1962, in answer to a letter from her concerning an Arabian stallion I had advertised for sale.

I rode about twenty-six miles the day the storm front passed, crossing to the north side of the Arkansas at Ford, camping alongside the river a few miles east of Dodge City. On May 20, I rode on through this cow town, where many thousands of Texas longhorns had been driven in the years following the Civil War. The trail drives that I was writing about had passed through this area before there was a Dodge City.

Helpful strangers tried to show me routes around Dodge City, but I was hungry and all the restaurants were uptown, so I rode Lad right down Wyatt Earp Avenue.

Lad's shoes were wearing thin, so I found a blacksmith, Leonel Padilla, and asked him to check them out. He thought I should get some more wear out of them. The problem of riding gravelly roadsides is that the steel shoes wear out before the hooves have grown out enough to provide places for new nails, so I heeded his advice to wait longer. The shoes put on in Arkansas by Andy Anderson were holding fine after almost five hundred miles.

Leonel, who was born and raised in Chihuahua, Mexico, is a good cowboy and a good roper. He anticipated my need for horse feed, and, learning the route I was taking through town, he overtook me with more grain than I could carry in my feed sack.

Two days west of Dodge City I tangled my tent in a Kansas thunder-and-wind storm. All afternoon the clouds had looked ominous, and no farms or ranches were showing up on the horizon, so I began looking for a good place to pitch my tent. Just before dark, I noticed an abandoned farmstead with a long row of bois d'arc trees (in Kansas they call them hedge apple) along one side so I set up my camp on the protected side of these. Before I finished securing the tent, black clouds with bulging undersides gathered over me, a strong wind was picking up, and the rumbling of thunder was increasing. I found some steel pins in a nearby junk pile and used these to secure my tarp over the tent.

I had already staked Lad on good grass, so I zipped myself inside the only protection I had. They say in a tornado you should never take refuge in an automobile, that you should stay by an interior wall or crouch by some sturdy furniture. I had the part about the automobile licked, but the wall and furniture were a problem. I partly solved it by placing my saddle on my left by my head and shoulders and my rather large saddlebags on my right. At the height of the wind, the popping and snapping was unbelievable. I felt like a mouse in a plastic bag with a dog shaking it. I was sure glad I had been to sea for a year when I was a kid because I'd learned to tie strong knots.

At one point I heard a loud roaring from the west; as it got closer I figured a funnel cloud was surely approaching so I pulled the saddle over my head and shoulders. Then I could distinguish a clickety-clackety sound and remembered that I had camped near the railroad. When the lightning flashed I could get a glimpse of Lad. He seemed relaxed, with his rear end, the only protection he had, turned toward the wind. He made me feel more secure. For the remainder of the ride across Kansas, the weather was fine, and as I rode along I completed the song that this state had started giving me at her border. Here are a few of the lines.

> Kansas, Kansas, I ride across your plains
> of wheat fields and cattle
> where the meadowlark sings.
> I can see the covered wagons
> that rolled across your past
> and the strength of your pioneers
> I hope will always last.

I stayed at my last stop in Kansas with a young cowboy, Rick Hinkel, who manages the twenty-eight-thousand-acre Tate Ranch, south of the Arkansas River near the Colorado border. Rick believes in ranching the old way, with horses, and he does a good job of it. He directed me along good, sandy dirt roads that lasted almost to Colorado.

12

The Long Horizons

*From the Colorado Plains
to the Rockies*

As I crossed the state line into Colorado, it was hard to realize that I had actually ridden Lad six hundred miles from Artist Point, Arkansas. At this stage I had established a more or less regular routine. I would always begin the day by giving Lad his grain. While he was eating I would have breakfast and fold up camp, counting the ten aluminum tent stakes twice as I could not afford to lose any.

After saddling Lad, I would ride about two hours and stop for a grazing break. If grazing had been good the night before or if he had had plenty of hay, I might limit this break to five minutes; otherwise, I might give him fifteen minutes or more. If I happened to be at a restaurant at noon, I could almost always give him an hour at least while I ate, but even if all I had was jerky and dried fruit, I would give him a long grazing break at noon. In the middle of the afternoon I would give him another short grazing period.

I tried to give Lad water each morning, at noon, and when we set up camp. The farther west we went, the more uncertain were my chances for doing this. After a while, grass as well as water had to be taken where it could be found. In Colorado and the other plains states alfalfa clumps were fairly common by the road. Buffalo grass and other native grasses were fairly plentiful in most of Colorado.

The plastic water pail was handy and sometimes necessary. I would find, for example, a water tank beyond a fence with no gate, and I had to pack Lad's water to to him. I could have used my hat but the plastic pail weighed only a few ounces. It also served sometimes as a wash basin.

My first day in Colorado, May 26, I made it to Holly, a small, friendly town. The Murrays, Martin and LeeAnna, invited me to spend the night with them. They and their three daughters keep several horses and had an empty corral for Lad. I will never take it for granted that people would allow me, a stranger, to share their homes.

Colorado gave me her song before I had ridden very far across the state. I added lines as I rode along and sang them to the beat of Lad's hooves. (At Lamar, incidentally, he finally got new shoes.) Here are a few verses:

> I ride my pony all across Colorado
> where the people have that old western way
> I ride the trails and the highways of our pioneers
> where a cowboy and his pony are O.K.
> Sometimes I find someone who speaks the cowboy lingo
> and we reminisce about the days of old.

> It seems so good when I can find an open door
> and a steaming coffee cup when days are cold.
> Colorado, Colorado, Colorado, oh the sights
> that I have seen, just drifting through.
> And I can see for one whole day
> where I'll be going,
> and I pitch my tent at night in yonder blue.

At Rocky Ford Lad seemed to be getting a little leg weary, so I thought I'd try to find a place to rest for several days. The old drovers and emigrant trains of the mid 1800s called this "recruiting the stock." At the post office in Rocky Ford, where I stopped to pick up my mail, I met Jose Lopez, a most valuable friend, who drove all over town until he found a place for me and some grain for Lad.

It was a marvelous place. Lad and I stayed a week with Kay and Charlie Lucero and their hogs, sheep, chickens, and horses. Kay had polio as a child and spends her days in a motorized wheelchair, but she is convinced (and almost convincing) that she is going to be America's first woman president. As we went uptown together in the hot June sun, with my long legs barely keeping up and her in an old straw hat with artificial flowers all over it—the same one she had worn when she and Charlie were married—we must have made quite a picture. The main planks to her presidential platform are that she's opposed to Devil worship, poverty, and drugs.

The rest in Rocky Ford did Lad a lot of good. He was prancing again when we rode out, and he had to be restrained. Saying goodbye to Kay and Charlie, I headed north across the long stretches of Colorado plains. After a few hours out I got my first glimpse of the Rockies. Two days later, on June 9, I could see Pikes Peak. Where these plains have never been plowed, the native buffalo grass grows in plenty. Buffalo grass is good feed; it reminds me of a small edition of Bermuda grass. Lad loved it.

South of Limon I had an unsettling experience that resulted in my putting in a lot of miles in one day. A cowboy friend of mine in Kansas had told me about a roping buddy of his who would probably put us up for the night. During the day a Colorado brand inspector stopped to chat awhile and inform me of the rules I would have to follow while riding in the state. Noticing the roper's name on my map, he said I'd enjoy meeting him and told me how to find his place.

When I rode in, there was no car by the house. I could hear the phone ringing, but no one answered it. I noticed a truck down by the barn and roping pens. There was no one with the truck, but I decided to wait. I wanted to meet the man and there was a nasty-looking thunderstorm coming up.

I was very sleepy from riding through country that looks like all God had to work with when he made it was a straight-edged ruler, so I decided to try to take a short nap. I was reaching to untie my bedroll from back of the saddle when a police car raced up with sirens going. Over a bullhorn a voice said, "Move away from your horse, sir, and keep your hands away from your body!" I felt like a character in a western movie. The man's wife had come home, as it turned out, parked her car on the other side of the house, and called the law. I told the policemen who I was and that I was a writing a book and was riding cross-country to research and publicize it. That didn't impress them. They asked to see my driver's license.

When a policeman brought the woman out to face me, I gave her the name of the cowboy who had told me about her husband. She didn't know him, maybe her husband did, but he wasn't home. The police advised me to get back on my horse and ride. I did.

A few miles south of Brush, a cowboy named Ralph Kline stopped to chat awhile. He had recently been hurt by a bucking horse and lost his summer job riding for a grazing association in the high country. He helped me with my route and turned his house in Brush over to me for a couple of nights.

During a one-day layover at Brush, I met a retired brand inspector named Joe Bowman. His small home was decorated with models of horses, wagons, saddles, and other souvenirs of a life spent as a cowboy in, among other places, southern Wyoming where my route lay. Together we studied my map, checking the probable locations of grass and water. This put me right on the old Cherokee Trail.

I would go through Brush again, on my way back from California, to learn that Joe Bowman had settled his earthly accounts and had died of cancer, taking a trail longer than mine over the great divide.

Out of Brush, I rode on dirt roads for most of the day. Around noon, I stopped at a farm to water Lad, and a woman arranged for the Fort Morgan newspaper to come out and interview me. When I was en route again after the interview and lunch, an elderly couple, sitting in the shade of their front porch, hailed me and told me to tie up my horse and give him a rest. As Lad grazed, I had another chance to visit.

Later that day, a storm began to brew, and I started looking for a shelter in a country where shelters can be far apart. Off to the left was the Fort Morgan Airport and to the right a farmer's barn, apparently deserted. As far ahead as I could see, nothing else broke the horizon. We reached the barn just as the storm struck in its full fury. The wheat bowed low, the wind blew the rain against the barn, and hail peppered the tin roof. The morning after the thunderstorm broke clear, and the rising sun on the snow-capped Rockies to the west made them look like a chain of jewels. I had coffee with some cropduster pilots gathered near the barn and then rode on.

After a freezing night and a sandstorm, I reached Fort Collins and was invited to use the bunkhouse at the stables of Vicki Donoho, who trains barrel-racing horses. At this point Lad had around a thousand miles behind him, but when he was turned loose in a corral, he ran, bucked, and kicked up his heels for a half hour or so. I rested out a storm front here and got all my legal paperwork in order—Lad's health certificate and other papers had to be checked by a state brand inspector before I could leave Colorado.

North from Fort Collins things changed rapidly. Snow-capped mountains were in full view and the air was cool. We followed the old Cherokee Trail much of the time. At Livermore, I stayed with a cowboy named Stan Brown, the first person I met who seemed familiar with the trail and where it went. We sat in Stan's house and talked of the old trail and cattle drives and trails we had ridden and looked out over some of the most beautiful country in this world. The next day I would ride out of Colorado into Wyoming. I looked forward to it, even though Stan took away the sense of adventure somewhat by calling Richard Borgman, a cowboy he knew at Tie Siding, to arrange for a place for me to stay the following night.

13

Wyoming

Wagon Ruts and Legends of the Cherokee Trail

On Sunday, June 25, I rode from Livermore, Colorado, to Tie Siding, Wyoming. A few miles south of the Wyoming border, near Virginia Dale, I was invited to a picnic lunch, where I learned that the road running nearby was the old Cherokee Trail.

As we climbed over the hump before descending to Tie Siding, we were at an elevation of around eight thousand feet. A fierce wind was building up and black clouds were forming. I pushed Lad into a trot and galloped him some to beat the storm to the small town, though speed was risky because of badger and gopher holes.

Richard and Inja Borgman live in a comfortable house that also serves as a grocery store and the Tie Siding post office. I had been telling people that my special cross-country saddle weighed only ten or twelve pounds, but I had never actually weighed it. Inja Borgman put it on the postal scales and the balance read twelve pounds and eight ounces.

Richard Borgman told me about the strong winds that blow in that part of Wyoming, sometimes reaching over a hundred miles per hour even when there's not a storm. Others in the area confirmed this, and I gained a deeper respect for those who ranch on those high plains and mountains. It was here that I started my song about Wyoming.

> There's a lot of Cowboys 'way out in Wyoming
> and they've got to be a special kind of breed
> 'cause they're living in a land
> that takes a tough kind of man
> and they've got everything a man could need.
> And they've got a lot of wind out in Wyoming
> it can blow a hundred miles per sometimes
> and they don't call it a storm
> they just say, "That's the norm,"
> but you may find that it can blow away your mind.

After I had written this, and before I had left Wyoming, I was told that a high suicide rate in one part of the state was blamed on the constant high winds in that area. Anywhere there are no trees, the wind seems to blow a lot.

Richard Borgman laid out a more or less direct route over dirt roads that would take me past the ranch of Clay Lilley, a friend of his who ranched on the Laramie River. The beautiful and fascinating antelope herds were becoming more numerous. I had heard of their curiosity and decided to experiment a little. Several times I lifted the red traffic-warning flag that hung from the left side of my saddle and let it flutter back down. The antelope would perk up their ears and move slowly toward me to investigate. Some would come quite close before stopping to stare at horse and rider, then bound away with their white rump hairs erect.

For most of the day I rode along a ranch road and didn't see a single automobile or even another person. To the north and on my right were undulating sage-covered plains. To the south, back toward Colorado, were rugged, snow-covered mountains. I could understand how this became an emigrant and cattle-drovers' route. Grass and water were more plentiful near the mountains. Further north and my route would have taken me through the Red Desert. I had been warned against it.

Another factor that may have made this route attractive to the original Cherokee Company was the relative security they may have felt in dealing with the mountain Indian tribes rather than the more warlike plains Indians.

Approaching the Laramie Valley, I was looking due west at the Medicine Bow Mountain Range, with the Snowy Range in view to the northwest. The valley floor itself, as I neared Clay Lilley's ranch, was at an elevation of around seven thousand feet. It is an upland wetland, with many wild ducks and the worst mosquitoes I had seen until then. The grass was very good, though, and thick hay meadows offered an abundance of prime feed for Lad.

On June 27, after I left Lilley's place, I was grazing Lad by the roadside when a local rancher, Bob Davis, stopped out of curiosity and invited me to stay at his place, the Mountain Meadow Ranch, a few miles up the road. I decided to accept because the following day we would be climbing to over nine thousand feet and a short day would make it easier on Lad.

At the ranch, Bob told me that he and his wife, Debbie, had to be in Laramie that night, as Bob was coach of a boys' softball team. I told them I would be willing to stay in the barn, but they insisted that I make myself at home until they returned. They showed me where all the food was and said to use the microwave oven to warm up anything I wanted to eat. I had the best chili I had ever eaten.

I was ridding myself of some of my preconceived opinions. I had never been completely comfortable with folks outside the Sun Belt. Now I was prepared to accept that Wyoming hospitality was among the best in the world. I don't think my prejudices were ever very deep, but it sure does one good to feel them evaporate.

Later the *Saratoga Sun* of Saratoga, Wyoming, said about my ride: "Although Arkansas receives little credit from other states for its contribution to the cattle industry, Denton said he doesn't want to bias his work. Written in his notebook were these words which came, undoubtedly, after much time in the saddle pondering on the ways and whys of life:

'The sweetest taste I ever had in my mouth and one that left no lingering bad after-effects was swallowing my prejudices.'"

I felt like the long days, weeks, and months in the saddle, along with the wide-open spaces, the high altitudes, and the high winds were blowing away my own impurities. Sometimes it seemed as if the hard Wyoming winds made the clothes I was wearing cleaner, even on days when I couldn't find a place to wash them.

At the Mountain Meadow Ranch I received a visit from Hap and Phyl Chisholm. I include parts of a letter sent by Mrs. Chisholm to my wife, back in Arkansas.

> Dear Mrs. Denton,
> We have had the most delightful visit with your husband, Ivan Denton. . . . I want to report first hand, he looks wonderful! Lad is sound, you can't even feel his ribs, and his feet look great! Ivan and Lad look as neat as if they were on the first day of the trip!
> Yesterday morning, my husband and I were driving southwest of Laramie and saw Lad at rest outside a building at the edge of town, saddled, with yellow slicker tied on, etc. "Someone's traveling!" we said.
> We live 25 miles out of town, out on the prairie. . . .

... Our son made a cross-country ride by himself in 1971 (when he was 15), and the sight of that horse and rider was too much for me!

My husband is a great-grandson of Jesse Chisholm. Hap and Ivan traded all sorts of stories about Jesse.

Ivan said [of the Davises] "I can't believe the hospitality of these folks. They just turned their house over to me last night!" I was not surprised, for the people in Laramie were just that kind of friendly to us when we first moved here. . . .

I certainly hope we do get to meet you, and to see Ivan again. We admire the work he's doing for his book, and its purpose, and even his saddle! . . . We wish him well on his trip!

          Sincerely,
          Hap and Phyl Chisholm

Leaving the Mountain Meadow Ranch on June 28, I rode on through Woods Landing, and then we climbed rapidly to around nine thousand seven hundred feet. That night was one of only two times during the ride that I rented a motel room. This was at Mountain Home, and the price of $15.00 included oats for Lad plus enough to take along for his next two-day supply. I was able to patch up an abandoned corral for his quarters. The abundance of spruce timber reminded me of the woods I'd seen in my teen years in Alaska.

Continuing west, I dipped back into Colorado, following an old cattle drovers' route. The original Cherokee Company may have circled the Medicine Bow Range to the north, but later the Arkansas cattle drovers probably took several slightly different routes. My thought at this point was to ride the distance the drovers went and to follow, in a general way, their route. To some extent, some of these old drovers' trails will always remain "lost trails."

During the next day, while I was back in Colorado, black clouds began to form just as I was passing a group of cowboys working a herd of cattle. I stopped for a short chat and was assured by one horseman that, "It'll thunder and lightning a little but it won't rain." In twenty minutes or less I got off Lad because of the thunder and lightning, and for about a quarter of an hour it rained, hailed, and snowed, all at the same time. I was glad that I had put my wool shirt on under my slicker.

At noon that day I happened to be at one of the rare restaurants in this country and enjoyed a hot meal. When I was ready to leave, the cook said, "It's already paid for." Someone I didn't know had paid for lunch and had left before I did, so I didn't even get to say my thanks.

On the ride to Encampment, Wyoming, I began to notice more gopher and badger holes. Badger holes are the worst. I'd heard many stories of cowboys in Colorado and Wyoming being hurt and some permanently crippled when their horses stepped into the holes. The gophers honeycomb the soft prairie soil (the word "gopher" means honeycomb, from the Old French *geufre*). Sometimes, fifty or a hundred times a day, Lad would fall through a few inches in the honeycombed gopher ground. This was never anything more than tiring or irritating to him, but once in Colorado he went down in a crusted-over badger hole so deep that *my* foot struck the ground. Also, incredibly, in some places power companies had taken up their poles and left yawning holes, a serious danger to horsemen riding the road shoulders.

The night before I got to Encampment, and for the first time since I had entered Wyoming, I slept in my tent. This was high prairie, around seven-thousand-feet elevation, and it was hard to keep warm. Grass was plentiful, though. Here I saw the biggest jack rabbits I have ever seen. Sometimes, if I got only a glimpse before they disappeared into the sagebrush, my first reaction was to think I had seen an antelope. I was told that these specimens would sometimes put up a pretty good scrap with a rabbit dog.

Even though the night was cold, it was a hot ride into Encampment on June 30. For several miles ahead I could see Riverside, with Encampment just beyond. I didn't know what to expect; I had seen so many towns of mostly abandoned buildings, a dot and a name on the map, but I was in for a pleasant surprise. It was early in the afternoon when I arrived, but I had already covered about twenty-four miles.

I will let the *Sun* tell it.

> July 5, 1989—*Saratoga Sun*
>
> On the Trail of Early Cattle Drives
>
> **Arkansas Cowboy Riding to California**
>   by Connie Patterson
>
> The cowboy, dusty and tired from the long ride, stopped in front of the saloon to quench his parched throat and, tying his horse, walked into the cool interior.
> The fellow sitting at the end of the bar called, "Howdy, mister! Can I buy you a beer?"
> "You don't even know me," the cowboy said, with suspicion in his voice.
> "Well, I'll buy you one anyway," the fellow said, grinning, "Welcome to Wyoming."
> This scenario was played out, not in the 1800's as one might imagine, but last Friday, June 30, 1989, at the Mangy Moose Saloon in Riverside.
> The cowboy, Ivan Denton, is just about at the halfway mark of an historic five-and-one-half month, 2,500 mile horseback journey he is taking to research and publicize his book. Entitled, "Old Brands and Lost Trails: A History of Arkansas Cattle Herds and Trail Drives West," the book is aimed at filling a major gap in the written history of Arkansas.

There was more hospitality shown here than the *Sun* reported. I was offered still more beer, but I said, "I don't think I can handle it on an empty stomach, I haven't eaten since early this morning and all I had then was jerky and dried fruit. I need to find a restaurant." The lady behind the bar asked, "Can I fix you a sausage sandwich?" I eagerly accepted, and when it came time to pay, she said, "There's no charge, it's on the house."

I hadn't given Lad a day off since we left Fort Collins, and as I had been planning to rest him before riding over the Continental Divide, I thought this would be a good time to do so. The fellow who had said "Welcome to Wyoming" offered me free pasture "for as long as you need it." He was Pat Bromley, the son of Joanne Bromley, who was recommended to me by her cousin Clay Lilley, with whom I had stayed back on the Laramie River. I turned Lad in the pasture with Pat's horse and spent the next four days resting and doing research at the Grand Encampment museum. It was a historical gold mine.

The first day in Encampment I met Earl Stokley, who gave me a room and told me about the local museum. Bill Saulcy, a realty agent I met in the museum said, "We here know a lot about the Cherokee Trail. I can take you out and show you the old wagon ruts, but we didn't know about these old cattle drives that you're telling us about. You're filling in a gap for us." Later, we did indeed see the faint traces of the trail.

Many of America's old trails can still be seen, but the Cherokee is so little known, so lost in a literal sense, that I never thought I would actually see it. Most of these Wyoming prairies have never been plowed; I could step from the written documents of the Grand Encampment Museum and in less than an hour view the reality written on the face of the earth.

What forms of sports and entertainment those old Arkansas cattle drovers may have enjoyed while encamped near present day Encampment, we have no way of knowing. But neither did they have any way of knowing that here in 1948 King Merrit, the famous Wyoming cowboy and rodeo star, would sponsor the first Laramie Plains Steer Roping Contest, as old drovers and modern cowboys mingled their tracks.

One day Bill Saulcy showed me where the old trail was thought to have crossed the Encampment River, and I could easily see the slight depression that led to a natural gravelly ford. I realized that when I had first tied Lad in front of the

Mangy Moose Saloon I was near enough to that old ford to have heard the rattling of the wagons and the creaking of the harness and saddles if the Cherokee Company had been crossing at that moment.

According to my mother, back in North Carolina, some of my forefathers were Cherokee, and I had been doing just what that 1849 Cherokee Company had been doing: looking for a good route, with good grass and water, and reasonably good terrain. Like those Indians, I had asked and listened and learned. In any event, the combination of research, instinct, and listening to locals was bringing to a focus the library dust and the trail dust.

Here is some of what I learned in the Grand Encampment Museum. All of these passages are taken from a paper entitled "Cherokee Trail," compiled by Elva Evans.

> The southerly route [of the Overland Trail] has often been thought to be that of the Cherokee Trail, so named as the Cherokee had used it on a westward trek in 1849, but actually the two routes are not the same. . . .The overland ran north of Elk Mountain, and the Cherokee went south of Elk Mountain."
>
> from *The Overland Trail of Wyoming*
> by Ed McAuslan

> . . . From its location it is evident that they had little fear of the Ute or Mountain Indians but desired if possible to avoid the plains or Arapahoe and Cheyenne Indians which were powerful tribes at that time. They probably also considered that the nearer they could keep to the mountains, the better, purer and more frequent would be a good water supply, timber and game and they may possibly have figured that they were making the landmark which exists to this day and which really defined the border line between the Plains and Mountain Indians, who were at war whenever a war party was caught over the foothill line.
> Many Indians and white men have traveled over

that trail, and during the cattle round-up days it was used extensively by men engaged in that business. It is therefore well marked to this day. During recent years a number of human skeletons have been discovered in that range of mountains on or near South Spring Creek and above the Cherokee trail. Great quantities of beads have been found near by indicating that sometime in the distant past a family or small party of Indians were snowed and starved to death, or were wiped out through poison, cholera or some other disease.

from *Frontier Days* (1917)
by Judge W. L. Kuykendall

This old trail crossed the Encampment River where the town of Riverside is now located. . . .

There had been some confusion among our late historians and map-makers about the exact locations of the Cherokee trail, but to many of us, who have lived and traveled the old road over endless years, there is no room for doubt or error. Personally, I was born beside it. It is a cornerstone of my early memories.

The real significance of this old thoroughfare is not so much in the story of its origin as it is in the use made of it by the immigrants in the ensuing years. In endless procession, in every type of vehicle, through all the summer months for a period of years, men and women wended their westward way from Arkansas, Oklahoma, and Missouri and even parts of Texas, seeking new lands, new homes and fresh adventures.

from Maude Jones Willford

The slight differences as to where the trail went are of no significance. Later, emigrants and especially the cattle drovers would be expected to make variations where they were needed.

Back at the Mangy Moose I was warned about the dangers of crossing the Red Desert to the west and northwest. One cowboy suggested I take the route through Brown's Hole, now called Brown's Park. He said that his mother, Belle Christensen, used to live there, in Butch Cassidy outlaw country, and that Belle Christensen's grandmother, Josey Bassett, had been one of Cassidy's girlfriends. The route sounded interesting even though it would be a hot, dry ride.

Later in the week I met Belle Christensen and learned that the Bassetts had come from Arkansas over the Cherokee Trail. Her great-grandfather, Herbert Bassett, had one of the oldest brands in Wyoming, a rafter "H" on the left side for cattle, and a lazy "B" on the left shoulder for horses.

On July 5, we left Encampment. The road wound its way up into the Sierra Madres and over Battle Pass. According to documents at the museum, the Cherokee had crossed south of Bridger Pass, a little to the north; I was not far off.

Sitting there on Lad and looking back down on the beautiful, peaceful town of Encampment, I had strange feelings. Its people were friends, good friends. I knew that back in Arkansas I had friends and a home and some land; I was not a saddle bum. But the reality was that everything I had at the moment was on that little gray Arabian horse. In the right saddlebag was my only home, my tiny tent. It weighed just three pounds. I had over a thousand miles of friends behind me, and the most recent of these would soon be out of sight. When I reined Lad back toward the west and touched my heels to his sides, we were heading into a thousand more miles of strangers.

The night before I left Encampment I felt insecure. I always did when I was leaving newly made friends. I was uneasy about tomorrow, about grass and water, about where the next night would find me. Would someone take me in? Would there be anyone to ask?

But there was another side to these emotions. At the beginning of each day, after my belongings were packed into the saddlebags, the words of an old song I don't really know kept going through my mind, "My bags are packed and I'm ready to go," and another line, "Already I'm so lonesome I could cry." I would hum and mumble these few words, but then as soon as I started grooming and saddling Lad, the words would change to my own song, "On down the road," which I had composed back in Oklahoma. My mood would lighten a little, and when I stepped up on Lad I felt secure. This was my world, this was where I belonged. I knew that if I were not careful I could get into some tough situations in the desert country to the west, but it was going to be all right. I was at home.

Climbing up the Sierra Madres I imagined that these spruce-covered mountains must have reminded the Cherokee of the Smokies of North Carolina.

Early in the day I began to see small patches of snow by the road. I was told that Battle Pass was at ten-thousand-feet elevation. Just as we passed a large snow field on our left we reached the barren, wind-swept crest. All the streams and rivers behind us drained into the Atlantic Ocean; all those before us drained into the Pacific.

The sign said "Battle Pass, Elevation 9,916 feet, Continental Divide." On the east side of the sign was printed "Atlantic," and on the west the word "Pacific." We had made it to the top! I tied Lad to the sign and took his picture. A national forest worker who was eating his lunch by the road asked me if I wanted to be in the picture, and took one with Lad and me together. We had over a thousand miles behind us and almost ten thousand feet beneath us.

From the pass we descended through the most beautiful stands of spruce and aspen I have ever seen. There was abundant grass between the groves and water was easy to find.

We camped at about eight thousand feet some twenty-seven miles past the divide. I was glad my little tent had a screen, because the mosquitoes were bad, even though it was cold at that elevation. As we worked our way farther down on succeeding days to a little over seven thousand feet, the daytime heat became more of a problem, so I took to resting during the middle of the day whenever I could.

When I got to Savery, Wyoming, I was still on the Cherokee Trail, according to Ed McAuslan's description of the route in *The Overland Trail of Wyoming*.

On Friday, July 7, I rode into Baggs, Wyoming, a little cow town where you can ride your horse down Main Street. I liked the town, but there seemed to be no way to go on. Local old-timers told me there were no routes going west where I could find grass and water. My map showed a dirt road to Powder Wash, but everyone I asked about the Powder Wash route told me it was insane. "There's nothing there," they said. I inquired about a route down the Little Snake River, one that would put me on a route through Brown's Park, and I was told that it was too hot and dry and that water and grass were not dependable. I had a sick feeling in my stomach.

As the degrees of longitude increased, rainfall decreased, and feed and water were harder to find. I began to feel that this could turn into a life and death situation. If I blundered blindly off into the desert I could become a bleached, white statistic.

I found someone to pasture Lad for an extra day or two and asked around for someone to drive me down the Little Snake River to Brown's Park to scout the territory.

Clint Weber, a young guide and former wild-horse roper, agreed to help me scout the country in his pickup. The route to Brown's Park didn't look as bad as it had been represented, so I decided to go that way. It interested me, since the Cherokees had been the first to winter a sizable herd of horses and cattle at Brown's Park.

Clint told me a story that helped me fill in part of the story of Arkansas's cattle drives. His great-great-grandmother, he said, was one of the survivors of the Mountain Meadows Massacre. He thought she had been around eleven years old at the time. Most accounts report that only seventeen little children, seven years old and under, were allowed to live, since they were considered too young to testify against the killers. But some historians do mention one older child surviving and being lost or left in Utah. The massacre had been kept so secret at first that reports of people turning up missing for asking too many questions persisted for years.

Clint took me a few miles north of Baggs to show me clear traces of the Cherokee Trail where it went between two hills called the Flat Tops. Just west of this landmark, he showed me a spring that was still running, and the clear tracks of the old wagon road. I saw wild horses near the trail and dozens of herds of pronghorn antelope.

As I rode southwest out of Baggs on July 9, I knew there would be little grass and water for at least two days. I would generally follow the Little Snake River, but it would be several miles away in most places and fenced off. Ranches would be practically nonexistent after the first day.

So, early in the hot afternoon, about fifteen miles out, I stopped at the ranch of Paul Evans. The typical Wyoming corrals were made of long pine poles which are rot-resistant in the extremely dry climate, and the buildings—except for Paul's dwelling—were low, sturdy log structures, some (as I learned later) over a hundred years old.

I found Paul in one of the corrals feeding stock and asked if I could water my horse and stay the night. He was agreeable, and we struck an immediate friendship. He suggested I get an early start the next morning, so as not to push my horse in the heat of the day through the long, dry, hot stretch ahead of me.

Paul was concerned about my route beyond Brown's Park and on into Utah. He put me in touch by phone with a friend who used to ranch in the Brown's Park area.

Conversations with men like Paul and his friend could save my life, but I had to pay attention to know whether a person was stringing a line or leveling with me. Pride can cause a person to tell more than he knows. What I heard from Paul's friend had the ring of truth: the Two-Bar Ranch was two days' ride; beyond that, the Solace Ranch would be the only water until I reached Vermillion Creek. From there to Brown's Park would be an easy day's ride, and a good stream of water was just across the Utah line. "Beyond that," he said, "you had better talk to someone else."

The next morning Paul suggested we look at one of his old wild horse traps. When we got out into the countryside, Paul stopped and said, "Now, Ivan, do you see anything that looks like a wild horse trap?" I didn't, so he told me to look some more. He was justly proud of his job. When he pointed it out to me, I admired how well he had worked the enclosure in among the native cedar trees and hidden the wings leading to the corral. It looked like it belonged to the landscape.

Paul said that before his mother passed away he had stationed her on a little hill overlooking the trap so that she could watch a wild bunch being run in. To me, that would be the ultimate gift from a cowboy to his mother.

He also told me of hiding on a fast horse near a waterhole while wild horses tanked up, then roping them while they were waterlogged. I will never forget the light in his eyes as he talked of roping wild horses.

"By the time you get to the Two-Bars," he said, "you will have ridden practically the entire length of the Little Snake River."

He invited me to stay at his place as long as I wanted to, but, like the drovers of olden times, I was geared to the seasons. I had to reach California before the fall snows caught me at high altitudes. Early in the morning of July 11, I rode southwest down the Little Snake.

My education in feeding a horse on desert grasses was about to begin.

14

Hopscotch on Four Corners

To Idaho, via Colorado, Wyoming, and Utah

It was sometimes quite a challenge for my friends in Arkansas to follow my route on the map. The route was not as complicated as the series of place names made it sound, but it did weave its way in and out and across state lines and corners. I entered and exited Colorado and Utah four times and Wyoming five times.

Almost immediately on leaving Paul Evans's ranch, I re-entered Colorado. Northwestern Colorado is not like the Rocky Mountain areas or the plains of eastern Colorado but resembles the arid sage plains of Wyoming or Nevada. The mountains have a beauty like those of Utah. The heat in these high dry areas is intense, and the flies and mosquitoes attacked in horse-eating swarms any time we got near the Little Snake River.

About noon on July 11 we came to an artesian well Paul had told me about. I watered Lad and refilled my canteen. I desperately wanted to noon up and rest out of the heat of the day, but there was no vegetation tall enough to shade anything larger than a rabbit, and the sun was too hot to lie out in the open. I realized as I never had before the importance of covered wagons.

In the 1850s, Capt. Randolph Marcy of the U.S. Army had recommended traveling through desert regions in the cool of the mornings and late afternoons and resting during the heat of the day; of course, you had to have shade to rest in. My tent would have been a baking oven. Whenever I found cedar trees, or even large sagebrush, I would spread a saddle blanket over the limbs and take a siesta. Lad would graze contentedly during these noon stops and usually catch a nap too. The heat didn't seem to bother him much.

It seemed we were forever curving to higher country away from the river. Ranch fencing prevented me from cutting across the river, so the road was overall the shortest distance. But now a nasty looking thunderstorm was brewing to the east of me, and I wanted to get off the ridges and find a campsite. I rode hard for about thirty or thirty-five miles and made a dry camp. The Little Snake lay several miles to the west.

Often, on this part of the ride, I couldn't find enough grass to stake Lad for any length of time; I would have to lead him about in the sage and allow him to pick here and there. On July 12, after passing the Two-Bar, I spent the night at the Solace Ranch, where Chet Solace identified several kinds of desert grasses for me and told me their relative merits as horse feed.

Later, in California, Jack Woods, a grandson of one of the

Arkansas cattle drovers, would show me the scientific names of these same varieties that had sustained Lad across these desert landscapes. Three of these were Indian rice, needle-and-thread, and crested wheat grass, the last introduced by the Bureau of Land Management. From western Wyoming on, these three grasses were the most important for us. The Indian rice was the most plentiful in extreme desert conditions.

Leaving the Solace ranch, I found that the heat and expanse of a semi-barren landscape can do strange things. If I talked or sang the sound seemed to die close to my lips, or blow away on the wind. Once when I was drowsy from heat and crossed a newly patched, jet-black section of road, I thought it was a patch of shade and felt cooler. When I perked up I felt foolish, but I realized how easily one can be deceived.

Back near Baggs, Wyoming, I had asked Paul Evans how far he thought I could get on a two-quart canteen of water. He thought about it for a few seconds, and then said, "It depends on how often you spit." So here I was learning not to spit, and my mouth was too dry to whistle. For the next thousand miles or so I just kept my mouth shut most of the time.

On the especially hot and dry stretch from the Solace Ranch to Vermillion Creek I was riding along feeling drowsy, not whistling, singing, or spitting, when several miles up ahead I thought I saw a crowd of people lined up on the bank. My first thought was that it might be a country baptism, but since it wasn't Sunday, I took it for a picnic. "Well," I thought, "how lucky can a saddle bum get?" All thoughts of the salty jerky and dried fruit in my saddle bag left me as I visualized cool lemonade, sandwiches loaded with juicy tomato slices, and who knows what else. I let myself sing and spit, and then I could see that there were no people there. It was only a line of rocks left by a construction crew.

The water in Vermillion Creek was thick and muddy. Lad drank his fill, and grass grew thick alongside, but I couldn't even refill my canteen. What's worse, Lad stepped on my toe getting down to the water.

As I rode on into Brown's Park I passed the old Bassett homestead and was reminded of all the stories I had read back in Encampment about Elizabeth, Herbert Bassett's wife, who was from around Hot Springs, Arkansas. Elizabeth was said to have been the head of the Bassett gang; her daughter, Josie, was fabled as one of Butch Cassidy's girlfriends; another daughter, Ann, was called the "Queen of the Cattle Rustlers." In the Brown's Park area I found a copy of *The Bassett Women*, a book by Grace McClure. It verified Elizabeth's birth in Arkansas in 1855. "She had the graciousness that marks a Southern gentlewoman," McClure wrote, "and an inborn magnetism . . . but when she lost her temper she was violent." She was raised in Arkansas by her maternal grandfather, Judge Crawford Miller, a breeder of Thorough-bred horses, a background that may explain why the Bassetts "made themselves a local reputation as good breeders" of fine horses.

In the early 1880s the historic Two-Bar Ranch, just east of Bassetts' ranch and the other small ranches of Brown's Park, had moved in between twelve and fifteen thousand cattle; the Flying VD, another of the big spreads, was also applying pressure. They wanted the better grazing of Brown's Park, and eventually committed several murders to force the "little guys" out.

Elizabeth, who rode sidesaddle like a lady, was said by McClure to have been as good a cowhand as any man, and any one of her cowboys would "willingly . . . have died and gone to hell for her." Two incidents described in *The Bassett Women* tell of her wild nature. Once when she was cornered with five hundred head of stolen Flying VD cattle, she "rim-rocked" them. This meant that she and her cowboys "drove them over the cliff into Lodore [now spelled Ladore] Canyon, thus destroying the evidence."

On another occasion, as McClure reports it, "Herb [Elizabeth's husband] heard a terrible bawling out in the corral and went out to find that it was full of calves. The calves were not yet weaned, so the corral was besieged on all sides by cows bearing various brands bellowing loudly for their young ones to be returned to them. In the middle of the uproar was Elizabeth, calmly using her branding iron. . . . Herb clicked his heels and walked away."

At a store at Brown's Park I got a sandwich and a cold drink. I set up my tent near the store. Grass was so sparse that I had to lead Lad about in the sagebrush, where needle-and-thread was scattered about with an occasional bunch of Indian rice.

At the Park store I met Keith Madsen, a young wildlife student, doing summer work at the wildlife refuge just twelve miles to the west. I stopped by there the following day. I was in need of grain and one front horseshoe for Lad. Keith located some grain at the refuge, but it was very moldy. We carefully scooped out the least moldy gallon or so. I used the refuge phone to call all the ranches nearby—there were a couple just over the line in Utah—but none of them had any grain or a horseshoe I could use. I mentally kicked myself for not replacing the shoe back at Paul Evans's ranch, but I had felt sure it would last to Manila, Utah. The left front shoe, being nearest the pavement where it shelves upward, would always wear out first, and this one Lad had worn so badly that the hoof was also rapidly wearing away.

I felt helplessly far from anywhere and close to despair. I had been on horseback so long that I was not thinking how easily an automobile could solve the problem. "I'll take you back to Maybell or Craig," Keith said, "where we can get a shoe."

I was allowed to turn Lad loose in about a thirty-acre pasture by Beaver Creek, which runs through the refuge. After I replaced the shoe I did some laundry by hand at Keith's cabin and followed him on some of his duties around the refuge. I also met Jerre Gamble, the refuge manager, who helped me see more clearly how wildlife interests do not have to clash with grazing interests.

On July 16, when I whistled for Lad (I couldn't see him in

the tall sagebrush along Beaver Creek) he came galloping up, and we crossed over into Utah. From Brown's Park to the Utah line, Indian rice had been abundant beside the road, but it soon gave out. I didn't dare feed Lad much of the moldy grain, so it was two hard days from Keith Madsen's cabin to Dutch John, Utah. We took grass where we could find it.

On a little-traveled dirt road we came to a small sign that said "Utah Line" and a cattle guard. The sagging barbed wire gate opened and closed by a simple loop of wire, like so many that I had opened and closed along the secondary roads the entire length of the ride.

The country was extremely dry and grazing scarce until we got to Green River. I ate a little jerky and dried dates, and let Lad water and graze the plentiful grass along the stream. Brown's Park and Green River were only at about five thousand feet of elevation, but we entered a narrow, steep canyon and climbed rapidly to around seven thousand feet before dropping over into Clay Basin. I had been warned that there would be no feed or water in the Basin, but I found a little needle-and-thread, a few bunches of Indian rice, and a small stream of clear water at the basin's upper end. Those who had warned me had driven through by car and so hadn't seen any of that.

As I climbed out of Clay Basin I found wheat grass in abundance. When I saw a couple of elk and a mule deer I thought conditions were permanently improving, but we soon passed through a narrow canyon lined with huge boulders on each side, and Lad snorted and spooked a little at the shadowy openings between the rocks. Beyond the canyon we were on the desert, with practically no grazing to be found. Lad ate dried cheat (one of the poorest of the desert feeds) as if it were alfalfa hay. That night I put up my tent by a stock pond with some growth for grazing by it. Lad was doing fine on desert grass and moldy grain.

The richly mineralized, highly colorful mountains, along with the cedars and pines of the higher altitudes, gave me my song of Utah.

> Mountains vermillion and green,
> rivers and canyons between,
> the smell of sage in the draw,
> and I ride alone through Utah.
> The ground is my floor and my bed,
> my horse feeds on needle-and-thread
> in a basin of clay and sand—
> no water for a horse or a man.
> The beauty I see in this land
> designed and made by God's hand—
> creations that touch me with awe,
> as I ride alone through Utah.

The next day we crossed the Wyoming line for a few miles, but we were soon back in Utah, where we passed by a long line of bluffs that appeared to be several hundred feet high. The lady in the store back at Brown's Park had told me about these and said I would see golden eagles here. I had forgotten about the eagles when suddenly I heard a loud scream in the sky. I looked up to see two golden eagles circling out from the rugged crest of the bluff. So I added these lines to my Utah song:

> Castles of stone in the sky
> High overhead eagles fly
> spirits that touch on the wing
> songs only wild things can sing.

At Dutch John there was a restaurant, but my first concern was grain for Lad. I was told by a fellow there that he would call his son at the Flaming Gorge Lodge and that he would have grain waiting for me.

On the way to the lodge I had to cross the Flaming Gorge Dam, which is five hundred feet high. I was a little apprehensive. I got off and led Lad across. He danced around a little, but he made it all right. The scenery around Dutch John is superb, and the country affords good grazing for the most part. Crested wheat and even occasional alfalfa clumps were plentiful.

Sure enough, when I got to the lodge, a lad of ten or eleven was waiting for me with a very generous amount of grain. This was T. J. Collett, and I was much impressed with him. He had the honest, straightforward look of western pioneer stock. He was working there at his dad's service station. He told me that he had his own horse and bought his own feed, which he was more than willing to share.

My last day in the Flaming Gorge area was spent in the lower sage flats alongside a creek that flows into Flaming Gorge Lake; the sage was tall enough that my camp was hidden. Grass was good beside the creek, and I took time out to bathe and do my laundry, hanging it on sagebrush to dry. The day after I left this camp I was back in Wyoming.

In unknown country one has to be careful of several things. At Lone Tree I found that just plain mud can be dangerous. In the dry West there is not enough rain to wash away the fine silt, and consequently the ground is usually not as solid as it is, say, in the rocky Ozarks of Arkansas. When I attempted to water Lad in an irrigation ditch at Lone Tree, his front feet suddenly sank deep into the earth. I reacted quickly and swung him around, but before he could extricate himself his hind legs went down. After we got out of that, we were both more careful, and Lad would always blow and snort a little when approaching irrigation ditches for a drink. On some streams, dangerously soft silt can wash in deep enough to pull down a horse or a cow (or a man). A thin, deceptively solid-looking layer of sand and even a fine gravel wash lying over the silt can set a trap for the unwary. In approaching those streams where we had to walk out on the stream bed to reach water, I would look for tracks to show where other large animals, either wildlife or range animals, were watering.

The Lone Tree area, along Henry's Fork of Green River, reminded me of the Alaska moose country and, indeed, I was then in Wyoming moose range. To the south lay the majestic Uinta Mountains, and Kings Peak, Utah's highest point at 13,528 feet, was less than thirty miles to the southwest. Many more rugged peaks, some snow covered, presented a striking panorama. I set up my tent at Lone Tree by good grass and water.

Past Lone Tree I crossed what the locals called the "blue clay badlands." I was told that the prominent material in that desert area was bentonite, a soft porous clay formed from weathering volcanic ash. I was also told that there would be nothing, no feed or water, for the many miles between Lone Tree and Mountain View, which is close to Fort Bridger. As with everything I had been warned about during the length of the ride, things were not as bad as they were represented to be. I found grass for Lad growing in the path of the water runoff from the road. There was no water, but we were able to take it all in one day.

And it was a hot day. There was no shade, and my canteen had developed a leak. In the hottest part of the afternoon I found it empty. It was on this day that I came close to developing some kind of mental problem. I became very drowsy and felt an overpowering need to lie down, but the ground was baking hot. I got off and led Lad several miles, hoping that walking would revive me. Lad seemed drowsy too. I tied him to a fence post and rested in his shadow. A striking thing about dry desert heat is that any shade seems cool. I was afraid to lie down underneath him, for fear he might stomp me in ridding himself of flies. But by sitting and resting my head on my knees, I got some rest.

Several miles from Mountain View a black thunderstorm started building in the southwest. As I reached the outskirts of town the wind rose to near gale force, so I didn't want to set up my tent. At the first likely looking place that I came to that had corrals, I asked for a place to stay. The wind was so high I had to shout to be heard. "I'm riding on horseback cross-country," I yelled, "and I don't want to put up my tent in this wind; if you can put up my horse, I can sleep in the barn or anywhere." This was the Lonnie Burch place. He gave me the best bedroom in the house. "Wyoming folks have sure been good to me," I said, and he said, "Well, I'm one of them damn Texans that moved up here."

In Mountain View I replaced my leaky canteen with a canvas water bag.

Fort Bridger was on the Cherokee Trail. Here the Cherokee Mining Company and the cattle drovers that followed joined the emigrant trail that ran from Independence by way of South Pass. Some went to Salt Lake City, where they would usually skirt the lake to the north and go on into Nevada to connect with the Humboldt River route. The Holmes herd evidently took this route and reportedly lost very few head.

Others would take the Bear River route on into Southern Idaho and swing farther away from the Great Salt Desert. Some went as far north as Soda Springs, Idaho, and then turned west to enter the Humboldt River by way of Thousand Springs Creek or even farther west to Mary's Fork of the Humboldt. I chose the route through southern Idaho simply because I wanted to extend my ride through that part of the country. Love of adventure had sent me on my ride in the first place, and anyway the interstate highway system looked as if it would be pretty complicated if I didn't.

On Friday, July 28, I crossed the Idaho border. Earlier I had sometimes felt insecure because ranches and other human habitations were so widely scattered. Here along Bear Lake in Utah and Idaho I felt insecure because houses were so close to one another. If I was refused hospitality, there would be no place to camp. But the problem never arose.

Lad seemed a little leg weary or trail worn, so at St. Charles, Idaho, I found a place to pasture him for a few days. Rose was born in Nevada, and she was planning a visit to relatives there while I rode that part of my route. At Lake Town, Utah, I had called her up to meet me at St. Charles. I wanted to use our pickup to scout ahead a little.

It was almost August when I got there, and I was mindful that I still had to cross a lot of high country where cold and snow come early. It was here that I wrote my Idaho song.

> To Idaho I'm gonna go.
> I've gotta get there before it snows.
> I'm gonna ride my pony all day long
> and I'll be there before too long.
> In Idaho
> the creeks are cold and the lakes are blue,
> blue as the skies in the Caribou.
> I rode in and I'll soon ride out
> Where the creeks are cold and full of trout,
> in Idaho.

15

Onward to California

High Deserts, Beautiful Rubies, and Wild Horses

Since April 14 I had crossed parts of seven states—Arkansas, Oklahoma, Kansas, Colorado, Wyoming, Utah, and Idaho—and I had covered well over fifteen hundred miles on one horse without any kind of back-up vehicle to accompany me, not even a pack horse. With Rose now following along in the pickup we could carry extra water and some other things I had been doing without. We had an old camper shell on the truck so we could sleep in that. I now had the luxury that some of the cattle drovers of the 1850s had: a chuck wagon to follow along with my bedroll and chuck. Lad still would live mostly on the desert grasses that grew beside the road, but now we could carry a sack of oats.

The four days' rest at St. Charles had done Lad a lot of good. When we resumed the trip he was acting like a bronc: he was snorty and sometimes even a little difficult to mount. He was becoming tough and trail hardened.

My itinerary across Idaho would take me through Preston, Dayton, Malad City, Holbrook, Malta, and along some back roads that generally followed the Raft River. I would cut across another corner of Utah before crossing into Nevada. Southern Idaho is semiarid and basically ranch country. There are frequent grass fires and high winds in some areas, so it was risky to start a fire for cooking. One late afternoon after I'd watered Lad we were invited to stay at the Eliason Ranch, one of the largest and oldest ranches in southern Idaho.

At Malta, Rose and I stayed overnight at a small motel owned by Ether Parke, a cowboy of the old school. He keeps a couple of his old cow horses, so I had a small pasture to turn Lad in for the night. When I turned him loose, he ran, kicking and bucking. He was feeling good.

It had seemed that we would never stop going north to follow the old drover trails, but here at Malta, Idaho, we had reached the northernmost point of the ride. From here I would rein Lad to the southwest and ride in a somewhat zigzag fashion for over two hundred miles before heading almost straight west to Woodfords Pony Express Station in California.

Even now, this close to the end of the trail, when I was asked the question, "Where're you headin'?" and I would answer "California," I would notice a flicker of an eyelash and a slight drop of the chin that meant to say, "On *that* horse?" Some were surprised that I could make the trip with only one horse of any kind.

One day southwest of Malta as we came to a clear swift-flowing stream. I led Lad to where he could get down to it, but when he lowered his nose almost to the water he started to snort and blow through his nostrils and refused to drink. I looked upstream across the sage-covered flat and saw steam rising from the water. I touched it. If it had been coffee it would have been hot enough to drink.

The country became extremely dry as we crossed a corner of Utah. Off to the south and southeast we could see the beginning of the Great Salt Flats we had avoided by circling north. We had begun to depend on sage for firewood, but here even that was sometimes hard to find.

Our first town in Nevada was Montello, population 199. I was to learn that these Nevada towns were a lot like those in Wyoming where the altitude figure is usually higher than the population figure. And in Nevada the bars and gambling casinos usually outnumber the grocery stores. Montello had two bars on its main street.

As I rode into the town, children playing in a park by the railroad yelled, "Hi, cowboy!" over and over as they jumped off their tricycles and ran toward me begging for a ride. Lad is too spirited for little children, so I had to refuse, but I asked them if they wanted to see him run. They yelled "Yes!" so I let him gallop a little.

Two families in Montello, the Nances and the Fourniers, opened their homes to Rose and me, giving us a few days to scout the country ahead in the pickup. We spent one night with the Nances and then left Lad with the Fourniers and drove over to Elko.

I found that I could not follow the historic Humboldt River route because the interstate highway follows it too closely. Horses are not allowed on interstate highways, even on the shoulders. So I decided to ride the railroad access road to Wells and then swing south to Highway 50 at Eureka. Mike Johnson, a saddle maker in Elko, recommended this route. It proved to be not only a good one but one of the highlights of the entire ride. It warmed my heart to learn that Mike owned a copy of my first book, *The Art of I. Denton*, and it meant he knew me well enough to cash a check for me. It was the first time in over a thousand horseback miles that anyone had known me well enough to cash my check.

Since I didn't know the country or how far apart the water holes would be, I decided to keep the chuck wagon—the 1970 Chevy pickup—and Rose, the chuck wagon driver, with me. Water was still scarce, and, besides, I was getting spoiled by all that convenience. We had an ice chest and so could carry fresh meat and tomatoes. But Nevada towns are so far-flung that even with the chuck wagon we had to be careful on some stretches, and the ice would melt between towns.

Still, I felt a little sad that the chuck wagon had so quickly spoiled me. Life now seemed too easy. The ride had returned to a soda pop ride, as it had been through western Arkansas, Oklahoma, and Kansas. I had loved those states and their people. Grass, water, and shade trees had been plentiful. Colorado had been like a mixed drink: I had to be a little more careful. But Wyoming and Utah had been pure whiskey: higher altitude, less water, grass that was sometimes hard to find, and towns far between. Now Nevada, which I had expected to be the biggest challenge, was a return to a soda pop ride. I no longer had to bum grain for Lad. We could carry an extra sack, and we had tomatoes and stuff like that to juice up a sandwich. I needed something to spike the drink, and despite my newfound conveniences Nevada was not going to let me down.

Sagebrush became even more plentiful, but it was separated enough by sand that in most cases, by being reasonably careful, we could safely build a cooking fire. The old, dead sagebrush will come apart in your hands and is always easy to start a fire with. We discovered the beautiful Rubies. Rose, having been born in northern Nevada, said she had always heard of the splendor of the Ruby Mountains but had never seen them. We were soon to cross them.

When I was a child in North Carolina, horses and mules, either ridden or hitched to wagons with iron-rimmed, wooden wheels, were sometimes the only means of transportation we had. I always loved riding in an old-fashioned wagon behind mules or horses. It gave me a feeling of peace and contentment just rattling along those old Carolina dirt roads. That was a long time ago, but on August 23, when we headed south out of Wells, Nevada, a feeling, a fantasy, settled over me, that I was the captain of a wagon train.

I was told that Nevada averaged only about three inches of rain a year, but I wore my slicker more in that state than I had in any other. As they would say at Reno, it was just the luck of the draw. The first day out of Wells it started to rain, and, not believing it would last, I got a little wet before I put on my slicker. It rained most of the day; a cold desert rain with a north wind on my back. I was following the Humboldts, whose peaks towered above the desert floor to around eleven thousand feet. When the rain stopped just before dark and the clouds cleared, it was a beautiful sight. The rough peaks were covered with new snow to about a fourth of the way down. We built a big sagebrush fire and cooked a good meal. We slept well.

The next day I rode on around the southern tip of the Humboldt Range and camped that night in the shadow of the Rubies. They are also around eleven-thousand-feet high. When I could, when ranch fences or terrain didn't prevent it, I would cut across through the sage. I came to love riding it. You don't have to crush it to release its wholesome aroma. As soon as my boots or stirrups would brush against it, even gently, I would notice the smell. A part of my song of Nevada, inspired by the sagebrush was quoted by the *Nevada Appeal*, in Carson City.

> It's a land of sagebrush perfume,
> mountains where wild flowers bloom,
> high deserts where the wild horse runs free,
> and a land that beckons to me.

On August 25 the rising sun on the Rubies was something to see. The aspens were turning yellow, and there was frost on the grass and sage. Rose had driven on ahead and found a place to build a fire for a fresh pot of coffee. When I caught up I decided to replace Lad's left front shoe, as it had worn completely through at the toe. I was shoeing Lad, using a rock for an anvil to shape the shoe, when a pickup stopped and out stepped Steve Sharp, a real Nevada buckaroo, with a Nevada buckaroo handlebar mustache.

He was dressed up in his going-to-town clothes. He told me he was the cowboss of the "7 H" Ranch, about twenty miles down the road. He invited us for supper and a night's lodging. Steve had been visiting his daughter in Malta, Idaho, who had shown him an article in the local newspaper about my ride, and he had recognized me there beside the road.

At the 7 H, Steve called up his wife, Maggie, in Salt Lake City to join us for the evening. Steve became one of the sponsors of my ride by purchasing one of the hand-carved figures of Lad. He wanted one that had been carved in Nevada, so I did one for him. Steve and Maggie told us they had been married only since June and that they had met through a magazine ad. Thanks to Steve, I added a line to my song of Nevada.

> I rode down the Rubies,
> a land of a cowboy's dreams,
> rode through some high passes,
> and camped by some clear mountain streams.
> I met a cowboy named Steve.
> It was real romantic scene—
> he had a beautiful bride
> He'd ordered from a horse magazine.

After leaving the 7 H, I followed streams over Harrison Pass. On the other side, we turned south toward Eureka and soon began to see "stud piles," mounds of defecation with which wild stallions mark their territory.

I also began noticing frequent wild horses' tracks, and it seemed to me that the "frog" imprint showed a more indistinct spreading structure than the domestic horse has. Elmer

Anderson, an old horseman back in Arkansas, had impressed on me the importance of shoeing Lad so that the frog—the soft mound in the center of the hoof—touched the ground. It was a vital organ, he said, acting as an extra blood pump to assist the heart. A Nevada veterinarian confirmed that the massage of the frog is necessary to the health of the horse. Seeing these imprints of the wild horse tracks, I was reminded of the marvel of these creatures, and of the one I was riding.

Now the mountains began to appear highly mineralized and grass was hard to find, though the wild horse tracks and stud piles continued to be in evidence. Wild horses can range farther from water than can range cattle. On August 29, we spotted two groups of wild horses. They looked larger than the old-time Spanish mustangs.

I staked Lad by some coarse grass the mustangs had bypassed after taking only a few bites out of the tops. Lad reluctantly grazed some of this grass. During the night I heard horses going by. Lad snorted and cavorted somewhat on his stake rope, but we had no trouble.

We continued to see occasional bunches of mustangs all through Nevada. Ranchers I talked to said the old-timers used to shoot the small Spanish stallions and turn out larger stallions to "improve the breed." We saw a few that looked as if they had some of the Spanish Barb blood.

From Eureka, I rode mostly along Highway 50 west to Carson City. *Life* magazine had called this the "loneliest road in America," but I've ridden several that were more lonely for sure. It's a dry desert road that passes through some beautiful country. A person who knows ahead of time where the water holes and creeks are could ride it without a backup vehicle.

Before climbing up the Austin summit, I met Bob Eddy, a rancher who used to run mustangs with an airplane. He had taught himself to fly and said that sometimes he flew so close to the ground, herding the wild ones, that he would come in with sagebrush on his landing gear. I asked him if he had ever bumped a wild horse with a wing tip. He said, "No, but I have run a wheel down their back," then added, "They'll buck when you do that."

My frequent mention of clear creeks and water in desert country may be surprising to some, but the very thing that causes a desert assures a fair supply of water. Extremely high mountains can create a desert in the country downwind to the prevailing winds, in this case the High Sierras to the west of the Nevada deserts. Cool air, as we know, holds less moisture than warm air, and loss of pressure causes cooling. As a moisture-laden storm system passes over the High Sierras, it has to rise, thin out, lose pressure, cool off, and dump its moisture in the mountains, leaving dry air to flow over the leeward land. These desert areas rely on mountain snowpack to furnish summer runoff, which keeps mountain streams flowing and provides irrigation water. In addition, moisture in the higher mountains may stock underground reservoirs and cause an occasional artesian well to appear in unlikely places in a desert. We saw one between Eureka and Austin. However, care must be taken or one can die of heat and thirst on dry stretches of desert.

Distances in the Nevada deserts are extremely deceiving. Alkali and salt flats are found on most valley floors. On one salt flat between Austin and Middle Gate—it was difficult to determine if it was salt water or a pure salt flat—we saw two tiny, dark specks, moving at a fair pace, which might have been birds. They appeared to be from a fourth to a half mile away. We stopped and waited to see what they were. They stopped, side by side on the opposite shore, then they began to move toward us, two automobiles racing across the flat.

In the middle of the desert a sign said "Middle Gate, Nevada, population 11." The only building, besides a few trailers and personal dwellings, was a bar. There were no electrical supply lines so a generator was run twenty-four hours a day. At night, everybody there, including little children, went to the bar. There was one horse, a mustang that one of the men had caught for his wife, and he was not fenced in. The mustang wanted to follow Lad away, and I thought he might be hit on the highway, so I asked the residents to corral him until I got away. The fellow that had caught the mustang said they had had him in the bar and he had drunk a beer.

Just beyond Middle Gate is what used to be called West Gate. There is nothing there now but a windmill and a large water tank. A tiny stream flowing past Middle Gate soon disappears in the desert; beyond West Gate there is nothing, or so I was told. Actually, there is much that a motorist never sees. I found plenty of grass for Lad. In some places there was only salt grass; if it was growing right in the alkali, Lad wouldn't eat it, but we could usually find some to his liking. Indian rice was becoming more abundant, and wheat grass and a few other varieties could be found occasionally. Lad never refused the Indian rice. I even ate some of the seed myself.

The night of September 11 we camped near Sand Mountain on a large alkali lake bed about twenty miles east of Fallon. There seemed to be absolutely nothing for Lad to graze there. What looked like grass of some kind would turn out to be thorny spikes of some unpalatable growth. Sage gave way to a prickly greasewood. There was a salt crust on most of the ground on the east side of the lake bed and a mushy alkali mess farther on. A little west of us, a trickle spring created a poisonous-looking purple mush. I was afraid Lad would nibble some poisonous plants, such as halogeton, which some said would drive him loco or kill him. Then I remembered that a rancher had said there was a spring just northwest of Sand Mountain Road. I wandered off through the greasewood brush and found two seep springs of good-looking water. Rusty remains of a barbed-wire fence testified to some kind of a ranching operation in years gone by. The water was covered with a green scum. I didn't let Lad drink it, but a fair-sized area around both springs was covered with lush grass up to a foot tall, and the spring overflow had carried the alkali away.

We visited the remains of an old pony express station just north of there. There was no guide, but there were markers for a self-guided tour. Seeing the station helps one see what was endured just to carry the mail. The remains of the walls of the old building still stand. You can see where the horses were kept, and signs point out the kinds of desert grasses that helped maintain them. A sign explains that the station attendants did not have to dig very far for water, but that it was so alkaline that it was necessary to add a little vinegar before drinking. In the remains of the rooms I visualized the lean, tired, teen-aged riders, eating and resting there. Looking east I could see where the trail came down the volcanic slopes, and when I was still and quiet I could almost hear the pounding of the pony's hooves and see the excitement on the young riders' faces as they rode in, exhausted.

Lad was holding up fine. Even his hooves were healthy. I had been warned to use sheep fat or some like substance on his hooves because he wouldn't be used to the dryness as we progressed westward, but this had not been a problem. At the Sand Mountain camp I had replaced his hind shoes, using the special rock I had picked up in the Rubies to shape them. I didn't think they would have much hard use before the ride's end. But I hadn't yet learned about the Virginia City One-Hundred.

On September 12 I rode the last part of the severe desert stretch into Fallon. It was weird, wonderful, fatiguing, and exhilarating at the same time. I felt that now the hard part was behind us. It was something like the final part of a sea voyage after you pass the breakwater.

At Fallon I was feeling trail weary. Lad and I had over two thousand miles behind us. It seemed as if all my life I had been a saddle tramp. It was hard to believe it had only been five months. It seemed that my main concerns had always been finding a good place to camp and good routes that would provide grass and water for my horse. It seemed, too, that the only friends I had ever had were new ones and that I would never see my old friends again.

The first ranch on the eastern outskirts of Fallon is the Bill Card place. We stopped there and got permission to put Lad up for a day or two of rest, and for me to relax and celebrate.

On September 13 I met Abe Nance, an endurance trail rider and ex-prizefighter who now calls himself the "redneck barber." Abe would hear nothing of my feeling trail weary. They were having their one-hundred-miles-in-one-day race that weekend at Virginia City, and he insisted that I enter it. This was on a Wednesday, which would give Lad Thursday and Friday to rest up. "You and your horse oughtta be the toughest ones there," Abe said. "We're having a steak dinner tonight, put on by the V.C. One-Hundred, and you can go as my guest." The steak sounded good, so I accepted. What the heck, I'd never been to Virginia City before. And anyway all I was accepting was the steak dinner.

The Virginia City one-hundred-miles-in-a-day race club is a pretty elite setup. A silver buckle is awarded to anyone who finishes the hundred miles in twenty-four hours. Abe introduced me to the club, held up my saddle, told about my ride all the way from Arkansas, and announced that I wanted to enter the ride.

They invited me to stand up and speak a few words. I told them that I felt honored, that I felt a little foolish about riding my horse over two thousand miles to ride a hundred miles with them. After a laugh, one of the riders stood up, said they would consider it an honor if I rode with them, and moved that the entry fee of $85.00 be waived. For some reason I may never be able to explain, I accepted.

I spent most of Thursday going over my saddle and other riding gear. I was excited about the ride, but I had no intention of hurting Lad. I would pull him from the ride if he needed it. He was looking good, though, and full of energy.

Friday night Abe trailered his horse and Lad to Virginia City. All was set for 5 o'clock Saturday morning. Some of the riders stayed up late and drank beer. I tried to get all the rest I could.

By 4 A.M. Saturday morning the area around the parked trucks and horse trailers was a beehive of activity. Fifty-one riders were saddling their horses and preparing for the ride. I knew I would have to ride close to someone, because I was a stranger to the territory. The one-hundred-mile course, marked with ribbons, was laid out in loops around Virginia City. Many of the riders lived near there, and some even trained their horses over those same trails, but I would have to keep up or get lost. I couldn't make time by riding on ahead.

I asked some of the riders if they were taking any kind of rain gear. Several of them, including my friend Abe, told me, "You won't need a raincoat. It never rains out here." While they were talking, I was tying my cowboy rain slicker to the pommel of my saddle.

We assembled in front of the Bucket of Blood Saloon in downtown Virginia City, and a pickup truck led us the few miles outside of town to the starting line. It was an exciting moment. Fifty-one horses, impatient to move faster, all iron-shod, prancing and trotting on the hard pavement, sounded like large hail on a roof. In the darkness I could see fire sparking from the shoes on the concrete.

It struck me that the electrically charged atmosphere was a part of the balancing act of a people with so many automobiles and other labor-saving devices that they are forced to use their energy sporadically in such a way. Our pioneer forefathers, who used horses practically every day of their lives, would make such long rides only in cases of emergency.

Lad and I both were caught up in the spirit of the V.C. One-Hundred. When the motorized escort peeled off outside of town, the horses hit a pace that I don't believe any kind of ATV vehicle could have kept up with, at least while the horses were fresh. As we reached the beginning of the sage-covered hills, we were an inspiring sight. So many hot-blooded horses fighting their riders for more speed. You would've thought it was a scene out of *Lawrence of Arabia*.

The moonlight cast a glow over the front-running Arabians with their tails held high and nostrils flared for maximum oxygen intake, speeding up through the sage.

I tried to hold Lad back. I wasn't riding to win. I just wanted to finish the ride, and I wanted to save his strength. But he would have none of it. I finally decided I was tiring him more by holding him back than I would if I let him out some, so we were breezing along at a pretty good clip. Virginia City, I believe, was at around a six-thousand-foot elevation. It seemed like only a short while until we were up on a high benchland and I could see city lights out on the flatland. I thought we may have circled more than we had, and I asked Dave Cootware, one of my riding companions, if those were the lights of Virginia City. "No," he said, "that's Reno." A little later I saw more city lights. He said, "That's Carson City." Distances in the desert can deceive, but the speed of our horses was no deception.

The first veterinary check station was in a valley with high mountains to the east. By the time the sun came up we were there. We had covered twenty-two miles from 5 A.M. until sunrise at 7:41. Lad had galloped a good part of the way. Lad's pulse and respiration and other checks cleared, and we completed the first fifty-mile loop back to Virginia by 2:36 P.M. Each of the loops took us up to around 7,400 feet. The trails were rugged. One section was honestly named the S.O.B.s. Most riders tailed their horses up that part (walking behind, holding the horses' tails for assistance), but after the first one I stayed on Lad. He's good on rocky slopes since he was raised in the Ozarks.

On the second loop it started to rain, a steady, soaking light rain at first. I put on my cowboy slicker that protects both me and the saddle, and I was comfortable.

Some of the riders fared badly until black plastic bags were handed out from a relief truck. As we climbed higher the rain became a steady downpour and later became mixed with snow. After dark, even riders who knew the trail found their way down the muddy dark slopes with difficulty. When we made it back to the starting point at Virginia City we had covered seventy-five miles. It was 9:05 P.M. The veterinarian cleared Lad for the final loop, but I pulled us from the race. In the extreme dark of a stormy night you can't always see the other riders, so several of us pulled out.

Dave Cootware, the rider I rode with the most, got lost on the last loop and came in too late to get a buckle. I was proud of Lad. He could have finished if I had known the area. Anyway, this experience wrote the final lines to my song of Nevada.

> I rode loops around the mountains
> of old Virginia City one time
> with some real good riders
> and now they're all friends of mine.
> It never rains out here,
> they told me at the "Bucket of Blood,"
> but something wet from the sky
> sure turned that old mountain to mud.
> But it's a land of sagebrush perfume,
> mountains where wild flowers bloom,
> high deserts where the wild horse runs free,
> and a land that beckons to me.

That some good people considered it an honor to have me ride with them through their beautiful country will always mean more to me than any silver buckle I might have won.

On September 12 we trailered Lad back to the Bill Card ranch to resume my ride from the exact point it had been left off. I gave him a couple of days' rest to recuperate from the Virginia City ride.

The road shoulders from Fallon to Carson City were generally broad and served well for a trail. In most of the little towns wild horse tracks led right on through town. One day I saw a wild bunch up ahead, and the stallion stopped to look us over. Lad was a little frisky that day, and I was more concerned about what he might do than I was about the wild stallion.

Because the news media wanted me to arrive at Woodfords on Tuesday, I spent Sunday and Monday at the ranch of Cliff Lewis, an endurance rider and publisher of *Trail Digest* magazine; the ranch is only twelve miles from the station. Incidentally, Cliff had scales for weighing livestock, so we weighed Lad. He weighed in at 780 pounds. He had gained twenty pounds since May 6 in Oklahoma. And this was after the seventy-five miles in one day in Virginia City. I guess the Wyoming cowboys were right in saying that the little bastard was tough as nails.

During my ride to Woodfords on Tuesday morning, September 26, I was filled with conflicting emotions. There was a strong feeling of victory, the fulfillment of a long-held dream, but also a feeling of disbelief that we were really finishing the trek. Trail fatigue was saying, "I'm glad it's over," but a stronger voice was saying, "I don't want it to end!" There were tears in my eyes.

And then we were there. A large, green sign said, "Welcome to California." There were five more miles to ride. Rose took a picture of Lad and me by the sign; I rode on.

Just east of the road, still within sight of the Nevada-California line, I noticed a set of ranch buildings. A cowboy and his daughter were out riding, and I rode by them just as they reached the end of the lane leading to the ranch. The man was dressed much the same as I was, including fringed chink chaps, and after the customary greetings he asked, "Where're you going?" After having answered that question hundreds of times since last April with "California," I realized that I couldn't say that now.

So I looked into his steady gaze and said, "I'm there."

After that, I felt refreshed. I no longer felt sad that I was finishing the ride. I rode on to Woodfords feeling that I had drunk the last drop from the cup.

The road began rising into the foothills of the Sierra Nevada. Tall pines began to appear, and the words of my California song were going through my mind to the beat of Lad's hooves.

> When I crossed the California state line
> my pony was feeling so fine.
> I've had my long ride,
> now I'm satisfied,
> and I ride through the Sierra pines.

Around a bend in the road, over a slight hill, stood the buildings of Woodfords Pony Express Station, now a combination restaurant, gift shop, and general store. The historic rest stop for pony express riders became a rest stop for an Arkansas cowboy. Hannah Phillips of the *Nevada Appeal* was there and Cliff Lewis of *Trail Digest*. After an interview and photo session, and an apple for Lad, the friendly folks of Woodfords gave me a free meal.

Cliff Lewis had offered to keep Lad until transportation arrangements could be made, so I returned to his place. As I rode back, the breezes from the High Sierras were blowing yellow aspen leaves across the trail, and I realized that it was a good time to end the ride. Soon snow would close the high passes. Lad was in a fine mood, feeling good, and I kept patting him on the neck and saying, "We made it!"

The road back to Cliff's had some sandy stretches on it, and Lad kept walking faster, so I decided to let him gallop a little. He couldn't seem to get enough, so I really blew him out for about a half mile.

I had not only drunk the last drop from the cup of my adventure; I had spent my last buck. Sandy McAuliffe of Los Angeles, daughter of Frank McAuliffe back in Arkansas, had anticipated this and had arranged several woodcarving seminars for me to teach.

One day while we were enjoying the royal hospitality of Sandy and her husband, Richard, I picked up a book of Robert Service poems and read my own feelings perfectly.

> It's good the great green earth to roam,
> Where sights of awe the soul inspire;
> But oh, it's best, the coming home,
> The crackle of one's own hearth-fire!

I thought of my place in the woods and the apple blossom given to me on April 14, at Artist Point, reminding me to return.

Then suddenly I felt like a deep-sea diver who had come up too quickly. I was in Los Angeles. Lad was four hundred miles away, and when I shut my eyes I could see him, especially that part from the saddle to his sensitive ears. I had watched him flick those ears at thousands of strange sights and sounds for a tenth of the way around the world. It seemed that forever I had saddled him every morning. For 2,500 miles we had searched for grass and water and good trails. I had learned to understand him when he'd seem to say, "Ask this rancher if we can stay here."

So down there in Los Angeles, I longed to reach out and touch him, to stroke him, even to cuss him and call him by that name Wyoming cowboys had given him—the "Little Bastard." So I decompressed. I wept.

Between carving seminars in the Los Angeles area, I was asked to speak to about a dozen classes in various schools. The children showed great interest in the story of the old cattle drives, and they had a lot of questions about my ride. Then they wanted to handle my special saddle. Once a group of about three hundred, as I walked toward them, yelled, "Hi, Cowboy!" It made everything right. I guess there are still a lot of people who feel a kinship with old cowboys who love to ride those old trails.

Bibliography

Fred W. Allsop. *Folklore of Romantic Arkansas.* 2 vols. New York: the Grolier Society, 1931.

Oren Arnold. *Irons in the Fire: Cattle Brand Lore.* Abelard-Schuman, 1965.

W. David Baird. *The Quapaw Indians: A History of the Downstream People.* Norman: University of Oklahoma Press, 1980.

Louise Barry. *The Beginning of the West; Annals of the Kansas Gateway to the American West, 1540–1854.* Topeka: Kansas State Historical Society

Juanita Brooks. *The Mountain Meadows Massacre.* Norman: University of Oklahoma Press, 1970.

Mattie Brown. "A History of River Transportation in Arkansas from 1819–1880." M.A. thesis. University of Arkansas, 1933.

Robert Brownlee. *An American Odyssey: The Autobiography of Robert Brownlee.* Patricia Etter, ed. Fayetteville: University of Arkansas Press, 1986.

Edward Everett Dale. *Cherokee Cavaliers: Forty Years of Cherokee History as Told in the Correspondence of the Ridge-Watie-Boudinot Family.* Norman: University of Oklahoma Press, 1939.

David Dary. *Cowboy Culture: A Saga of Five Centuries.* Lawrence, Kans.: University Press of Kansas, 1989.

J. Frank Dobie. *Mustangs and Cow Horses.* Denton, Tex.: University of North Texas Press, 1982. Reprint of 1940 edition.

Clement Eaton. *A History of the Southern Confederacy.* New York: Macmillan, 1954.

John L. Ferguson and J. H. Atkinson. *Historic Arkansas.* Little Rock, AR: Arkansas History Commission, 1966.

John Gould Fletcher. *Arkansas.* Fayetteville: University of Arkansas Press, 1989.

John B. Friend. *Cattle of the World.* Poole, Dorset: Blandford Press Ltd., 1978.

Garcilaso de la Vega. *The Florida of the Inca* . . . Translated and edited by John Grier Varner and Jeannette Johnson Varner. Austin: University of Texas Press, 1951.

"Gentleman of Elvias." *True Relation of the Hardships Suffered by Governor Hernando De Soto and Certain Portuguese Gentlemen during the Discovery of the Province of Florida.* Translated by James A. Robertson. Northford, Conn.: Eliott's Bks., 1933.

Frederich Gerstaecker. *Wild Sports in the Far West: The Narratives of a German Wanderer beyond the Mississippi.* London, New York: G. Routledge & Co., 1854.

Henri Joutel. *A Journal of La Salle's Last Voyage.* Boston: Applewood, reprinted 1986.

Jim Lair. *Mountain Meadows Massacre: An Outlander's View.* With Collaboration by O. Klute Braswell. Marceline, MO: Walsworth Publishing Co., 1986.

John Doyle Lee. *Mormonism Unveiled* . . . St. Louis: M. E. Mason, 1891.

Letter Book of the Arkansas Trading House 1805–1810. U. S. National Archives, Washington, D.C.

Randolph Marcy. *The Prairie Traveler.* New York: Harper & brothers, 1859.

Theodore Maynard. *De Soto and the Conquistadores.* London, New York, Toronto: Longmans, Green and Co., 1930.

Priscilla McArthur. *Arkansas in the Gold Rush.* Little Rock, Ark.: August House, 1986.

Grace McClure. *The Bassett Women.* Athens: Swallow Press/Ohio University Press, 1985.

A. B. Nichols (?). *The Mormon Menace: Being the Confession of John Doyle Lee.* New York: Home Protection Publishing Co., 1905.

Thomas Nuttall. *A Journal of Travels into the Arkansas Territory during the Year 1819.* Norman: University of Oklahoma Press, reprinted 1980.

Harold Oppenheimer. *Cowboy Arithmetic: "Cattle as an Investment."* Danville, Ill.: The Interstate Printers & Publishers, Inc., 1971.

Waterman Ormsby. *The Butterfield Overland Mail*. Lyle H. Wright and Josephine M. Bynum, eds. San Marino, Calif.: The Huntington Library, 1942.

Tate Page. *The Voices of Moccasin Creek*. Point Lookout, Mo.: School of the Ozarks Press, 1972.

James W. Raine. *Land of Saddle-Bags: A Study of the Mountain People of Appalachia*. Detroit: Omnigraphics, reprinted 1990.

John Hugh Reynolds. *Makers of Arkansas History*. New York: Silver, Burdett and Co., 1911.

Hope Ryden. *America's Last Wild Horses*. New York: Dutton, 1970.

Henry Schoolcraft. *Journal of a Tour into the Interior of Missouri and Arkansaw* . . . London: Printed for R. Phillips and Co., 1821.

Kenneth L. Smith. *Sawmill: The Story of Cutting the Last Great Virgin Forest East of the Rockies*. Fayetteville: University of Arkansas Press, 1986.

John Upton Terrell. *La Salle, the Life And Times of an Explorer*. New York: Weybright and Talley, Inc., 1968.

C. W. Dub West. *Among the Cherokees*. Muscogee Pub. Co., 1981.

Jaunita Wilson. *Cincinnati, Arkansas, 1836–1986, Illinois Township*. Siloam Springs, Ark.: Siloam Springs Printing, 1986.

William Wise. *Massacre of Mountain Meadows: An American Legend and a Monumental Crime*. New York: Crowell, 1976.

Manfred R. Wolfenstine. *The Manual of Brands and Marks*. Norman: University of Oklahoma Press, 1970.

Walker D. Wyman. *The Wild Horse of the West*. Lincoln: University of Nebraska Press, 1963.

One of the pioneering Ozarks woodcarvers, Ivan Denton has long been fascinated by western subjects and landscapes. His carvings have often been compared to the works of Russell and Remington and were the subject of his first book, *The Art of I. Denton*, published by the University of Arkansas Press in 1988. Denton lives with his wife, Rose, on their farm north of Mountainburg, Arkansas.